CIVIL WAR

OSPREY
PUBLISHING

CIVIL WAR

FORT SUMTER to APPOMATTOX

GARY GALLAGHER, STEPHEN ENGLE, ROBERT KRICK,
AND JOSEPH GLATTHAAR

FOREWORD BY JAMES MCPHERSON

First published in Great Britain in 2003
by Osprey Publishing
PO Box 883, Oxford, OX1 9PL, UK
PO Box 3985, New York, NY 10185-3985, USA
Email: info@ospreypublishing.com

Osprey Publishing is part of the Osprey Group

A CIP catalog record for this book is available from the British Library.

ISBN: 978 1 4351 5698 2

Typeset in Berling, Rosewood and Trade Gothic
Index by Sharon Redmayne
Cartography by The Map Studio
Origination by PDQ Digital Solutions, Suffolk, UK
Printed and bound in China through World Print Ltd.

2 4 6 8 10 9 7 5 3 1

Osprey Publishing is supporting the Woodland Trust, the UK's leading woodland conservation charity, by funding the dedication of trees.

www.ospreypublishing.com

Front cover: *First day at Gettysburg* by James Walker. (US Military Academy)
Endpapers: Map of the Battle of Gettysburg. (LOC)

CONTENTS

CHAPTER 1:
THE WAR IN THE EAST 1861-MAY 1863

CHAPTER 2:
THE WAR IN THE WEST 1861-JULY 1863

CHAPTER 3:
THE WAR IN THE EAST MAY 1863-1865

CHAPTER 4:
THE WAR IN THE WEST JULY 1863-1865

FOREWORD

BY JAMES McPHERSON

The centrality of the Civil War to American history is indisputable. At least 620,000 soldiers lost their lives from 1861 to 1865. This number constituted 2 percent of the American population. If the same percentage of Americans were to die in a war fought today, the number of war dead would be five and a half million. The war also wreaked havoc and destruction in the South. It wiped out two-thirds of the assessed value of Southern wealth (including slaves), destroyed more than half of the region's farm machinery, consumed two-fifths of Southern livestock, and killed a quarter of Southern white males between the ages of 20 and 40. In 1865 the South presented a bleak landscape of desolation. Burned-out plantations, fields growing up in weeds, and railroads without tracks, bridges, or rolling stock marked the trail of conquering and defeated armies.

The consequences of the war for the country as a whole, however, were more positive than negative. Northern victory resolved two festering issues that had plagued the United States since its founding: whether this fragile experiment of a democratic republic could survive in a world where most republics through the ages had been swept into the dustbin of history; and whether the house divided would continue to endure half slave and half free. Many Americans had doubted whether the republic would survive; many Europeans regularly predicted its demise; some Americans believed in the right of secession and periodically threatened to invoke it; 11 states did invoke it in 1860–61. As Abraham Lincoln said in his address at Gettysburg in 1863, the conflict was a test whether a nation "conceived in Liberty, and dedicated to the proposition that all men are created equal" could "long endure" or would "perish from the earth." It did endure, and in such a way as to give promise of long life. Since 1865 no state or region has seriously threatened secession, not even during the South's "massive resistance" to desegregation from 1954 to 1964.

The war also gave America "a new birth of freedom," as Lincoln put it at Gettysburg. Before 1865 the United States, a boasted "land of liberty," was the largest slaveholding country in the world. "The monstrous injustice of slavery," Lincoln had said in 1854, "deprives our republican example of its just influence in the world – enables the enemies of free institutions, with plausibility, to taunt us as hypocrites." With the abolition of slavery by Northern victory, that particular "monstrous injustice" and "hypocrisy" came to an end. As Mark Twain wrote in 1873, the Civil War "uprooted institutions that were centuries old, changed the politics of a people, transformed the social life of half the country, and wrought so profoundly upon the entire national character that the influence cannot be measured short of two or three generations."

How did all this happen? That is the question the four authors of this volume undertake to answer. In four sections that weave together the story of military campaigns in the Eastern and Western Theaters with the impact of the war on the home front, spiced with stories of individual men and women who experienced the conflict, this book sets forth the essential history of the war. The four authors are in the top rank of Civil War historians. Their lucid prose, the clarity of the maps, and the well-selected illustrations offer a rich feast for readers, who will take away an understanding of how and why the war came out as it did.

The authors make clear that this outcome was not inevitable. Although the North had superior numbers and resources, these did not assure victory. To win the war, Union forces had to invade, conquer, occupy, and control key parts of the South's 750,000 square miles (1,942,500 sq km) and destroy its armies and infrastructure. The Confederacy, by contrast, began the conflict in political and military control of this territory. To win the war, it needed only to defend what it already had in 1861 and to wear out the will of its enemy to continue fighting. In these terms the Confederacy came close to winning on several occasions, as this book makes clear.

There were many twists and turns in the four years of war, many reversals of momentum that frustrated imminent victory by one side or the other. This book identifies the four major turning points of the war. The first came in the summer of 1862 when counteroffensives by Confederate commanders Robert E. Lee and Stonewall Jackson in Virginia and Braxton Bragg and Edmund Kirby Smith in Tennessee and Kentucky reversed the previous four months of Union naval and military success. These Northern victories had gained control of much of the vital interior network of the Cumberland, Tennessee, and Mississippi Rivers and of the South Atlantic coast, had captured New Orleans, Nashville, and Memphis, and had approached to within 5 miles of the Confederate capital of Richmond, whose fall seemed imminent in May 1862.

The Southern counteroffensives prolonged and intensified the war and created the potential for Confederate success, which appeared imminent before each of the next three turning points. The first of these occurred in the fall of 1862, when battles at Antietam and Perryville blunted Confederate invasions, forestalled European mediation and recognition of the South, perhaps prevented a Democratic victory in the Northern congressional elections that might have inhibited Lincoln's ability to carry on the war, and set the stage for the Emancipation Proclamation which enlarged the scope and purpose of the war.

The third critical point came in the summer and fall of 1863 when Gettysburg, Vicksburg, and Chattanooga turned the tide toward ultimate Northern victory. But one more reversal of that tide seemed possible in the summer of 1864 when appalling Union casualties and apparent lack of progress, especially in Virginia, brought the North to the brink of peace negotiations and the election of a Democratic president. However, Sherman's capture of Atlanta and Sheridan's victories in the Shenandoah Valley turned the tide one last time. Only then did it become possible, after Lincoln's reelection, to speak of the inevitability of Northern victory.

The consequences of that victory have profoundly affected the course of American history – indeed, world history – since 1865. This volume provides the essential foundation for an understanding of those consequences.

James McPherson

INTRODUCTION: THE NATION IN CRISIS

America in the mid-19th century was a nation of conflicting ideological and cultural identities attempting to forge out of its agrarian traditions and industrial impulses a republic that remained committed to the ideals of its founding fathers. Bound by a common belief in freedom and independence as realized through democratic principles and republican virtues, Americans came to believe that their nation was God's chosen nation. However, although the country had been unified for more than 60 years, political, economic, social, and cultural differences stretching back to the nation's origins brought about a crisis for the young republic in 1861.

THE DEVELOPMENT OF AN INDUSTRIAL SOCIETY

In the early 19th century, the United States was predominantly an agrarian society. Land was fundamental to freedom, self-sufficiency, and independence. Most Americans believed that owning land and tilling the soil nurtured freedom and independence, and that those without land, engaged primarily in manufacturing, posed the greatest threat to that freedom. So long as land was plentiful, Americans believed, they could maintain the virtues granted them as the rightful beneficiaries of republican liberties. They could therefore escape

The antebellum South was a land of prosperous cotton plantations. Even after the war, cotton remained king of agriculture. (Edimedia)

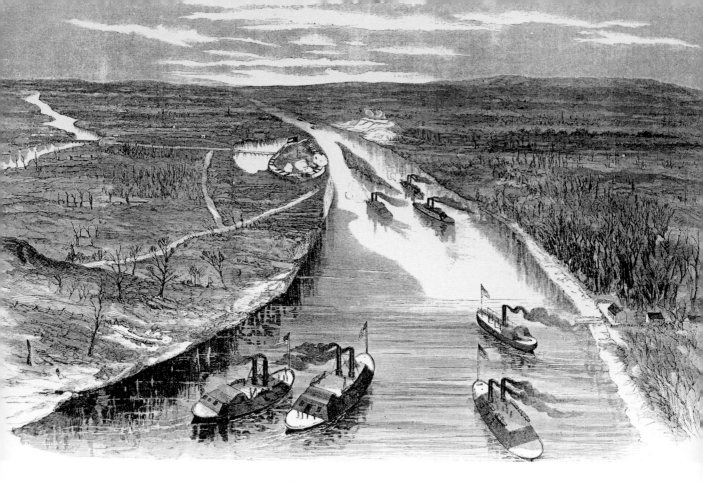

Like the Mississippi and Ohio Rivers, the Tennessee and Cumberland Rivers had been arteries of economic exchange in the decades before the Civil War, but the outbreak of war changed them into routes of military invasion. (*Harper's Weekly*, public domain)

poverty, dependency on others, and overpopulation produced by a manufacturing society. Thus, the desire to own land was at the core of the initial republican vision, as conceived by revolutionary leaders such as Thomas Jefferson.

Few Americans of Jefferson's generation, however, could have imagined that the quest for land that sparked the settlement of the west would actually accelerate rather than deter urban and industrial development. The very nature of the migration west was as much a cause as it was a consequence of the ideological differences and sectionalism that prevailed in the decades before the Civil War. Significantly, the migration and settlement of the west transformed an agrarian society that defined itself as a virtuous farming republic into an industrial society that came to accept the free-labor ideology as paramount in achieving republican dreams of a truly free and democratic society.

Beginning in the 1820s, westward expansion flowed along America's natural arteries, such as the Ohio and Mississippi Rivers and their tributaries, which allowed western farmers to channel goods south to New Orleans. After the 1830s, however, steamboats, canals, and railroads redirected western trade to the flourishing urban markets of the northeast. The cumulative impact of more effective transportation resulted in widening market opportunities. Simultaneously, the small manufacturing initiatives shifted from artisan shops to small factories, and merchant capitalists in the northeastern cities assumed the lead in organizing production for the expanding markets. In the four decades before the Civil War, urbanization and manufacturing reinforced each other in their growth patterns and came to shape the character of the North.

Although Southern whites moved west for basically the same reasons that Northerners did, slavery provided a different experience. The cotton industry was directly linked to the size and substance of slave plantations. Between 1790 and 1860, cotton production exploded from 3,000 bales to 4,500,000 bales. Like the farmers of the Old Northwest who responded optimistically to market opportunities, planters and ambitious slaveholders responded to market incentives. Still, the slaveholder had little incentive to invest in labor-saving machinery and instead invested in land and slaves.

The antebellum wests, North and South, played integral roles in the economic development of the nation because they were linked to eastern markets. By the 1840s, the west had become a principal market for manufactured goods and provided food for factory workers who were being pulled to Northern cities by employment. Still, cotton dominated American exports after the mid-1830s and served as the basis for national credit. As the northeastern economy continued to develop and diversify, the economy of the South remained predominantly agrarian.

These east–west connections brought about by economic changes galvanized and shaped antebellum American culture and spawned a transportation revolution that brought not only numerous Americans into the market place, but also new expectations. The revolution in transport encouraged economic diversification, ethnic diversity, and an emphasis on free labor. These gave rise to an American middle class characterized by a materialism and moralism that sought to democratize the market place. Middle-class ideals harmonized with the Protestant work ethic to shape an environment conducive to capitalist expansion. This Protestant ethic prompted many Northerners to embrace reform movements that sought to regulate society by helping persons who lacked self-control. By the 1850s, they had targeted the containment of slavery as one of their primary interests.

Though there was a small aspiring middle class of merchants, professionals, and tradesmen in the South, the region was bound to an agricultural slave society that repudiated the wage earner. Consequently, middle class reform remained predominantly a Northern phenomenon.

THE CHALLENGE TO SLAVERY

In a republic that lacked any uniform concept of citizenship, an interpretive consensus of the Constitution, and a large standing army and navy, and where liberty and slavery coexisted, perhaps the only clearly defined aspect was that states possessed the exclusive rights to regulate slavery within their jurisdiction. By 1820, however, even those rights were being challenged. The congressional

South Carolina Senator John C. Calhoun, who devised the theory of nullification, was also an ardent defender of slavery. "I hold that in the present state of civilization," he once argued, "the relation now existing in the slave-holding states between the two [races] is, instead of an evil, a good – a positive good." (Ann Ronan Picture Library)

sessions of 1819 and 1820 concerning Missouri's admission to the Union as a slave state attested to the unsettling aspects of territorial expansion. The debates over slavery brought Northern frustrations about the institution to a climax and for the first time disclosed a bipartisan Northern majority determined to contain the institution. The conclusion of the debates produced the Missouri Compromise, which admitted Missouri as a slave state and Maine as a free state. Still, Missouri's southern boundary, the infamous 36–30 line, was extended westward through the remainder of the Louisiana Purchase territory. Above the imaginary line slavery was prohibited and below it the institution was permitted.

The combination of the financial panic of 1819 and the Missouri Compromise forced the fracture of the Republican Party. What emerged in its place was a Democratic Party that spoke to those who considered themselves victims of the ever-changing market place, and a Whig Party that spoke to those who considered themselves the winners or benefactors of the changing market place. By and large, Democrats, largely rural, championed a negative use of the government in the economy, attacked banks, opposed tariffs, and wanted to be left alone in their manners and morals. Whigs promoted a favorable and progressive use of the government in promoting economic change, and endorsed banks, higher tariffs, and free labor.

Ironically, in the pre-Civil War decades, these conflicting beliefs formed a strong concept of Union. However, they also allowed a significant degree of sectional strife to emerge. In 1832–33, in response to the tariff of 1828, South Carolina Planters led by John C. Calhoun forced a theory of nullification on the presidency of Andrew Jackson, whereby an individual state could nullify a federal law: that is, declare the law void within its borders. A crisis was averted as both sides compromised and claimed victory, but the significance of nullification was that Southerners came to believe they were a permanent minority. On the heels of Nat Turner's bloody slave uprising in Southampton, Virginia, in the summer of 1831, Southerners convinced themselves that their worst fears were before them. In the context of the Missouri Crisis, the Southern populace came to believe that the horror of losing independence could not be escaped. Concern over economic decline, combined with alarm over slave uprisings and the rise of abolition in the North, encouraged several Southern states to tighten slave codes and pass laws to suppress abolitionist speeches in the South.

The expansionist impulses of Americans, or "Manifest Destiny" as it came to be known, continued in the 1840s with the admission of Florida and Texas as slave states. The crisis over Texas's admission erupted in a war with Mexico that lasted two years and ended with the acquisition of Mexican territory. By gaining a land mass that nearly doubled the size of the United States, Americans faced the continuing dilemma of making the Federal government responsible for protecting the baggage of slavery that accompanied expansion.

By mid-century, American republicanism was facing a national crisis. The acquisition of Mexican land forced Americans to consider whether the newly expanded Union would be one with or without slavery. Land was losing its value in terms of promising freedom and self-sufficiency because the freedom to earn a wage was gaining national prominence. Because the Democrats were the primary spokesmen for the original definition of freedom and advocates of the farmers, they came to the defense of Southern traditions. Whigs, on the other hand, supported free labor. As a prewar Whig, Abraham Lincoln espoused the virtues of free labor, remarking that, "There is no such thing as a man being bound down in a free country through his life as a laborer."

In general, beginning in the 1840s, Northerners viewed the South as an impediment to realizing the full democratic principles that the market had to offer. Most antislavery Northerners opposed slavery not because of its effect on blacks, but because of the institution's effect on whites. It degraded the value of free labor. Southerners, however, came to believe that their fundamental rights were being usurped because they were a political minority. The Wilmot Proviso, which in 1846 unsuccessfully attempted to prohibit slavery in any territory acquired from Mexico, confirmed Southern fears that individual rights were no longer a constitutional matter, but a political matter. The emergence in the election of 1848 of the Free Soil Party, which promoted the containment of slavery, also helped to confirm these fears.

By the 1850s, Americans were searching for common ground that no longer existed in their political culture. Such a center had deteriorated because of economic and social change. The Compromise of 1850 was representative of the nature of congressional responses, attempting to placate both Northerners and Southerners. Although it admitted California as a free state, which offset the balance in the Senate in favor of Northern states, it also imposed a tougher Fugitive Slave Act. In many respects the Compromise of 1850 was at best an armistice to an American political culture attempting to wrest itself from permanent divisions along sectional lines.

The publication in 1852 of *Uncle Tom's Cabin*, a best-selling antislavery novel by Harriet Beecher Stowe, further intensified the emotionally charged atmosphere surrounding slavery. It hardened Northern middle-class attitudes regarding slavery's incompatibility with the

Harriet Beecher Stowe, author of *Uncle Tom's Cabin*, spent just one weekend in a slave state and yet from Maine wrote the most popular novel of slavery of the nineteenth century. (Ann Ronan Picture Library)

nation's democratic principles. So popular and offensive was the book that, at one point during the Civil War when Abraham Lincoln finally met Harriet Beecher Stowe, he referred to her as "the little lady who made this big war."

Sectional tensions erupted in 1854 when the Kansas–Nebraska Act repealed the Missouri Compromise and allowed the ambiguous concept of "popular sovereignty" (let the people of the territories decide) to settle the question of whether or not slavery would exist. When it passed, Illinois Senator Stephen A. Douglas prophesied that the Kansas–Nebraska Act would "raise a hell of a storm." Although it opened the landscape for the construction of a transcontinental railroad, it signaled the collapse of the Whig Party, served as a catalyst for the new Republican Party, and was instrumental in the growth of the one-party Democratic South.

In 1857, the Supreme Court attempted to settle the issue that Congress had failed to solve. By ruling in the Dred Scott case that Congress had no right to single out slave property for prohibition in the territories (areas owned by the US government but not yet divided into states), the Court endorsed what Southerners had believed all along – slavery was protected by the Constitution. Many Northerners concluded that politically a slave power did exist and that it had won a triumphant victory over the forces of free soil and free labor.

Territorial conflicts were so central to the future of the republic that the religious culture divided into factions. Parishioners came to believe in an antislavery God in the North and a pro-slavery God in the South. As institutional centers fragmented, the election of 1856 signaled a departure from an American culture forced to compromise repeatedly on issues of vital significance to the nation's future. Although James Buchanan won, the Democrats became unavoidably divided. Republicans employed the rhetoric of complete prohibition of slavery in the territories, and many white Southerners interpreted this as simply a disguise for the true intentions of the party to eventually abolish the institution.

In the debate over the territories, both parties claimed to be defending republican standards of individual freedom, liberty, honor, and moral righteousness. Yet, such fundamental disagreements, whether moral or political, over how these standards should be applied to the problems confronting the nation gave rise to hardened perceptions of each other. They became consumed by seeing one another as enemies.

By the end of the 1850s, hardened perceptions, emotionally charged legislative disputes, and vicious recriminations cast a mold of uncompromising attitude. In 1858, running for the Illinois senate, Lincoln perhaps best summed up the young republic's crisis in his famous "House Divided" speech. "I believe this government cannot endure, permanently half *slaves* and half *free*," he concluded. The Civil War that erupted in 1861 revealed that Southerners and Northerners were fighting to preserve the fundamental patterns and practices of their economic and social life. What Americans had failed to solve during peacetime, they would now settle by war.

A MODERN WAR

In many respects, the Civil War was a watershed in the history of warfare, as it ultimately took shape as a total or modern war. The warring sides voiced the rhetoric of ideology and cause, they employed conscription, simplified strategies and tactics to create armies of unparalleled size and power, and they used these armies to strike at the enemy and destroy their possessions. At first, Northern commanders anticipated a limited, short, and bloodless war that would restore the Union without alienating the Southern populace. They attempted to prevail quickly by blockading Southern ports and by capturing principal cities, including the Confederate capital, Richmond. By the end of 1861, however, Northern political leaders had come to believe that Union armies were actually losing the war because they were trying to win the peace.

Perhaps more than any other aspect of the war, rifled weapons gave rise to a longer and more protracted war. These rifles gave the armies a defensive advantage, and Northern soldiers soon realized that they could neither easily destroy Southern armies nor capture fortified positions. By early 1862, commanders fully understood the lethal implications of such firepower, at a time when Northern political leaders came to embrace an expansive war to be waged against the South's institutions. Northern political leaders and commanders sought not only to reduce Confederate forces in campaigns of attrition, but also to deplete the South's ability to wage war by liberating slaves, destroying the region's farms and factories, and, most significantly, breaking the spirit of the Southern people.

The Civil War ravaged the American landscape for four years and instead of conserving the old America it steadily and profoundly reshaped the political, economic, and social contours of the nation. By the time it ended, the original American republic was gone. The postwar republic would be carved out of a world that the war made.

CHRONOLOGY

1820 Missouri Compromise admits Missouri as a slave state, but prohibits slavery elsewhere in Louisiana territory above latitude 36 30' N

1828 South Carolina politician John Calhoun urges nullification in response to the 1828 tariff

1831 Nat Turner's slave rebellion sends shock waves through the South; William Lloyd Garrison founds abolitionist newspaper *The Liberator*

1836 Congress adopts the Gag Resolution on slavery, preventing discussion surrounding the subject, or antislavery petitions

1845 Texas and Florida are admitted to the Union

1846–48 War between the United States and Mexico

1846 Wilmot Proviso calls for barring slavery from lands acquired from Mexico

1848 Free Soil Party fields presidential candidate

1850 Compromise of 1850 includes admission of California as a free state and enactment of a tough Fugitive Slave Act

1852 Whig Party fields its last serious presidential candidate, signaling breakdown of the two-party system; publication of Harriet Beecher Stowe's *Uncle Tom's Cabin* makes many Northerners sensitive to the issue of slavery

Lincoln's inauguration ball, March 4, 1861. (Ann Ronan Picture Library)

1854	Kansas–Nebraska Act repeals the Missouri Compromise and inflames sectional tensions	July 21	Battle of First Manassas or Bull Run
1857	The Supreme Court's Dred Scott decision opens Federal territories to slavery and outrages many people in the North	July 25	US Senate passes Crittenden Compromise that the Union is not fighting to interfere with slavery
1859	John Brown's raid on Harpers Ferry intensifies sectional tensions	August 10	Battle of Wilson's Creek or Oak Hills, Springfield, Missouri

1860

November 6	Abraham Lincoln elected President
December 20	South Carolina secedes from the Union

1861

January 9–February 1	The remaining six states of the Lower South secede
February 4–March 11	Convention of delegates from the seceded states in Montgomery, Alabama, writes a Constitution and selects Jefferson Davis and Alexander H. Stephens as provisional President and Vice-President of the Confederate States of America
March 4	Lincoln's First Inauguration
April 12–13	Confederate bombardment results in the surrender of Fort Sumter
April 17–June 8	Four states of the Upper South secede in response to Lincoln's call for volunteers
Early May	Winfield Scott briefs President Lincoln about a strategy later known as the "Anaconda Plan"
May 10	Camp Jackson affair, St Louis, Missouri
May 20	Confederate Congress votes to move national government from Montgomery, Alabama, to Richmond, Virginia; Kentucky declares neutrality

August 30	John C. Fremont declares martial law and declares slaves in Missouri free
September 3	Confederate forces under Gideon Pillow enter Kentucky, ending neutrality in that state
September 10	Confederate Albert Sidney Johnson is appointed to command Tennessee, Missouri, Arkansas, and Kentucky
November 1	Winfield Scott resigns as general-in-chief of the United States army and is replaced by George B. McClellan
November 6	Jefferson Davis is elected as the Confederate States President
November 9	Don Carlos Buell and Henry Halleck are appointed to departments in Kentucky and Missouri

1862

January 19	Battle of Mill Springs or Logan's Cross Roads, Kentucky
February 6	Union gunboats force the surrender of Fort Henry, Tennessee
February 13–16	Battle of Fort Donelson, Tennessee, results in the Union's capture of 15,000 Confederates
February 22	Jefferson Davis inaugurated as President of the Confederacy
February 25	President Lincoln signs the Legal Tender Act, which creates national Treasury notes soon dubbed "greenbacks"; Don Carlos Buell captures Nashville, Tennessee
March 7–8	Battle of Pea Ridge or Elkhorn Tavern, Arkansas

March 11	Lincoln's War Order No. 3 relieves McClellan as general-in-chief and consolidates western commands under Halleck
March 17	McClellan begins movement of Union troops to Virginia Peninsula
April 6–7	Battle of Shiloh or Pittsburg Landing
April 16	Confederate Congress passes the first National Conscription Act in American history
April 26	Union gunboats force New Orleans to surrender
May 8	"Stonewall" Jackson wins the Battle of McDowell, the first of several victories in his Shenandoah Valley campaign; other victories follow at Front Royal (May 23), First Winchester (May 25), Cross Keys (June 8), and Port Republic (June 9)
May 29/30	Confederates evacuate Corinth, Mississippi
May 31–June 1	Battle of Seven Pines or Fair Oaks
June 1	Robert E. Lee takes command of Confederate Army at Richmond
June 6	Confederates surrender at Memphis, Tennessee
June 19	Lincoln signs a law prohibiting slavery in the territories
June 25–July 1	Seven Days battles reverse a tide of Union military success as Lee drives McClellan away from Richmond in action at Mechanicsville (June 26), Gaines's Mill (June 27), Savage's Station (June 29), Glendale or Frayser's Farm (June 30), and Malvern Hill (July 1)
July 11	Halleck is named general-in-chief of the United States army
July 13	General Nathan Bedford Forrest captures Murfreesboro, Tennessee

July 17	Second Confiscation Act approved by US Congress; Congress approves Militia Act
August 9	Battle of Cedar Mountain
August 28–30	Battle of Second Manassas or Bull Run
September 17	Battle of Antietam or Sharpsburg ends Lee's first invasion of the North; Battle of Munfordville, Kentucky
September 19	Battle of Iuka, Mississippi
September 22	Lincoln issues his preliminary Emancipation Proclamation
October 3–4	Battle of Corinth, Mississippi
October 8	Battle of Perryville or Chaplin Hills, Kentucky
October 20	Lincoln orders John McClernand to raise troops for an expedition against Vicksburg, Mississippi
October 24	William Rosecrans replaces Buell as commander of Union forces in Kentucky and Tennessee
November 5	Ambrose E. Burnside replaces McClellan as commander of the Army of the Potomac
November 24	Joseph E. Johnston is assigned to the Confederate command in the west
December 13	Battle of Fredericksburg
December 20	Confederates under Earl van Dorn raid Holly Springs, Mississippi
December 31–January 2	Battle of Murfreesboro or Stone's River, Tennessee

1863

January 1	Lincoln issues final Emancipation Proclamation
January 11	Federal gunboats capture Fort Hindman, Arkansas
January 26	Joseph Hooker replaces Burnside as commander of the Army of the Potomac
January 30	Ulysses S. Grant assumes command of the expedition against Vicksburg, Mississippi

February 25	US Congress passes the National Bank Act
March 3	US Congress passes the Enrollment Act, which institutes a national draft
March 7	Nathaniel Banks's Federal force moves to Baton Rouge to cooperate with Grant's Vicksburg expedition
April 2	Women take to the streets in Richmond "bread riot" to protest against food shortages
April 16	Porter's flotilla runs past Vicksburg batteries
April 17	Confederate Benjamin Grierson launches a raid into Mississippi to draw attention from Grant's expedition
April 24	Confederate Congress enacts the Tax-in-Kind Law, a highly unpopular measure requiring agricultural producers to give a portion of various crops to the national government
April 30	Porter ferries part of Grant's army across the Mississippi River
May 1–4	Battle of Chancellorsville
May 2	Grierson's raiders reach Baton Rouge, Louisiana
May 10	"Stonewall" Jackson dies
May 12	Grant defeats Confederates at Raymond, Mississippi
May 14	Engagement at Jackson, Mississippi; Grant defeats Confederates
May 16	Battle of Champion's Hill, Mississippi; Grant defeats Pemberton
May 17	Battle of Big Black River; Grant defeats Pemberton
May 18–July 4	Siege of Vicksburg, Mississippi
May 27	Banks attacks and besieges Port Hudson; first major engagement for black soldiers
June 7	Confederate attack on Milliken's Bend
June 9	Cavalry battle at Brandy Station
June 11	Banks's attack repulsed for a second time at Port Hudson
June 14	Banks's attack repulsed for a third time at Port Hudson
June 14–15	Second Battle of Winchester
June 23	Rosecrans advances on Tullahoma, Tennessee
June 28	General George G. Meade replaces Joseph Hooker in command of the Federal Army of the Potomac in the midst of the campaign, just before the war's largest battle
July 1–3	Battle of Gettysburg
July 3	Bragg retreats to Chattanooga, Tennessee
July 4	Pemberton surrenders Vicksburg to Grant
July 9	Port Hudson falls
July 13–14	Lee's Confederates recross the Potomac River into Virginia, ending the main phase of the Gettysburg campaign. At the same time, frenzied mobs in New York City riot in opposition to conscription, killing or wounding hundreds of victims, many of them black citizens resented as a visible cause of the war and the draft
July 19	Union attack on Fort Wagner led by 54th Massachusetts (Colored) Infantry
August 15	Burnside begins campaign for Knoxville, Tennessee
August 16	Rosecrans begins campaign for Chattanooga
August 21	Quantrill raids Lawrence, Kansas
September 2	Burnside occupies Knoxville
September 8–14	Lee detaches General Longstreet with a third of the army's infantry to go west and reinforce Confederate operations in Georgia and Tennessee. Meade moves south against Lee, but only heavy skirmishing results
September 9	Rosecrans occupies Chattanooga
September 18	Longstreet's men begin to reinforce Bragg's army

September 19   Battle of Chickamauga, Tennessee begins

September 20   Longstreet breaks Rosecrans's line

September 23   Bragg lays siege to Chattanooga

September 24   Hooker leaves for Chattanooga with XI and XII Corps

October 14   Battle of Bristoe Station

October 17   Grant made commander of all the Union forces in the west

October 19   Thomas replaces Rosecrans

October 23   Grant arrives at Chattanooga

November 4   Longstreet detached to attack Burnside at Knoxville

November 7   Battle of Rappahannock Station

November 19   President Lincoln delivers the Gettysburg Address

November 20   Sherman arrives at Chattanooga with reinforcements

November 23   Thomas seizes Orchard Knob

November 24   Hooker drives Confederates off Lookout Mountain

November 25   Sherman's attack stalls; Thomas's men storm Missionary Ridge

November 28   President Lincoln issues a Proclamation of Amnesty and Reconstruction, offering pardons to any Confederate willing to take an oath of allegiance

November 29   Longstreet repulsed by Burnside at Knoxville

December 1   Bragg resigns as Army of Tennessee commander

December 27   Johnston assumes command of Army of Tennessee

1864

February 3   Sherman leaves Vicksburg on Meridian campaign

March 12   Grant is commissioned lieutenant-general and general-in-chief, to command all Federal armies. He would make his headquarters with the Army of the Potomac and soon exert virtually direct command over it. Halleck becomes chief-of-staff

March 18   Sherman assumes command of Union forces in the west

March 25   Banks begins Red River campaign

April 8   Banks defeated by Richard Taylor at Sabine Crossroads, Louisiana

April 12   Forrest massacres of black soldiers at Fort Pillow, Tennessee

May 5–7   Battle of the Wilderness

May 6   Sherman opens Atlanta campaign

May 8–21   Battle of Spotsylvania Court House

May 9   McPherson's flanking movement stalls; General John Sedgwick killed

May 11   Battle of Yellow Tavern; General J. E. B. Stuart is mortally wounded and dies the next day

May 13–16   Battle of Resaca

May 15   Battle of New Market

May 18   Battle of Yellow Bayou, Lousiana, the last battle of the Red River campaign

May 19   Johnston's attack at Cassville never develops

May 23–27   Battle of the North Anna River; Sherman attempts to outflank Johnston's position at Allatoona, Georgia

May 25–28   Battle around Dallas, Georgia

June 1–3   Battle of Cold Harbor

June 5   Battle of Piedmont

June 8   Lincoln renominated for president

June 14   Army of the Potomac starts to cross James River; Lieutenant-General Leonidas Polk killed at Pine Mountain

June 15–18   Opening engagements around Petersburg, while Confederate General Jubal Early arrives near Lynchburg to launch his long and crucial campaign in the Shenandoah Valley

June 21–23	First Battle of the Weldon Railroad near Petersburg
June 27	Sherman's assault on Kennesaw Mountain repulsed
July 4–9	Sherman maneuvers across Chattahoochee River
July 9	Battle of Monocacy
July 11–12	Early's Confederate stand on the outskirts of Washington; President Lincoln comes under long-range fire
July 17	Hood replaces Johnston as commander of Army of Tennessee
July 20	Hood repulsed at Peachtree Creek
July 22	Hood fails to turn Sherman's army at Battle of Atlanta; Major-General James B. McPherson is killed
July 24	Second Battle of Kernstown
July 28	Hood's attack at Ezra Church is repulsed
July 30	Dramatic explosion of mine at Petersburg turns into the Battle of the Crater
August 5	Farragut wins Battle of Mobile Bay
August 18–25	Battles of the Weldon Railroad and Ream's Station
August 23	Lincoln submits to his cabinet a sealed memo stating that, "it seems extremely probable that this Administration will not be re-elected," and pledging support after the election to the President-elect
August 29	McClellan nominated for President
August 31	Battle of Jonesboro, Georgia
September 1	Battle of Jonesboro concluded; Hood evacuates Atlanta
September 2	Sherman occupies Atlanta
September 14–17	The Beefsteak Raid
September 19	Third Battle of Winchester; Price crosses into Missouri with 12,000 men
September 22	Battle of Fisher's Hill

September 27	Anderson's attack on Centralia, Missouri
September 28	Hood moves to strike at Sherman's supply line
September 29–October 7	Fighting around Richmond and Petersburg at Fort Harrison, Chaffin's Bluff, New Market Heights, Darbytown Road, and Boydton Plank Road
October 9	Cavalry fights at Tom's Brook
October 19	Battle of Cedar Creek
October 23	Price defeated at Westport; begins retreat
October 27	Battle of Burgess Mill
October 30	Sherman shifts Schofield's troops to support Thomas in Middle Tennessee
November 8	President Lincoln reelected with 55 percent of popular vote
November 15	Sherman's troops burn Atlanta; begin March to the Sea
November 19	Hood opens push into Middle Tennessee
November 23	Milledgville, capital of Georgia, falls to Sherman
November 29	Schofield escapes at Spring Hill, Tennessee
November 30	Schofield repulses Hood at Franklin; Lieutenant-General Patrick Cleburne killed
December 13	Sherman captures Fort McAllister
December 15–16	Battle of Nashville; Thomas routs Hood's army
December 21	Sherman occupies Savannah
December 25	Butler repulsed at Fort Fisher, North Carolina

1865

January 15	Fort Fisher falls to Porter and Terry; Hood relieved of command of Army of Tennessee
January 31	Thirteenth Amendment abolishing slavery passes in Congress

February 1	Sherman begins Carolinas campaign
February 5–7	Battle of Hatcher's Run
February 6	Lee appointed general-in-chief of all Confederate armies by Congress, against President Davis's wishes – far too late to affect the prosecution of the war
February 17	Columbia falls to Sherman
February 18	Charleston seized by Union troops
February 22	Wilmington surrenders to Schofield; Johnston recalled to command Confederate forces against Sherman
March 2	Early's last remnant destroyed at the Battle of Waynesboro
March 4	Lincoln's Second Inauguration
March 13	Confederate Congress approves raising of black troops
March 16	Sherman pushes back Hardee at Averasborough, North Carolina
March 19–21	Sherman repulses Johnston's attack at Bentonville, North Carolina
March 24	Sherman occupies Goldsboro, North Carolina, ending the Carolinas campaign
March 25	Attack on Fort Stedman near Petersburg
March 27–28	Lincoln, Grant, Sherman, and Porter confer on peace terms
March 29–31	The final campaign in Virginia begins with fighting around the Dinwiddie Court House
April 1	Battle of Five Forks
April 2	Confederate government evacuates Richmond
April 8	Sherman resumes march on Johnston
April 9	Lee surrenders to Grant at Appomattox Court House
April 12	Mobile falls to Canby; Johnston tells President Jefferson Davis resistance is hopeless
April 13	Raleigh falls to Sherman
April 14	Lincoln assassinated at Ford's Theater in Washington

April 18	Sherman and Johnston sign broad surrender agreement
April 21	President Johnston and cabinet reject Sherman's terms
April 26	Johnston surrenders to General William T. Sherman and accepts same terms as Grant gives Lee
May 10	President Davis is captured at Irwinsville, Georgia
May 13	Last battle of the war, at Palmito Ranch, Texas
May 23–24	Grand Review in Washington, DC
May 26	General Edmund Kirby Smith surrenders Confederate forces west of the Mississippi River

1866

April 2	State governments having been installed to meet Unionist directives, President Andrew Johnson officially proclaims, "that the insurrection … is at an end and is henceforth to be so regarded"

1877

The last enforced military government in the ex-Confederate states is removed and home rule is restored at the state level

CHAPTER 1

THE WAR IN THE EAST 1861-MAY 1863

OUTBREAK: ELECTION, SOUTHERN SECESSION, AND CREATION OF THE CONFEDERACY

The opening scene of the crisis of 1860–61 took place in the autumn of 1859. On October 16, John Brown and a small band of followers seized the federal arsenal at Harpers Ferry, Virginia, as part of a plan to gather slaves in a mountain stronghold, arm them, and wage war on the South's slaveholders. Robert E. Lee and a detachment of United States Marines quickly suppressed the raiders, and Brown himself was tried, sentenced to die, and hanged. Comporting himself with dignity and courage at his trial and execution, Brown won the admiration of much of the North. As he went to the gallows, he handed one of his jailers a note that read, "I John Brown am now quite *certain* that the crimes of this *guilty land: will* never be purged *away*; but with Blood." In the North, a number of newspapers praised Brown, church bells peeled his honor, and other such demonstrations underscored that a substantial element of the Northern public shared, at least to a degree, Brown's hatred of slavery.

White Southerners, in contrast, reacted in horror at both Brown's actions and the Northern response. Here was a man who had planned to incite a full-scale slave rebellion that would trigger a bloodbath and leave the South in chaos. Assurances from Northern Democrats that they repudiated Brown's raid fell on deaf ears. White Southerners equated Brown with abolitionists,

Depiction of the Second Battle of the Bull Run. (Ann Ronan Picture Library)

HARPER'S
FERRY.

MARYLAND HEIGHTS.

abolitionists with Republicans, and Republicans with the whole North. A wave of near hysteria swept the South, the greatest since Nat Turner's rebellion nearly 30 years earlier. Slave patrols were increased, volunteer military companies drilled more seriously, and talk of secession mushroomed. William L. Yancey of Alabama, one of the extreme advocates of Southern rights known as "fire-eaters," used heightened fears of Northern aggression to persuade his state's Democratic Party to instruct delegates to the 1860

LOUDON
HEIGHTS.

national convention to demand a plank calling for protection of slavery in all national territories. Other states of the Lower South (Florida, Georgia, Louisiana, Mississippi, South Carolina, and Texas) might be expected to follow Alabama's lead.

Election of Abraham Lincoln

The Democratic convention met in Charleston, South Carolina, in April 1860. A hotbed of secessionist sentiment, Charleston witnessed a contentious series of debates. Northern Democrats rejected a proposed platform that embodied Yancey's demands, several dozen Southern delegates walked out, and the convention adjourned without a nomination. The Democrats reconvened in Baltimore in mid-June, but failed again to agree on a platform. The regular Democrats, who comprised the majority of the party, ultimately nominated Senator Stephen A. Douglas of Illinois, a supporter of popular sovereignty, while Southern rights Democrats selected slaveholder John C. Breckinridge of Kentucky to bear their standard. As the election approached, the Democratic Party, long the dominant force in American national politics, lay in a shambles.

The Republicans had met in Chicago in mid-May and chosen Abraham Lincoln as their presidential candidate. A moderate, Lincoln fully supported a platform that would prohibit slavery in the territories but accept the institution in states where it already existed. The platform further called for measures that expressed the mercantile, pro-business, free labor sentiments of many in the North.

A fourth candidate, nominated by voters calling themselves the Constitutional Union Party, also entered the field. He was John Bell, an old Whig from the state of Tennessee. Hoping to avoid the poisonous influence of issues related to slavery, the Constitutional Union Party based its campaign strictly on support of the Constitution, the laws of the United States, and the sacred Union.

The election broke down into a contest between Lincoln and Douglas in the North and Breckinridge and Bell in the South. The Republicans did not appear on the ballot in ten slave states, and Bell and Breckinridge stood no chance of winning any of the free states. During the course of the campaign, many leaders from the Lower South threatened secession in the event of

"Without the shedding of blood there is no remission [of sin]" was John Brown's favorite biblical passage. It inspired him to seize the Federal Armory and Arsenal at Harpers Ferry in mid-October 1859. The attempt failed and Brown went to the gallows. (Ann Ronan Picture Library)

29

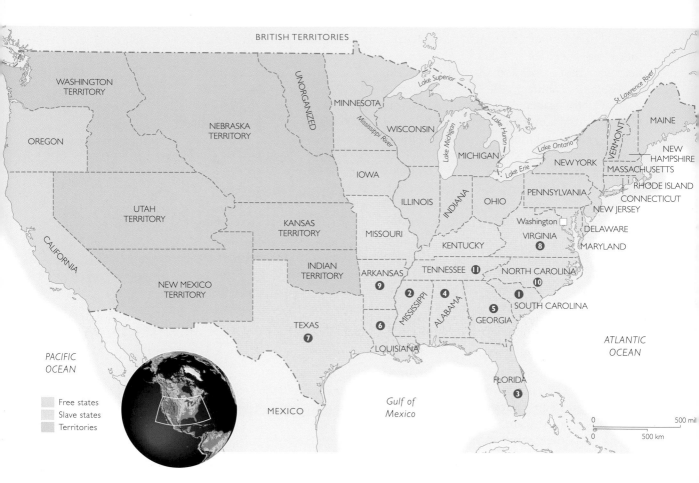

The United States in 1860. Of the 15 slave states, Missouri, Kentucky, Maryland, and Delaware remained loyal to the Union. Numbers in the 11 Confederate states indicate the order in which they seceded.

a Republican victory. Republicans responded that the South had postured about secession in the past, and they vowed not to give in to any Southern demands. Outpolled by nearly a million popular votes, Lincoln and the Republicans achieved a decisive victory in the Electoral College, taking 180 votes to the other three candidates' 123. Lincoln did especially well in the upper sections of the North, where antislavery sentiment was strongest, polling about 60 percent of the vote, but he managed a bare majority elsewhere in the North. Breckinridge carried the Lower South and four states of the Upper South. Bell won in Virginia, Kentucky, and Tennessee. Douglas showed poorly, winning just 12 electoral votes in New Jersey and Missouri – which showed how sectionalism had ravaged the proud old Democratic Party.

Secession begins

Contrary to those who believed they were bluffing, secessionists in the Lower South moved quickly after Lincoln's election. South Carolina led the way, calling a convention that voted unanimously on December 20, 1860 to leave the Union. Over the next six weeks, following debates of varying intensity between those for and against secession, Mississippi (January 9, 1861), Florida (January 10), Alabama (January 11), Georgia (January 19), Louisiana (January 26), and Texas (February 1) also seceded. The seven states created the Confederate States of America at a convention in Montgomery, Alabama, in February and March 1861. Adopting a constitution much like that of the United States but with explicit guarantees for slavery and stronger provisions for state powers, the founders of the new nation selected Jefferson Davis of Mississippi and Alexander H. Stephens of Georgia as President and Vice-President respectively.

Davis and Stephens emphasized the centrality of slavery to the process of secession. In a speech delivered on March 21, 1861, Stephens averred that the Confederate constitution "has put at rest *forever* all the agitating question relating to our peculiar institutions – African slavery as it exists among us – the proper *status* of the negro in our form of civilization. *This was the immediate cause of the late rupture and present revolution.*" Five weeks later, Davis observed in a message to the Confederate Congress that slave labor "was and is indispensable" to Southern economic progress. "With interests of such overwhelming magnitude imperiled," added Davis, "the people of the Southern States were driven by the conduct of the North to the adoption of some course of action to avert the danger with which they were openly menaced."

The secession of the Lower South represented a gambling effort to protect the institution of slavery in the face of a striking defeat at the polls. Many slaveholders looked down the road and saw ever-larger numbers of free states controlling both houses of Congress, Republican justices on the Supreme Court, and a national government willing to tolerate or even encourage agitators such as John Brown.

Fort Sumter

Democratic President James Buchanan remained in office nearly two and a half months after the secession of South Carolina. Eight slave states remained in

Abraham Lincoln was elected President of the Union on November 6, 1860; his first inauguration followed in March. It was after this electoral win that the Southern states began to secede. (Library of Congress)

Jefferson Davis believed ardently in slavery and Southern rights, but he was not a "fire-eater." These qualities, together with his stature as a prominent United States senator, made him an attractive figure to the delegates in Montgomery, Alabama. Although frequently compared unfavorably to Abraham Lincoln, Davis proved to be an able chief executive for the new slaveholding republic. He lacked Lincoln's genius with language, but dealt forcefully with the staggering challenge of simultaneously launching a nation and waging a war. (Gary Gallagher)

the Union, all of them disinclined to join their Lower South brethren. Buchanan refused to accept the legitimacy of secession, but also said he would do nothing to force the wayward states back into the Union. He watched helplessly as the Confederate states seized federal installations and property, prompting a furious barrage of criticism from Republicans. Many of Buchanan's critics overlooked the fact that Unionists in the Upper South typically made it clear that they would remain loyal only as long as the incoming Lincoln administration guaranteed the safety of slavery in states where it already existed and, more ominously, employed no coercion against the seceded states.

The question of coercion came into focus on Fort Sumter, a federal stronghold in Charleston harbor. In his inaugural address of March 4, 1861, Lincoln sought to place responsibility for the start of hostilities on Jefferson Davis and the Confederates. Lincoln announced his intention to "hold, occupy, and possess the property, and places belonging to the government, and to collect the duties and imposts; but beyond what may be necessary for these objects, there will be no invasion – no using of force against, or among the people anywhere." Turning directly to the question of responsibility for any aggressive moves, Lincoln added: "In *your* hands, my dissatisfied fellow countrymen, and not in *mine*, is the momentous issue of civil war. The government will not assail *you*. You can have no conflict, without yourselves being the aggressors." What Lincoln meant by "occupy and possess" was left deliberately murky – most federal holdings in the Confederate states had long since been lost. Lincoln mainly sought to gain time in the hope that Unionist sentiment would assert itself across the South and reverse the secessionist tide.

But time ran out. President Buchanan had previously refused to abandon Fort Sumter and sent a ship with reinforcements for the small garrison commanded by Major Robert Anderson. Southern batteries had fired on that vessel on January 9, 1861, prompting both sides to bluster and posture before drawing up short of open hostilities. Since that incident, Sumter had become a tremendously important symbol. Northerners saw it as the last significant installation in the Confederacy still in national hands, and Republicans adamantly refused to give it up. Confederates just as adamantly insisted that it stood on South Carolina soil and must be transferred to their control.

Major Anderson informed Lincoln in early March that the garrison's supplies would soon be exhausted. Convinced that the North would not tolerate loss of the fort, the President decided to send an unarmed ship with provisions. A full-scale effort to supply and reinforce the fort, Lincoln believed, would cast the North as the aggressor and almost certainly send the Upper South out of the Union. If Confederates fired on the unarmed ship, the North would appear as the injured party. Lincoln informed the governor of South Carolina that provisions were on the way and that the United States would not fire unless fired upon by Southern batteries around Charleston harbor.

Jefferson Davis and the Confederate cabinet faced a serious dilemma. They also hoped to avoid the label of aggressor, yet public opinion in the Confederacy overwhelmingly favored seizing Fort Sumter. Davis decided to request surrender of the fort before the relief vessel arrived. Anderson refused to capitulate, however, and shortly after 4.30am on April 12 Southern guns opened fire. Anderson and his men surrendered 36 hours later. They left the fort with colors flying and to the accompaniment of a 50-gun salute, climbed aboard ships and sailed for the North. The next day, Lincoln issued a proclamation that declared a state of insurrection and called out 75,000 militia from the Northern states.

War fever

War fever swept across the North and South. In four states of the Upper South, all of which had previously decided against secession, Lincoln's call for militia galvanized sentiment. Virginia left the Union on April 17, Arkansas on May 6, North Carolina on May 20, and Tennessee on June 8. The Confederacy soon moved its capital from Montgomery to Richmond, Virginia, and the loss to the Union of these four states virtually assured a long and difficult war. Virginia, Tennessee, and North Carolina ranked first, second, and third in white population among the Confederate states. They also possessed more than half of the new nation's manufacturing capacity, produced half its crops, contained nearly half its horses and mules and, most tellingly, would provide nearly 40 percent of the Confederacy's soldiers.

Eleven of the 15 slave states had reacted decisively to the seismic events that had rocked the nation between the election of 1860 and Lincoln's call for volunteers. In withdrawing from the Union, white Southerners set the stage for a war that would test the strength of the American republic and destroy for ever the social structure they had hoped to preserve.

WARRING SIDES

The North entered the war with seemingly decisive advantages in almost every measurable category. This has led to a common perception, often rooted in analysis that begins with the Confederate surrender at Appomattox and works

Confederates occupied Fort Sumter immediately after Robert Anderson's small garrison surrendered. In this engraving based on a photograph, the "stars and bars" float atop a makeshift flagpole attached to a derrick used for hoisting cannons to the fort's upper tier. Fort Sumter remained a defiant symbol of Confederate nationhood until the very last days of the conflict. (Gary Gallagher)

backward, that the South faced such overwhelming odds as to make victory impossible. A corollary to this idea suggests that the Confederacy managed to fight as long as it did only because of superior generalship and a gallant effort on the part of its common folk inside and outside the army. In fact, either side could have won the war, as an assessment of the contestants' strengths and weaknesses suggests.

Strengths of the North

The North did enjoy a number of advantages. The 1860 census placed the population of the United States at about 31,500,000. Of these, the 11 Confederate states had roughly about 9,100,000 – 5,450,000 of whom were white, 3,500,000 slaves and 130,000 free black people. The North boasted a population of about 22,400,000. However, a number of factors somewhat altered these basic figures. A number of white people in states remaining loyal to the Union – especially the slaveholding Border states of Missouri, Kentucky, Maryland, and Delaware – supported the Confederacy. Conversely, many white residents of the Confederacy – especially in the mountain areas of western Virginia, western North Carolina, eastern Tennessee and parts of Alabama, Texas, and Arkansas – remained loyal to the Union. Moreover, about 150,000 black men from the Confederate states eventually served in the Union army. That slaves did not carry arms for the Confederacy was offset by the fact that their labor freed a disproportionate number of white Southern males to fight. With all factors taken into consideration, the North enjoyed about a five-to-two edge in manpower. Roughly 2,100,000 men fought for the Union (around 50 percent of the military-age male population), while between 800,000 and 900,000 served in the Confederate army (nearly 80 percent of the 1860 military-age males).

Hundreds of thousands of men volunteered on each side during the first few months of the war, after which enlistment fell off sharply. Both sides eventually resorted to national conscription (the Confederates a year earlier than the United States), though some men continued to enlist freely until the end of the conflict. Little separated the two sides in terms of the quality and potential of their volunteers. Haphazard training left many thousands

of men woefully unprepared for the rigors of active campaigning. Units led by West Point graduates or other officers with military experience fared better than those commanded by volunteers whose enthusiasm far exceeded their expertise. Volunteer officers and enlisted men learned their craft together in camp, on the march, and in the unforgiving crucible of combat.

The North far outstripped the Confederacy in almost every economic category. A few comparative figures suggest the degree of Northern superiority. In 1860, there were 110,000 Northern manufacturing establishments employing 1,300,000 workers; in the Confederate states, just 18,000 establishments employing 110,000 workers. Northern railroad mileage totaled nearly 22,000 compared with just over 9,000 in the Confederacy, and the Northern roads generally were more modern and better maintained. The North produced 97 percent of the nation's firearms in 1860, held more than 80 percent of the national bank deposits, accounted for more than 85 percent of capital invested in industry, and manufactured 15 times as much iron as the Confederate states and virtually all of the nation's textiles (though these were heavily dependent on Southern cotton) and shoes and boots. There were 800,000 draft animals in the North compared with just 300,000 in the Confederate states – a tremendous logistical advantage in an era when armies moved by horse and mule power. In agricultural production, the two sides stood roughly at parity in terms of the ratio of production to overall population.

A third Northern advantage lay in the area of professional military forces. Lincoln's government began the conflict with an army and a navy, while the Davis administration had to build theirs from scratch. However, the United States army numbered only about 14,000 in the spring of 1861 (many Southern officers had resigned to support the Confederacy) and lay scattered across the country in small posts, many of them in the vast trans-Mississippi territories. Like the Confederacy, the North had to build huge armies of volunteers with no previous military experience. The North initially kept the regular units together rather than parceling out veterans among volunteer units, thus limiting the nation's soldiering expertise to a handful of regiments.

These members of the Sumter Light Guards of Americus, Georgia, were typical of the hundreds of thousands of men who joined infantry companies following the outbreak of war. The photographer posed them in Augusta, Georgia, in April 1861, while they were en route to join the Confederate army in Virginia. The Guards became Company K of the 4th Georgia Infantry and saw extensive action. (Library of Congress)

The United States navy began the conflict with only 42 ships in commission, most of which patrolled waters far from the American coast. In the spring of 1861, when Lincoln declared a blockade of the Confederacy, only three vessels were available for immediate service along the southern coast. Moreover, the United States navy was a deep-water force with little expertise in the type of coastal and offshore operations that would be required to suppress the Southern rebellion. Still, the navy must be reckoned a Northern advantage because the Confederacy possessed no naval force at the opening of the conflict and lacked the industrial base to construct modern warships.

Strengths of the South

The Confederacy also entered the war with decided advantages. Perhaps the greatest lay in requisite conditions for victory. The Confederacy had only to defend itself to achieve independence, whereas the North faced the prospect of invading the South, destroying its capacity to wage war, and crushing the Confederate people's will to resist. The Confederacy could win by default if the Northern people chose not to expend the human and material resources necessary to fight a war. If the North did commit to a major conflict, the Confederacy could triumph by prolonging the contest to a point where the Northern populace considered the effort too costly in lives and national treasure. The American War of Independence offered an obvious example of how the colonies (with vital assistance from France) had faced daunting material disadvantages against Great Britain, but had won by dragging the war out and exhausting the British commitment to win.

Defending home soil conveyed other advantages to the Confederates. Soldiers protecting hearth and family typically exhibit higher morale than invaders, and Confederates often had a better grasp of topography and local roads. Friendly civilians provided information to Southern officers, as when a local man helped Thomas J. "Stonewall" Jackson find a route that would allow his command to launch its famous flank attack at the Battle of Chancellorsville on May 2, 1863.

Geography promised an overall military advantage to the South. The Confederacy spread over more than

General Pierre Gustave Toutant Beauregard commanded the bombardment of Fort Sumter and became an early Confederate military idol. A native of Louisiana whose first language was French, he graduated second in the West Point class of 1838 and served with distinction in the war with Mexico. (Gary Gallagher)

GEN. P. G. T. BEAUREGARD.

750,000 square miles (1,942,500 sq km), much of it beyond the reach of good roads or rail lines. A 3,500-mile (5,630km) coastline contained nearly 200 harbors and navigable river mouths, and Texas shared an open border with Mexico – features that rendered a truly crippling Union blockade nearly impossible. In Virginia, the Shenandoah Valley offered a protected corridor through which Confederate armies could march to threaten Washington and other parts of the North, and several rivers that flowed generally west to east presented potential barriers to Union overland movements against the Southern capital. On the negative side for the Confederacy, the North could use these same rivers as waterborne avenues of advance.

Aware that material factors favored their opponents, many Confederates nevertheless understood their own strong points and appreciated the magnitude of the North's challenge. For example, George Wythe Randolph, a Virginian who served as a brigadier-general and Secretary of War, commented in the autumn of 1861 that Union forces "may overrun our frontier States and plunder our coast but, as for conquering us, the thing is an impossibility." Randolph believed that history offered no instance of "a people as numerous as we are inhabiting a country so extensive as ours being subjected if true to themselves." General P. G. T. Beauregard similarly remarked after the war that no "people ever warred for independence with more relative advantages than the Confederates," among which he noted geography well suited to blocking Union invasions. "If, as a military question, they [the Confederate people] must have failed," concluded Beauregard, "then no country must aim at freedom by means of war."

A persistent myth about the Civil War holds that the Confederacy enjoyed better generalship. Such a view makes sense if applied only to the Eastern Theater in the first two years of the war. The Army of Northern Virginia, under the guidance of Robert E. Lee and a talented cast of subordinates who included Stonewall Jackson and James Longstreet, won a series of dramatic victories in 1862–63 that created an aura of magnificent accomplishment. Overall, however, North and South drew on very similar pools of officers. West Pointers held most of the top positions in all Civil War armies, and they shared a common heritage. They took the same courses from the same professors at the academy, learned the same lessons in class and on battlefields in Mexico, and tended to subscribe to the same strategic and tactical theories. They understood the dominance of the tactical defensive because of the increased killing range of rifle muskets and the value of field fortifications. They therefore tried to avoid direct assaults by turning an enemy's flank (which often proved impossible). They also sought to operate on interior lines both strategically and tactically. Some generals proved more adept at translating these ideas into action, but most Civil War campaigns and battles were based on them. Apart from the West Pointers, both sides appointed some political generals and saw a few untutored officers achieve substantial fame.

The Confederacy seemed to have a clear advantage in their commander-in-chief. Jefferson Davis was a West Point graduate who had commanded a regiment in the war with Mexico and later served as Secretary of War. Abraham Lincoln's military credentials consisted of a short stint as a volunteer junior officer during the Black Hawk war of the 1830s. But Lincoln learned quickly, and he and Davis both exhibited a sound grasp of strategy as well as military theory and practice.

One variable could throw off the entire equation. The possibility of foreign intervention, particularly by Great Britain or France, received enormous attention from both governments and the Northern and Confederate people. The example of the American War of Independence once again stood out. Intervention along the lines of French participation in the Revolutionary War could yield profound military and economic consequences.

In summary, the North entered the war with a range of considerable advantages, but the Confederacy by no means faced a hopeless struggle. Other nations had won against longer odds. In the end, it would come down to which side mustered its human and material resources more effectively, found the better military and political leaders, and managed to sustain popular support for the war effort.

THE FIGHTING: FROM FIRST MANASSAS TO CHANCELLORSVILLE

After the secession of Virginia and the transfer of the Confederate capital to Richmond, both sides sought to mobilize men and resources and devise their military strategies. The North faced the prospect of mounting an active campaign to compel the Confederate states to return to the Union, while the Confederacy had the easier task of responding to Northern movements. If Lincoln and his government proved unable to launch a major offensive, the Confederacy would win its independence by default.

Volunteers poured into both armies. The Confederate Congress passed laws in March and May 1861 authorizing the enrollment of 500,000 men (from a pool of roughly one million military-age white males), and hundreds of thousands stepped forward. About half volunteered for three years and the rest for 12 months. The North drew roughly 700,000 men into its forces during the initial rush to the colors, most of them for three years' service.

The basic unit of organization on both sides was the company, which on paper contained 100 men. Ten companies made up a regiment, four or more regiments a brigade, two or more brigades a division, and two or more divisions a corps (the Confederacy did not officially have corps until the autumn of 1862). Companies tended to be raised from a single locality, and many regiments came from one town or county. Locally prominent individuals served as company and regimental officers. In terms of drill and discipline, regiments with a West Pointer, a graduate of military colleges such as the Virginia Military Institute, or a veteran of the war with Mexico typically progressed far more rapidly than those dependent entirely on civilian officers.

A native of Virginia who remained loyal to the Union, Winfield Scott ranks among the most accomplished soldiers in United States history. Scott's brilliant march from Vera Cruz to Mexico City in 1847 impressed the Duke of Wellington. "His campaign was unsurpassed in military annals," observed the Duke. "He is the greatest living soldier." (Gary Gallagher)

Irvin McDowell impressed many of his contemporaries more as a gourmand than as a military leader. Often tentative in the field, he acted more decisively at the table. A staff officer who dined with the general in 1861 described him as "so absorbed in the dishes before him that he had but little time for conversation … he gobbled the larger portion of every dish within reach" (Gary Gallagher)

A West Point classmate of Robert E. Lee, Joseph E. Johnston compiled a dazzling record during the war with Mexico and left the United States army in 1861 as a brigadier-general of staff. Always envious of his fellow Virginian Lee, Johnston garnered neither the public adulation nor the professional acclaim he believed his Confederate service deserved. (Gary Gallagher)

Strategic planning proceeded apace with volunteering. General-in-Chief Winfield Scott coordinated Union planning. Born in 1786, hero of the second war against Great Britain in 1812 and the war with Mexico in the 1840s, and the Whig Party's nominee for President in 1852, Scott was in the final stage of an illustrious career. He had cut an imposing figure as a younger man, a full 6ft 5in (2m) tall, immaculately dressed and of flawless military bearing. Ulysses S. Grant described him in the 1840s as, "the finest specimen of manhood my eyes had ever beheld, and the most to be envied." By 1861, Scott suffered from an array of ailments and weighed more than 300lb (135kg), but his mind remained strong and in April and May he formulated a long-range plan for defeating the Confederacy.

Known as the "Anaconda Plan" because it aimed to squeeze the Confederacy to death, Scott's strategic blueprint called for a vigorous movement down the Mississippi River by a naval flotilla and an army of 80,000. Union control of the Mississippi would split the Confederacy into two pieces, while other naval forces would blockade Southern ports and cut off supplies from the outside

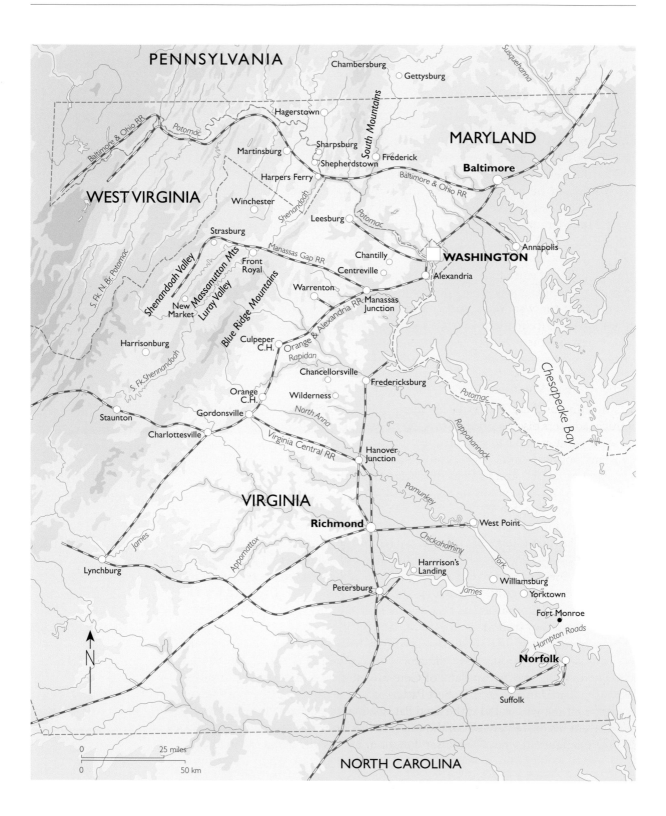

world. Should the Confederacy continue to resist after losing the Mississippi and its key ports, Scott believed a major invasion would be necessary. Such an operation would consume two or three years and require a force of up to 300,000 soldiers. Scott took a realistic view of campaigning with volunteer soldiers. The initial strike down the Mississippi could not begin earlier than the autumn of 1861, he insisted, due to the need to muster the recruits, train them for several months, and prepare the logistical effort.

The old general's planning, which in many respects anticipated the way the war would be conducted, soon ran foul of politics and public opinion. Scott worried that the Northern people would demand an immediate invasion of the Confederacy to extinguish the rebellion, and his fears soon proved to be well grounded. When the Confederacy moved its capital to Richmond, just 100 miles (160km) separated the two seats of government. Ignorant of the staggering task of equipping and training an army, Northerners clamored for an immediate campaign against Richmond. This began a pattern that held for the remainder of the war. Many in the North, both civilians and political leaders, exhibited a preoccupation with Richmond rooted in a belief that its capture would destroy the Confederacy. This preoccupation in turn helped make northern and central Virginia by far the bloodiest battleground of the war.

Battle of First Manassas or Bull Run

At a meeting on June 29, 1861, Abraham Lincoln listened to his military and political advisers discuss strategy. Brigadier-General Irvin McDowell, a 42-year-old West Pointer who had served his entire career in staff positions and enjoyed excellent political connections, commanded Union troops near Washington. He urged an attack against a Confederate force known to be in position 25 miles (40km) southwest of Washington near Manassas Junction. Scott opposed McDowell, arguing for "a war of large bodies" rather than "a little war by piece-meal." Lincoln and the cabinet supported McDowell, approving an advance to begin on July 9. Meanwhile, Northern newspapers called for a quick movement into Virginia. The *New York Tribune* trumpeted: "Forward to Richmond! Forward to Richmond! – The Rebel Congress must not be allowed to meet there on the 20th of July! By that date the place must be held by the National Army!" On July 16, a week past the date originally set, McDowell put his army in motion toward Manassas Junction.

Four armies played roles in the campaign. Near Winchester in the lower Shenandoah Valley,* Joseph E. Johnston commanded about 12,000 soldiers who guarded the north-west flank of Confederate forces in Virginia. Opposite Johnston, near Harpers Ferry, Robert Patterson led nearly 18,000 Union troops. A veteran of the war of 1812, the aged Patterson had orders to watch Johnston and prevent his movement out of the valley to link up with P. G. T. Beauregard's 20,000 Confederates near Manassas Junction. McDowell's 35,000 men, the

OPPOSITE PAGE:
Eastern Theater of Operations, May 1861–June 1863. Note: 50 counties of Western Virginia broke away from the rest of the state in 1861–1862 to form the new state of West Virginia, which was admitted to the Union in June 1863.

---

*   Rivers flow southwest to northeast in the valley, so the northern section is called the lower valley.

largest American field army to that point in history, marched to strike Beauregard before Johnston could reinforce him. The Confederate forces enjoyed the strategic advantage of the Manassas Gap Railroad, which ran from Beauregard's position to a point slightly south of Johnston's.

McDowell's green troops moved slowly toward Manassas, exhibiting lax discipline while taking two and a half days to cover a 20-mile (32km) march to Centreville. Confederate civilians alerted Beauregard to the Union advance, and on July 17 he sent a message asking Johnston to join him and help "crush the enemy." Johnston had become convinced that the timid Patterson, who imagined himself badly outnumbered and refused to take decisive action, posed no serious threat. When orders arrived from Richmond early on July 18 urging him to support Beauregard if practicable, Johnston began shifting his troops toward a loading point on the Manassas Gap Railroad. The bulk of Johnston's force made the trip to Manassas over the next 48 hours, completing the first large-scale movement of troops by rail in an active campaign.

After inconclusive skirmishing on July 18, Beauregard and McDowell each developed plans to hit the other's left flank on the 21st. Beauregard had placed the Confederates along the western bank of Bull Run, a sluggish stream to the north and west of Manassas Junction. Although outranked by Johnston, Beauregard maintained tactical control and planned to hold his left with a light force while massing his strength against McDowell's left. McDowell planned a demonstration against the Southern right as a strong flanking force crossed Bull Run in the vicinity of Sudley Ford and sought to roll up the enemy's line along the creek.

The Union soldiers, or Federals, struck first on July 21. After a fumbling advance toward Sudley Springs, Northern troops under General David Hunter collided with Colonel Nathan G. Evans's brigade of South Carolina and Louisiana troops. Reinforcements came forward to support both sides, and a bitter struggle for control of Matthews Hill, a prominent knob on the Manassas–Sudley road, raged between about 10.00 and 11.30am. The arrival of Union brigades under colonels William Tecumseh Sherman and Erasmus Keyes eventually compelled the Confederates to abandon Matthews Hill and take up a position south of the Warrenton Turnpike on Henry Hill.

Beauregard and Johnston had abandoned all thoughts of a blow against McDowell's left. As Federals gathered themselves along the Warrenton Turnpike for a final push against Henry Hill, Confederates sought to knit together a stable defensive line. Among the Southern troops going into position was a brigade of five Virginia regiments led by Brigadier-General Thomas Jonathan Jackson. This dour Virginian, a graduate of West Point in 1846, had fought with distinction in Mexico and later taught at the Virginia Military Institute. As Jackson's soldiers went into position on Henry Hill, Brigadier-General Barnard Bee of South Carolina, whose brigade had fought on Matthews Hill, remarked that the enemy "[is] beating us back." "Sir," replied Jackson, "we will give them the bayonet."

Fighting swayed back and forth across the crest and along the slopes of Henry Hill between about 1.30 and 3.30pm. Near the eye of the storm stood the home of Judith Carter Henry, an 85-year-old bedridden widow who became the only civilian killed during the battle (various accounts place the number of wounds she suffered as high as 13). Jackson's brigade played a major part in the action. At one point, General Bee approached a group of soldiers standing some distance behind Jackson's position and asked, "What regiment is this?" "Why General, don't you know your own men?" replied an officer. "This is what is left of the 4th Alabama." The men said they would follow Bee back into the fight, whereupon he pointed toward his left and shouted: "Yonder stands Jackson like a stone wall; let's go to his assistance." Thus was born the most famous soubriquet of the Civil War.

The climax on Henry Hill came at about 4.00pm. Confederate brigades under colonels Jubal A. Early, Arnold Elzey, and Joseph B. Kershaw had hurried forward from Manassas Junction. The weight of their bayonets turned the tide, propelling exhausted Federals away from the high ground. "We scared the enemy worse than we hurt him," remarked Early later. "He had been repulsed, not routed. When, however, the retreat began, it soon degenerated into a rout from the panic-stricken fears of the enemy's troops." Beauregard next ordered a general advance. Hungry, thirsty, hot, and without experience in such situations, thousands of Union troops decided they had seen enough. "The men seemed to be seized simultaneously by the conviction that it was no use to do anything more," observed a Northern officer, "and they might as well start home."

The tide of humanity sweeping away from the battlefield included a number of people who had ridden out from Washington to watch the action. Soldiers discarded their weapons and pressed eastward in the midst of cannons, caissons, and wagons, jostling for position among civilians in fine carriages. Congressman Alfred Ely of New York was taken prisoner, barely escaping death at the hands of an infuriated South Carolina colonel who tried to shoot him. "He's a member of Congress, God damn him," raged the colonel. "Came out here to see the fun! Came to see us whipped and killed! God damn him! If it was not for such as he there would be no war. They've made it and then come to gloat over it! God damn him. I'll show him."

The Confederates made only a feeble effort to harry the retreating Federals. Although this failure would prompt a great deal of criticism, the Southern army almost certainly lacked the discipline to mount an effective pursuit. Victory had left Johnston's and Beauregard's soldiers nearly as disorganized as their foe. By the end of the following day, McDowell's army had gathered itself near Washington. Any chance for a Confederate counterstroke had passed.

The Battle of First Manassas or Bull Run (Confederates called it the former, Federals the latter) set a new standard for bloodletting in American history. Union casualties totaled 2,896, and the Confederates lost 1,982 men. Carnage at later battles would dwarf these figures, but in July 1861 the respective

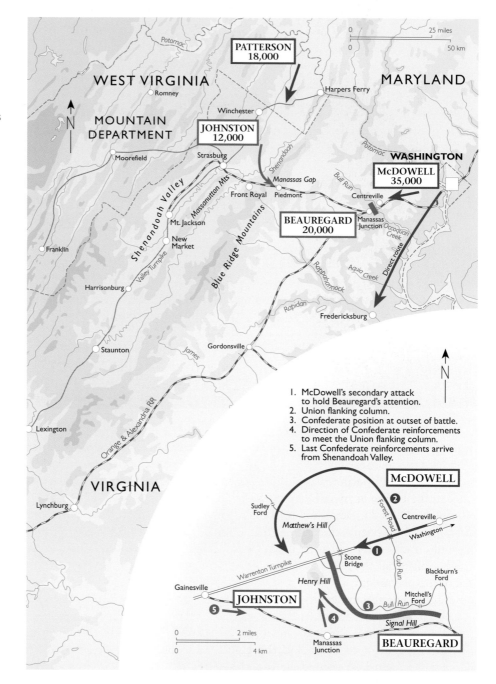

Campaign and Battle of First Manassas or Bull Run, July 16–21, 1861. The strategic situation showing J. E. Johnston's movement from the Shenandoah Valley to reinforce P. G. T. Beauregard at Manassas Junction.

1. McDowell's secondary attack to hold Beauregard's attention.
2. Union flanking column.
3. Confederate position at outset of battle.
4. Direction of Confederate reinforcements to meet the Union flanking column.
5. Last Confederate reinforcements arrive from Shenandoah Valley.

nations viewed the battle as a ghastly affair. It foreshadowed later engagements in a number of respects. Both commanding generals sought to avoid frontal assaults by launching flank movements. The side with interior lines held an advantage, as the Confederates used the Manassas Gap Railroad to effect a

strategic concentration and later shifted troops from their right to their left along shorter tactical lines. Finally, the battle demonstrated the difficulty of achieving a truly decisive tactical triumph. Although battered and forced to retreat, the Union army remained intact.

The battle had a major impact on the home fronts. Northerners abandoned all hopes of a speedy end to the war. Subduing the Rebels would be more difficult and costly than many had imagined. Confederates took heart, celebrating what they saw as the superiority of their fighting men. The battle remained prominent in the national consciousness for many months because no other major action occurred in Virginia until the spring of 1862.

Abraham Lincoln knew he had to replace McDowell after the ignominious result of First Bull Run. He selected 34-year-old Major-General George Brinton McClellan to command the Union army near Washington. A West Pointer who finished second in the class of 1846, McClellan had earned distinction as an engineer during the war with Mexico, studied European military thinking and policies in the 1850s, and retired from the army to go into business in 1857. He returned to military service in April 1861 and won some modest victories in western Virginia early in the war. A man of medium height with large shoulders and a barrel chest, he dressed carefully and

British artist Frank Vizetelly witnessed the Union retreat at First Manassas, making this sketch for the *Illustrated London News*. "The terror-stricken soldiers threw away their arms and accoutrements," wrote Vizetelly disdainfully, "herding along like a panic-stricken flock of sheep, with no order whatever in their flight. Those who had been fortunate enough to get placed in the baggage-waggons thrust back others with their bayonets and musket-stocks." (Mary Evans Picture Library)

Major-General George B. McClellan won the hearts of soldiers in the Army of the Potomac, but he lacked the stomach for the harsher aspects of war. "I am tired of the sickening sight of the battlefield," he wrote to his wife following his first real engagement at Seven Pines, "with its mangled corpses & poor suffering wounded! Victory has no charms for me when purchased at such cost." (Gary Gallagher)

presented a thoroughly professional appearance. The Northern press lauded him as a brilliant commander, which fed his considerable ego and led him to believe no one else could save the republic.

As a Democrat, McClellan opposed much of the Republican Party's legislative agenda and reserved some of his harshest criticism for Radical Republicans and abolitionists who sought to turn the war into a crusade against slavery. McClellan joined virtually all other Northern Democrats (and most Republicans as well) in defining the conflict as a struggle to restore the Union rather than to free slaves. A member of his staff recalled McClellan's saying that anyone who expected him to wage war against the South "to *free the slaves* … would be mistaken, for he would not do it."

McClellan quickly revealed a deep contempt for most of his civilian and military superiors. He complained to his wife that General-in-Chief Scott got in his way. He called three members of the President's cabinet "an incompetent little puppy," a "garrulous old woman," and "an old fool." He dismissed Lincoln as "an idiot" and a "well-meaning baboon." On one occasion, he returned home to find that Lincoln and Secretary of State William Henry Seward had been waiting to see him. The general proceeded to go upstairs, sending word 30 minutes later that he had gone to bed and the two could come back another time.

Thomas Jonathan Jackson in November 1862, in a photograph his wife considered an excellent likeness. During a two-month visit to the Confederacy in 1862, British traveler W. C. Corsan heard stories about the Presbyterian Jackson that reminded him of "Cromwell, or some old Covenanter. The same silent, brooding self reliance – the same iron will – the same tenacity of purpose … all surrounded and tinged by the same almost fanatical mingling of incessant devotions with arduous duties." (Gary Gallagher)

Obnoxious personal qualities did not prevent McClellan from turning McDowell's demoralized soldiers into a formidable force. He christened them the Army of the Potomac in August 1861, having expanded their number to more than 100,000, put them through a strict regimen of drill and instilled in them a strong sense of pride. Soldiers and officers alike responded with an outpouring of affection that made McClellan by far the most popular of all the generals who fought with the army.

Promotion came McClellan's way in early November 1861. A combination of infirmities and aggravation with McClellan prompted Winfield Scott to resign on November 1. "Little Mac," as the men called him, took Scott's place and added overall planning responsibility to his role as field commander of the Union's largest army. When Lincoln cautioned the general about juggling the many responsibilities of his two positions, McClellan answered, "I can do it all."

What he proved unwilling to do was move against Joseph E. Johnston's 45,000 Confederates in northern Virginia. McClellan grotesquely overestimated Johnston's strength, insisting that he needed 200,000 men to launch an offensive. To the end of his time in field command, McClellan inflated Southern numbers and devised innumerable excuses for not advancing. In truth, he lacked the mental or moral courage to risk his great army in a major contest with the Rebels. He always hedged his bets, refused to take chances, sought to have every detail perfect before engaging in battle, and thus cannot be counted among the war's leading generals.

Lincoln and McClellan engaged in a struggle of wills throughout the late summer and autumn of 1861. Under pressure from Republican politicians and newspaper editors to capture Richmond, the President pressed McClellan to no avail. Months slipped by with no action. McClellan surrounded himself with officers who shared his conservative political beliefs, triggering dark rumors in Washington that he and his subordinates did not want to smite the enemy.

Confederate President Jefferson Davis suffered through a similarly trying period with Joseph Johnston. The two men quarreled bitterly after Johnston learned in September 1861 that he would be the fourth-ranking full general in the Confederacy. Johnston insisted that he should be the Confederacy's senior commander, engaging in an acrimonious correspondence that highlighted pettiness on both his and Davis's parts. During the ensuing months, Johnston, like McClellan, constantly requested more men and sniped at his civilian superiors.

A diplomatic crisis erupted as Lincoln and Davis labored to manage their principal commanders in Virginia. On November 8, Captain Charles Wilkes of the USS *San Jacinto* stopped the British vessel *Trent* and removed James Mason and John Slidell, a pair of Confederate diplomats bound for London and Paris respectively. The Northern public lauded Wilkes's action, but the British government issued a strongly worded protest to the United States, demanded an apology and took steps to strengthen its military presence in Canada and the North Atlantic. After several tense weeks, during which Lincoln sought to find a graceful way to defuse the issue, the United States freed Mason and Slidell to travel to their original destinations. Anglo-American diplomatic relations had survived an initial stressful test.

The winter of 1861–62 passed without significant action in Virginia. McClellan devised a plan to turn Johnston's flank by moving his army by ship to the Rappahannock River and taking Fredericksburg. That would isolate Johnston in northern Virginia, forcing him to attack McClellan in order to reach Richmond. McClellan tarried, however, and a frustrated Lincoln finally ordered him to commence his campaign on February 22, 1862 – George Washington's birthday. When that date came and went without a movement and the first days of March slipped by, Lincoln ended McClellan's stint as general-in-chief.

Shenandoah Valley campaign

Now just commander of the Army of the Potomac, Little Mac changed his plans when word arrived that Johnston had retreated to the Rappahannock line. On March 17, the Army of the Potomac began a larger turning movement toward Fort Monroe, situated at the tip of the finger of land between the York and James Rivers known as the Peninsula. By the end of April, Confederate planners faced a range of threats in Virginia: the bulk of the Army of the Potomac lay on the lower Peninsula; another 30,000 Federals under Irvin McDowell near Fredericksburg; 15,000 under Nathaniel P. Banks in the lower Shenandoah Valley, and nearly 10,000 under John C. Fremont in the Allegheny Mountains west of the valley.

The Confederates responded by concentrating forces near Richmond and mounting a diversion in the Shenandoah Valley. Johnston fell back to the Peninsula, where he contested a slow Union advance toward the capital. As the forces under Johnston and McClellan sought to gain an advantage over each other, the ironclad CSS *Virginia* (popularly called the "Merrimac") was scuttled on May 11. The *Virginia* had raised hopes in many a Confederate breast after its historic victories over several wooden warships on March 8, before fighting the Union ironclad USS *Monitor* to a draw at Hampton Roads the next day. "No one event of the war," remarked Confederate ordnance chief Josiah Gorgas from his post in Richmond, "created such a profound sensation as the destruction of this noble ship." Heavy rains drenched the Peninsula during May, adding to Confederate gloom over the *Virginia* and affording McClellan a good excuse for making little headway. The end of the month found the two forces – more than 100,000 Federals and about 70,000 Confederates – arrayed opposite one another along the Chickahominy River just east of Richmond.

By that time, the first major Southern response to McClellan's Peninsula offensive had come in the Shenandoah Valley. General Robert E. Lee, acting as principal military adviser to Jefferson Davis, proposed to reinforce Stonewall Jackson's small force in the valley with Richard S. Ewell's division, bringing it to about 17,500 men. He wished for Jackson to pin down all the troops belonging to Banks and Fremont so that they could not join in the advance against Richmond. Jackson had gained attention with an offensive movement in late March that resulted in a sharp action at First Kernstown. Although a tactical defeat, that fight had prompted the Federals to hold Banks and Fremont in the valley, which in turn set up Jackson's subsequent campaign.

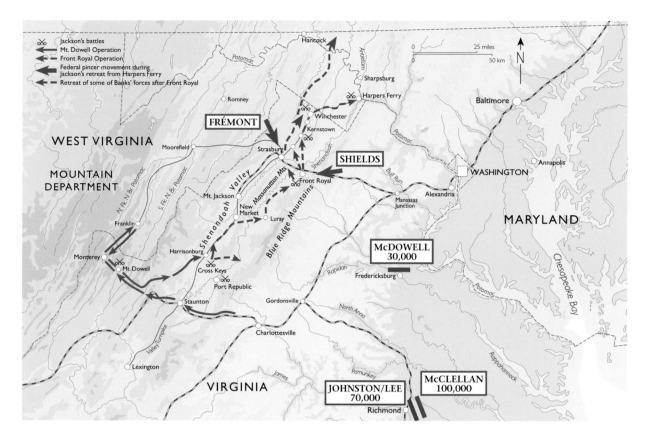

Jackson's Shenandoah Valley campaign, March–June 1862.

Jackson stands as one of the most arresting military figures in United States history. Thirty-eight years old in May 1862, he was a devout Presbyterian of odd personal attitudes and characteristics. A British traveler in the Confederacy wrote in 1863, "I heard many anecdotes of the late 'Stonewall Jackson.' When he left the US service he was under the impression that one of his legs was shorter than the other; and afterward his idea was that he only perspired on one side, and that it was necessary to keep the arm and leg of the other side in constant motion in order to preserve circulation." Secretive, stern, and unyielding, Jackson took a very hard view of war. Above all, he fought aggressively, moved rapidly (his infantry became known as "foot cavalry"), and pressed his soldiers to the limit in search of decisive victories.

The outline of Jackson's valley campaign may be sketched quickly. He took part of his force westward from Staunton to strike the advance element of Fremont's force under Robert H. Milroy at McDowell on May 8, 1862. With these Federals retreating into the wilds of the western Virginia Alleghenies after a largely inconclusive engagement, Jackson hastened back to the valley. He then moved north toward New Market, while Ewell's division paralleled his march to the east in the Luray Valley (the Massanutten Range divides the Shenandoah Valley into western and eastern sections for 50 miles (80km) between Harrisonburg on the south and Strasburg on the north; the Luray or Page Valley constitutes the eastern portion of the valley). Crossing to the Luray Valley at New Market Gap, Jackson joined Ewell and captured a Federal garrison at Front Royal on May 23, defeated Banks in the Battle of First Winchester on May 25, and pursued retreating Federals all the way to the Potomac River.

Jackson had placed himself in an exposed position in the extreme northern reaches of the valley, and the Federals planned a three-pronged offensive designed to cut him off north of Strasburg. Fremont would march east out of the Alleghenies, a division under James Shields would move west from Front Royal, and Banks would pursue southward from near Harpers Ferry. Jackson responded by driving his men to the limit. Aided by incredibly lethargic movement on the part of the Federals, he escaped the trap and marched southward to the southern end of the Massanutten Range near Harrisonburg. There he turned on his pursuers, defeating Fremont at Cross Keys on June 8 and Shields at Port Republic on June 9.

In a whirlwind of action, Jackson's Army of the Valley had marched more than 350 miles (560km), won a series of small battles, immobilized 60,000 Union troops, inflicted twice as many casualties as it suffered, and captured a great quantity of military supplies. After the twin victories on June 8–9, the Federals retreated northward down the valley, and Jackson joined the Confederate forces defending Richmond.

Perhaps most importantly, Jackson's campaign inspirited a Confederate populace starved for good news from the battlefield. A North Carolina woman named Catherine Ann Devereux Edmondston wrote a typical reaction, in which she pointedly contrasted Jackson's accomplishment with Joseph Johnston's performance. "Jackson has gained another victory in the Valley of Va.," she wrote on June 11. "He has beaten Shields & holds Fremont in check, who fears to attack him singly… He is the only one of our generals who gives the enemy no rest, no time to entrench themselves. Matters before Richmond look gloomy to us outsiders. McClellan advances, entrenching as he comes. Why do we allow it?"

The situation at Richmond did look serious for Confederates in early June. Relatively inactive during much of Jackson's Valley campaign, the armies under McClellan and Johnston had fought their first major battle on May 31 and June 1 at Seven Pines (also called Fair Oaks). Johnston had retreated as far as he could without reaching the defensive works of Richmond. Faced with the prospect of a siege that would inevitably favor McClellan, he attacked on the 31st. Wretched coordination, a poor grasp of local terrain, and other factors plagued the Southern army in a battle that ended in tactical stalemate. More than 6,000 Confederates and 5,000 Federals fell in the two days, most notably Johnston, who suffered a severe chest wound. On June 1, Jefferson Davis named Robert E. Lee to succeed Johnston. Thus did the man who would become the greatest Confederate general step into the limelight.

Lee possessed impeccable credentials. Fifty-five years old, he belonged to one of the nation's first families and had compiled an exceptional record at West Point, as an engineer in the antebellum years and as a member of Winfield Scott's staff in Mexico. Superintendent at West Point for several years in the 1850s, Lee followed his native Virginia out of the Union in April 1861. He began the war as a figure from whom much was expected, before plummeting in the public's estimation following his activities in western Virginia and along the South Atlantic coast during the autumn and winter of 1861–62 – service that lacked what the Confederate people considered a suitable offensive component. Diarist Catherine Edmondston responded unfavorably to reports of Lee's assuming command of the army after Seven Pines. In words echoed in many quarters across the Confederacy, Edmondston stated, "I do not much like him, he 'falls back' too much. He failed in Western Va owing, it was said, to the weather, has done little in the eyes of outsiders in S C. His nick name last summer was '*old-stick-in-the-mud*' … pray God he may not fulfil the whole of his name." Armistead L. Long, who served on Lee's staff during the war, recalled the winter of 1861–62 as a time when the press and public were "clamorous" against his superior, and Edward Porter Alexander, another staff member in June 1862, remembered that when Lee assumed command "some of the newspapers – particularly the Richmond *Examiner* – pitched into him with extraordinary virulence," insisting that "henceforth our army would never be allowed to fight."

Fitz John Porter, whose Fifth Corps bore the brunt of Union fighting at Mechanicsville, Gaines's Mill, and Malvern Hill. A conservative Democrat and supporter of McClellan, Porter attracted the ire of congressional Republicans. Court-martialed for his role in the Second Manassas campaign, he was stripped of command and dismissed from the army in January 1863. Sixteen years later, a military board cleared him of all charges. (Gary Gallagher)

The Seven Days battles

The next five weeks proved Lee's critics wrong. No general exhibited more daring than the new Southern commander, who believed the Confederacy could counter Northern numbers only by seizing and holding the initiative. He spent June preparing for a supreme effort against McClellan. When Jackson's Valley troops and other reinforcements arrived, Lee's army, at 90,000 strong, would be the largest ever fielded by the South. By the last week of June, the Army of the Potomac lay astride the Chickahominy, two-thirds south of the river and one third north of it. Lee hoped to crush the portion north of the river then turn against the rest. Confederates repulsed a strong Union reconnaissance against their left on June 25, opening what became known as the Seven Days battles and setting the stage for Lee's offensive.

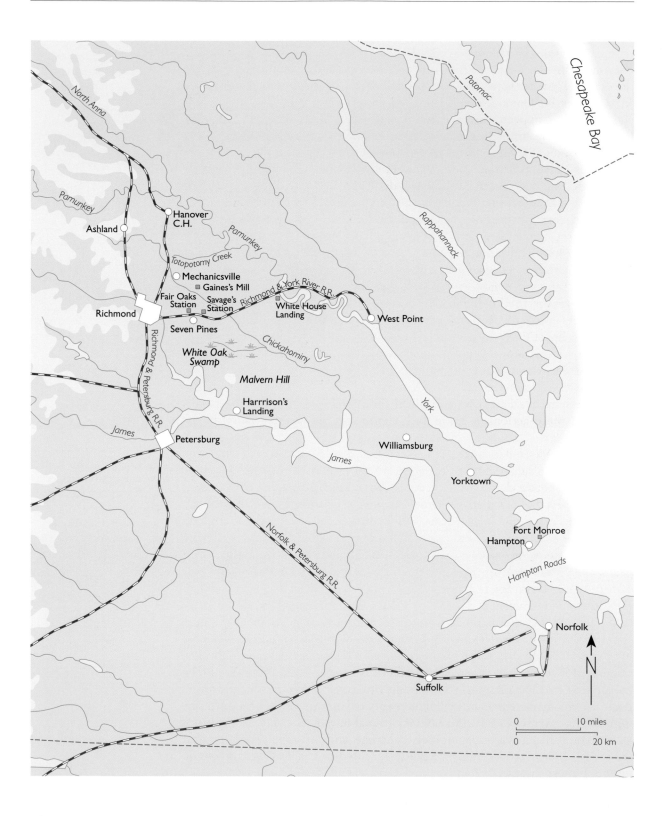

Chesapeake Bay

Potomac

North Anna

Pamunkey

Rappahannock

Ashland

Hanover C.H.

Pamunkey

Totopotomy Creek

Mechanicsville

Gaines's Mill

Richmond & York River R.R.

Fair Oaks Station

Savage's Station

White House Landing

West Point

Richmond

Seven Pines

White Oak Swamp

Chickahominy

Malvern Hill

York

Harrrison's Landing

Richmond & Petersburg R.R.

James

Williamsburg

Petersburg

James

Yorktown

Norfolk & Petersburg R.R.

Fort Monroe

Hampton

Hampton Roads

Norfolk

N

Suffolk

0   10 miles

0   20 km

Heavy fighting began on June 26, 1862 at the Battle of Mechanicsville and continued for the next six days. Lee consistently acted as the aggressor, but never managed to land a decisive blow. At Mechanicsville, he expected Jackson to strike Union General Fitz John Porter's right flank. The hero of the Valley failed to appear in time, however, and A. P. Hill's Confederate division launched a futile frontal assault about mid-afternoon. Porter retreated to a strong position at Gaines's Mill, where Lee attacked again on the 27th. Once again Jackson stumbled, as more than 50,000 Confederates mounted savage attacks along a wide front. Late in the day, John Bell Hood's Texas Brigade spearheaded an effort that broke Porter's lines and pushed the Federals across the Chickahominy to rejoin the bulk of McClellan's army. Jackson's poor performance, most often attributed to exhaustion verging on numbness, joined poor staff work and other factors in allowing Porter's exposed portion of McClellan's army to escape.

In the wake of Gaines's Mill, McClellan changed his base from the Pamunkey River to the James River, where Northern naval power could support the Army of the Potomac. Lee followed the retreating McClellan, who insisted that the Rebels badly outnumbered his army. He sought to inflict a crippling blow as the Federals retreated southward across the Peninsula. After heavy skirmishing on June 28, the Confederates launched ineffectual attacks on the 29th at Savage's Station and far heavier ones at Glendale (also known as Frayser's Farm) on the 30th. Stonewall Jackson played virtually no role in these actions, as time and again the Confederates failed to act in concert.

By July 1, McClellan stood at Malvern Hill, a splendid defensive position overlooking the James. Lee resorted to unimaginative frontal assaults that afternoon. Whether driven by vexation at lost opportunities or by his natural combativeness, he had made one of his poorest tactical decisions. Southern division commander Daniel Harvey Hill said of the action on July 1, "It was not war, it was murder." As evening fell, more than 5,000 Confederate casualties littered the slopes of Malvern Hill. Some of McClellan's officers urged a counterattack against the obviously battered enemy; however, Little Mac retreated down the James to Harrison's Landing, where he awaited Lee's next move and issued endless requests for more men and supplies.

Casualties for the entire Peninsula campaign exceeded 50,000, more than 36,000 of whom had fallen during the Seven Days. Lee's losses from Mechanicsville to Malvern Hill exceeded 20,000 killed, wounded, and missing, while McClellan's surpassed 16,000. Gaines's Mill, where combined losses exceeded 15,000, marked the point of greatest slaughter. Thousands of dead and maimed soldiers brought the reality of war to Richmond's residents. One woman wrote that, "death held a carnival in our city. The weather was excessively hot. It was midsummer, gangrene and erysipelas attacked the wounded, and those who might have been cured of their wounds were cut down by these diseases."

OPPOSITE PAGE:
Area of operations for the Peninsula campaign, April–July 1862.

The campaign's importance extended far beyond setting a new standard of carnage in Virginia; Lee had seized the initiative, dramatically altering the strategic picture by dictating the action to a compliant McClellan. Lee's first effort in field command lacked tactical polish, but nevertheless generated immense dividends. The Seven Days saved Richmond and inspirited a Confederate people buffeted by dismal military news from other theaters. On the Union side, the campaign dampened expectations of victory that had mounted steadily as Northern armies in Tennessee and along the Mississippi River won a string of successes. McClellan's failure also exacerbated Northern political divisions, clearing the way for Republicans to implement harsher policies that would strike at slavery and other Rebel property. The end of the rebellion had seemed to be in sight when McClellan prepared to march up the Peninsula; after Malvern Hill, only the most obtuse observers failed to see that the war would continue in a more all-encompassing manner. "We have been and are in a depressed, dismal, asthenic state of anxiety and irritability," wrote a perceptive New Yorker after McClellan's retreat. "The cause of the country does not seem to be thriving just now."

The campaign underscored the degree to which events in the Virginia Theater dominated perceptions about the war's progress. Despite enormous Northern achievement in the western campaigns, most people North and South, as well as observers in Britain and France, looked to Virginia. Lincoln spoke to this phenomenon in a famous letter to a French diplomat in early August, complaining that "it seems unreasonable that a series of successes, extending through half-a-year, and clearing more than a hundred thousand square miles of country, should help us so little, while a single half-defeat should hurt us so much." Lincoln did not exaggerate the impact of McClellan's failure. However, taken overall, the ramifications were such that the Richmond campaign must be reckoned one of the turning points of the war.

Yet victory in the Seven Days battles had not removed the Union threat from Virginia. McClellan's host remained just a few miles below Richmond, and Major-General John Pope commanded the newly consolidated troops of Fremont, Banks, and McDowell in north-central Virginia. Denominated the Army of Virginia, Pope's force could operate against the railroads between Warrenton and Gordonsville, thus endangering the flow of supplies from the Shenandoah Valley to Richmond and imperiling Lee's western flank.

Pope descended from a prominent family in Kentucky, had collateral ties to George Washington and was connected by marriage to Mrs Lincoln's family. A West Pointer and veteran of the war with Mexico, he had won victories along the Mississippi River earlier in 1862. Unlike most senior officers in McClellan's army, Pope agreed with Republicans who sought to wage a tougher war against the Rebels. Pope promised to hang guerrillas, arrest citizens who aided them, confiscate all Rebel property, and displace civilians who would not take the oath of allegiance to the United States. Although he neither engaged in mass hangings nor drove many people from their homes, his soldiers did seize or

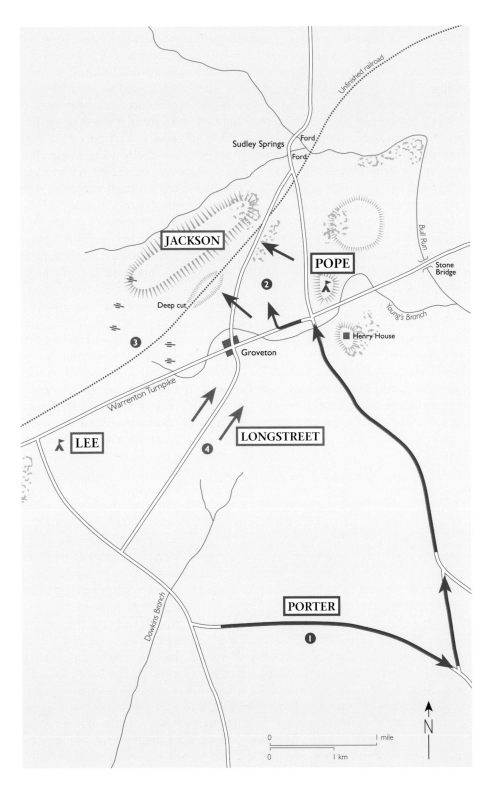

Battle of Second Manassas or Bull Run, August 30, 1862.

destroy an enormous amount of property. Pope also manifested personal arrogance in issuing several bombastic statements about how he would thrash Lee's army. His actions and pronouncements earned the enmity of white Southerners and provoked Lee to write in late July that he hoped to destroy "the miscreant Pope."

Pope rather than McClellan emerged as Lee's principal Union opponent in the next campaign. This stemmed partly from Lee and Jefferson Davis's determination to protect their fragile rail links to the Shenandoah Valley. But McClellan's behavior also figured in the equation. Little Mac showed no inclination to resume active operations against Richmond, preferring to whine about reinforcements and lecture Lincoln on the need to refrain from seizing Rebel property or forcing emancipation on the South. A visit to McClellan's headquarters at Harrison's Landing on July 8–9 convinced Lincoln that he could expect no aggressive action in that arena. Later that month, McClellan received orders to leave the Peninsula and unite in northern Virginia with Pope's 55,000 men.

Lee kept an eye on both Pope and McClellan throughout a tense July. During this period, he reorganized his Army of Northern Virginia, dividing the infantry into two wings commanded by Stonewall Jackson and Major-General James Longstreet. He sent Jackson and 24,000 troops to Gordonsville during July, granting his lieutenant wide latitude in responding to any movement from Pope. On August 9, Jackson defeated part of the Army of Virginia in the Battle of Cedar Mountain, fought north of Culpeper between the Rapidan and Rappahannock Rivers. Shortly thereafter, having decided that McClellan was withdrawing from the Peninsula, Lee ordered Longstreet's wing to join

James Longstreet committed nearly 30,000 Confederates to his impressive counterattack against the Army of Virginia on the afternoon of August 30. His wing lost more men in a few hours of hard combat than Jackson's had in three days of fighting. This postwar painting shows Union officers trying to form a line of battle to stem the Confederate tide. (Gary Gallagher)

Jackson's near Gordonsville. The Confederate chieftain hoped to defeat the Army of Virginia before it could unite with McClellan's Army of the Potomac. A period of maneuvering and probing along the Rappahannock River ensued, during which Lee and Pope sought to catch each other off guard.

Battle of Second Manassas or Bull Run

Lee took control of the campaign in late August 1862 when he ordered Jackson to make a sweeping march around Pope's right flank. On August 25–27, Jackson's infantry covered 56 miles (90km) in brutal heat and captured Pope's massive supply base at Manassas Junction. Lee's army now offered a tempting target, with its two main pieces separated by Pope's army. Pope reacted to the threat in his rear by concentrating against Jackson, who formed a defensive line near the Warrenton Turnpike on the battlefield of First Manassas. The initial clash of the Battle of Second Manassas or Bull Run took place on August 28 at the Brawner Farm. There the Stonewall Brigade and the Union's Iron Brigade engaged in a famous stand-up fight at a distance of less than 100 yards (92m). A series of Union assaults the next day pressed Jackson's defenders, whose line ran along an unfinished railroad bed, to the limit. More than once the attackers broke through, only to be driven back by reinforcements. In the course of the long day's action, Jackson grimly told A. P. Hill, "If you are attacked again, you will beat the enemy back."

While Jackson's troops tenaciously held their ground, Lee and Longstreet arrived with the rest of the Army of Northern Virginia. Longstreet's left joined Jackson's right, and by about noon the whole line approximated an open V – Jackson's men facing generally southeast and Longstreet's nearly due east. Lee initially wanted Longstreet to attack, but consented to postponements when intelligence suggested a Union movement toward the Southern right. Other than a brief clash at about 7.00pm, Longstreet's soldiers remained inactive on the 29th.

Pope planned additional attacks against Jackson on August 30. Despite the protestations of Fitz John Porter and others, he clung to the idea that Longstreet's wing had not reached the field and insisted that a final push would drive Jackson away. After a series of delays, the Federals advanced at about 3.00pm. Jackson's weary soldiers, ably supported by Southern artillery that fired directly into the Union flank, repulsed the attackers. At about 4.00pm, Longstreet launched a spectacular counterstroke that yielded a second stunning Confederate success at Manassas. Tenacious Union units, some of them fighting on Henry Hill, helped slow Longstreet's attackers long enough for Pope to organize an effective withdrawal. One Confederate soldier graphically described firing at a group of retreating Federals "so near and so thick" that "every shot took effect… We shot into this mass as fast as we could load until our guns got so hot we had at times to wait for them to cool." A few days after the battle, a Union survivor described his experience amid the chaos of Longstreet's attack. "I saw the men dropping on all sides," he wrote, "canteens struck and flying to pieces, haversacks cut off, rifles knocked to pieces, it was a perfect hail of bullets. I was expecting to get it every second, but on, on, I went, the balls hissing by my head."

Pope withdrew to Washington in good order, blocking a Confederate blow at Chantilly on September 1 and reaching the city's formidable entrenchments the next day. His successful escape did little to soften the impact of another Federal defeat. The campaign had cost Pope 16,000 casualties out of approximately 75,000 engaged (some units from the Army of the Potomac had reinforced the Army of Virginia). Lee lost about 9,200 out of 50,000 engaged. Lee's bold decision to split his army, swift marching, and hard fighting had paid off for the Confederates. Pope had proved to be aggressive but inept, and Lincoln removed him from command on September 2. For the second time in 13 months, George B. McClellan stepped forward to restore order following a Northern defeat in Virginia.

Lee lost little time in preparing his next movement. He had accomplished a remarkable strategic reorientation in Virginia, shifting the military frontier from Richmond to the banks of the Potomac River. Seeking to maintain the strategic initiative and improve his logistical situation, he decided to take the war across the Potomac into the United States. He knew the Army of Northern Virginia had suffered enormously during the preceding ten weeks. As one veteran wrote, by early September the army's "divisions had sunk to little more than brigades, & brigades nearly to regiments." Indeed, the average Southern regiment would number fewer than 175 men during the upcoming campaign. Still, Lee wrote to Jefferson Davis on September 3 that he considered it "to be the most propitious time since the commencement of the war for the Confederate Army to enter Maryland."

Lee's invasion of Maryland represented the final act in a three-part drama that opened at the Seven Days, continued with the Battle of Second Manassas, and closed with the fearful slaughter at Antietam. The entire campaign from June to September dramatically reoriented the war in the Eastern Theater. *Harper's Weekly* depicted Confederates crossing the Potomac into Maryland on a brightly moonlit night. (Gary Gallagher)

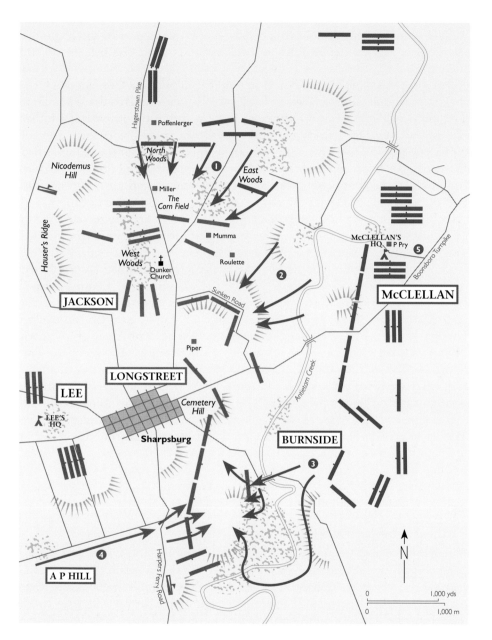

Battle of Antietam, opposing forces at daybreak, September 17, 1862.

Several factors influenced Lee. Logistically, he wanted to collect food and forage in Maryland and Pennsylvania, remaining north long enough to allow Virginia farmers to gather their autumn harvest. The enemy would have to follow him into Maryland, thus sparing Richmond from a fresh Federal advance. His presence above the Potomac during the North's autumn elections also might hurt the Republicans and bolster advocates of peace. Moreover, if he stayed north until late autumn, he might forestall another Union offensive in

Virginia until the spring of 1863. Finally, his army's presence might inspire slaveholding Marylanders to flock to the Confederate colors. Although Lee did not expect help from abroad, a victory north of the Potomac could prove decisive in persuading leaders in London and Paris to extend formal recognition to the Confederacy. Prime Minister Palmerston had interpreted the Seven Days as evidence of impending Confederate success, suggesting to the Queen on August 6 that Britain consider proposing an armistice in October.

The Army of Northern Virginia began crossing the Potomac on September 4, 1862, and events unfolded rapidly over the next two weeks. Lee divided his army while at Frederick, Maryland, on September 9. He assigned the majority of it to Stonewall Jackson, who was to capture Harpers Ferry (control of that point would give Lee a secure supply line to the lower Shenandoah Valley) while Longstreet and the rest of the army marched toward Hagerstown. McClellan had followed cautiously. Lincoln saw Lee's invasion as an opportunity to punish the Rebels. On September 12, his greatest fear was that the Rebels would escape to Virginia unscathed. Late that afternoon the President urged McClellan not to let Lee "get off without being hurt."

The next day, in an incredible stroke of luck, Union soldiers rummaging through abandoned Confederate camps at Frederick found a copy of Lee's operational blueprint. The document quickly made its way to Union headquarters, where McClellan instantly grasped its importance. Turning to a subordinate, he said, "Here is a paper with which if I cannot whip Bobbie Lee, I will be willing to go home." But precious hours ticked by before the Federal chief bestirred himself to press the invaders. While Jackson laid siege to Harpers Ferry on September 14, McClellan's troops forced Lee's defenders out of the gaps of South Mountain in sharp fighting. Lee briefly thought about abandoning Maryland, then decided to concentrate his army near Sharpsburg. Two days passed with little action on Lee's and McClellan's front, but Harpers Ferry and its 12,000-man garrison surrendered on the 15th, freeing Jackson to hasten to Lee's support.

Battle of Antietam or Sharpsburg

The climactic clash came on September 17 at the Battle of Antietam (called Sharpsburg by most Confederates). Straggling and desertion had reduced Lee's army to fewer than 40,000 men. McClellan's army numbered more than 80,000, though a quarter had been in service only a few weeks. The battle unfolded from north to south in three distinct phases. Between about 6.00 and 9.30am, Federals from three corps pounded the Confederate left under Stonewall Jackson. Lee shifted troops from his right, commanded by Longstreet, to shore up his harried left. Particularly vicious action occurred in a 23-acre (9.3ha) cornfield owned by a farmer named David R. Miller. Some 8,000 men, including more than 80 percent of one Texas regiment, fell in the midst of cornstalks cut down by musketry and cannon fire. This part of the fighting ended with the near destruction of a Union division that stumbled into a deadly crossfire in woods near a modest brick church that served a Dunker congregation.

The second phase focused on the middle of Lee's position and lasted from 9.30am until about 1.00pm. Two Confederate brigades situated in a sunken country lane held this section of the line. Together with other units that came to their aid, these brigades beat back a series of Union attacks before being flanked and driven out at great loss. Lee had no reinforcements at hand, and his army teetered on the edge of utter defeat. Union division commander Israel Richardson, whose soldiers had broken the Rebel line, pleaded with McClellan to send in reinforcements. Thousands of uncommitted Federals stood nearby, but McClellan chose not to send them forward lest he leave himself without a substantial reserve. A staggering opportunity slipped away as action died down along what the soldiers later christened the "Bloody Lane."

The battle closed on the Confederate right, where Major-General Ambrose E. Burnside orchestrated an unimpressive tactical offensive against a handful of Southern defenders. Fighting on this part of the field began just as the action in the Sunken Road subsided. Two Federal regiments crossed a stone bridge over Antietam Creek (later dubbed "Burnside's Bridge") under fire, after which Burnside took his time preparing for a final advance. If successful, Burnside's soldiers could cut Lee and his army off from the only available ford over the Potomac. By about 3.00pm, Union attackers had approached to within 250 yards (230m) of the road to the ford when elements of A. P. Hill's division slammed into their left flank. A difficult 17-mile (27km) march from Harpers Ferry had

Northern photographers reached the battlefield at Antietam before the Confederate dead had been buried. Their studies of Southern corpses created a sensation in the North. An article in the *New York Times* remarked that the photographs "bring home to us the terrible reality and earnestness of war." The pictures did not lay bodies "in our door-yards and along streets" but accomplished "something very like it." This view shows Confederates, most likely from William E. Starke's Louisiana brigade, along the Hagerstown Pike. (Gary Gallagher)

carried Hill's leading brigades to the field just in time to disrupt Burnside's attacks. The battle closed as the Federals fell back toward Antietam Creek.

The exhausted armies had waged the costliest single day's combat in United States history. McClellan's loss approached 12,500, and Lee's exceeded 10,300. Another 2,300 Federals and 2,700 Confederates had fallen at South Mountain on September 14. One Southerner remarked that the "sun seemed almost to go backwards" during the fighting on the 17th. A Union soldier counted himself fortunate that his regiment did not have to view the shattered landscape in full daylight. "We were glad to march over the field at night," he told his parents, "for we could not see the horrible sights so well. Oh what a smell[,] some of the men vomit as they went along."

The Army of Northern Virginia remained on the field during September 18, after which McClellan permitted Lee to recross the Potomac unmolested. A Federal foray across the river at Shepherdstown late on the 19th promised to disrupt Lee's withdrawal, but A. P. Hill's division counterattacked the following day and drove the Northerners back to the left bank of the Potomac. The campaign closed without a determined Union effort to pursue the Confederates.

McClellan's handling of the campaign inspired heated debate. While some applauded his success in stopping Lee's invasion, others inside the Army of the Potomac and behind the lines in the North believed he had lost a tantalizing opportunity. A newspaper correspondent voiced a common criticism in wishing McClellan had attacked again on September 18: "We could have driven them into the river or captured them… It was one of the supreme moments when by daring something, the destiny of the nation might have been changed." No one experienced more bitter disappointment than Abraham Lincoln. Although he used Lee's retreat as a pretext to issue a preliminary emancipation proclamation on September 22, a step that signaled a profound shift in the course of the war, he nevertheless believed his commander had once again shown insufficient aggressiveness.

Thousands of Union soldiers had remained out of the action on September 17 (Lee, in contrast, had committed every available man) and reinforcements had reached the field on the 18th, yet still McClellan refused to advance. He insisted that his men were worn out, too few in number to harass the Rebels, and poorly supplied. Secretary of the Navy Gideon Welles likely mirrored Lincoln's attitude when he wrote on September 19 that he had no news from the army, "except that, instead of following up the victory, attacking and capturing the Rebels," McClellan was allowing Lee to escape across the Potomac. An obviously unhappy Welles added: "McClellan says they are crossing, and that Pleasonton is after them. Oh dear!"

McClellan typically lavished praise on himself. "I feel some little pride," he wrote to his wife on September 20, "in having, with a beaten and demoralised army, defeated Lee so utterly and saved the North so completely. Well – one of these days history will I trust do me justice in deciding that it was not my fault that the campaign of the Peninsula was not successful." The next day he complained that Lincoln and the Secretary of War had not congratulated him sufficiently. But he assured his wife that a higher power had blessed his work: "I have the satisfaction of knowing that God has in His mercy a second time made me the instrument for saving the nation & am content with the honor that has fallen to my lot."

If McClellan erred on the side of caution in September 1862, Robert E. Lee might have been too audacious. Thousands of Confederates had fallen at Antietam when Lee stood to gain very little either tactically or strategically. The decision to remain on the field on the 18th, with a powerful enemy in his front and just a single ford available to reach Virginia, might have jeopardized his entire army. He had driven his worn army relentlessly, misjudging the men's physical capacity and watching thousands fall out of the ranks from hunger, debility, or a simple unwillingness to be pushed any further. The army had survived, however, and as it lay in camps near Winchester, Lee congratulated the soldiers who had discharged their duty. History offered "few examples of greater fortitude and endurance than this army has exhibited," he assured them, "to your tried valor and patriotism the country looks with confidence for deliverance and safety."

Lee did not exaggerate how important his soldiers' activities would be to future Confederate morale. No one could claim a clear-cut success for the army. Marylanders had not rushed to the Confederate colors, and the army fell back to Virginia long before Lee had expected. Yet he had accomplished many of his logistical goals by virtue of McClellan's failure to press him after September 17. More significantly, between June and September 1862, the Army of Northern Virginia had crafted spectacular victories that helped cancel the effects of defeats in other theaters. The retreat from Maryland, itself counterbalanced by the capture of thousands of Federals at Harpers Ferry and the tidy success at Shepherdstown, did not detract appreciably from laurels won at Richmond and Second Manassas. Similarly, the bitter contest at Sharpsburg, seen by most Confederates as a bloody drawn battle, confirmed the gallantry of Lee's soldiers. In the space of less than three months, the Confederate people had come to expect good news from Lee and the Army of Northern Virginia, investing ever more emotional capital in them. That investment led to a belief in possible victory that would be as important as any other factor in lengthening the life of the Confederacy.

Lincoln visited the Army of the Potomac in early October, hoping to prod McClellan into advancing against Lee's army. As he and a companion looked over the army's headquarters camp one morning, Lincoln asked the man what he saw. The Army of the Potomac, came the answer. "No, you are mistaken," said Lincoln, "that is General McClellan's bodyguard." In this photograph, Lincoln and McClellan sit stiffly in the general's field tent. (Library of Congress)

Abraham Lincoln lost all patience with McClellan in the wake of Antietam. The outspoken general reiterated his opposition to emancipation, angering Republican politicians already eager to see him relieved. The principal problem from Lincoln's standpoint lay in McClellan's refusal to mount a new campaign into Virginia. In mid-October, an exasperated Lincoln asked whether his general was "over-cautious when you assume that you can not do what the enemy is constantly doing? Should you not claim to be at least his equal in prowess, and act upon the claim?" McClellan finally began crossing the Potomac on October 26. His army took six days to make the passage (Lee's had done it in one night after Antietam) and then marched slowly toward Warrenton. Nearly seven weeks had elapsed since Lee's retreat, and Lincoln had reached his breaking point. On November 5, the day after the Northern off-year elections (elections held in between presidential elections), Lincoln issued orders replacing McClellan with Ambrose E. Burnside. Little Mac received the orders late in the evening on November 7. He took an emotional leave from the army three days later, having played his final scene in the war's military drama.

Ambrose Everett Burnside in a wartime engraving. Although primarily remembered for losing the Battle of Fredericksburg, Burnside had previously earned a favorable reputation for overseeing successful operations along the North Carolina coast that employed land and naval forces. In February 1862, a New York diarist wrote: "Burnside is pushing on, up Albemarle Sound, it would seem. Hurrah for Burnside!" (Gary Gallagher)

AMBROSE E. BURNSIDE.

Battle of Fredericksburg

Burnside doubted his capacity for high command. At 38 years old, he could look back on a largely unexceptional career. He graduated from West Point in 1847 and served a few uneventful years in the army before resigning to enter civilian life. Trying unsuccessfully to market a carbine he had designed while in military service, he later worked for the same railroad that employed his friend McClellan. In 1861, he led a brigade at First Bull Run before winning several victories along the North Carolina coast. Powerfully built and bald, he affected luxuriant whiskers that swept down the sides of his face and joined to form a bushy moustache – the famous "Burnside cut" (from which the word "sideburns" derived). Personally brave and widely popular, he lacked the intellectual ability of a great commander.

His government expected him to organize a campaign against Richmond before the end of the year. Burnside knew that Lee's army was divided, with Jackson's Second Corps in the Shenandoah Valley and Longstreet's First Corps near Culpeper (the Confederates had replaced wings with corps after Antietam). He proposed marching his 130,000 soldiers from northern Virginia to Fredericksburg, seizing that important city and striking south along the Richmond, Fredericksburg, and Potomac Railroad. Lincoln and

Major-General Henry W. Halleck, who had earned a high reputation in the Western Theater and been named general-in-chief after the Seven Days, approved Burnside's plan and recommended that he move quickly.

Burnside reached the eastern bank of the Rappahannock River opposite Fredericksburg on November 19, 1862, but he could not cross into the city because necessary pontoon bridges had not arrived. Several days passed, affording Lee time to hurry Longstreet's soldiers to high ground west and south of Fredericksburg. Jackson's corps followed in early December, extending Lee's position along the Rappahannock below Fredericksburg.

Jackson's presence foreclosed the option of a Union crossing downstream, so Burnside settled on several points near the city. On December 11, engineers oversaw construction of pontoons at two points opposite the city and one about a mile (1.6km) downstream. Confederates resisted the two upper crossings, firing on the bridge builders from the shelter of houses and other structures. Union artillery bombarded the city, driving civilians into the countryside and destroying a number of buildings. A Confederate artillerist described the memorable scene:

> The city, except its steeples, was still veiled in the mist which had settled in the valleys. Above it and in it incessantly showed the round white clouds of bursting shells, and out of its midst there soon rose three or four columns of dense black smoke from houses set on fire by the

George Gordon Meade's division of Pennsylvanians achieved the only Federal offensive success at Fredericksburg. Shortly after the battle, Meade told his wife that his "men went in *beautifully*, carried everything before them, and drove the enemy for nearly half a mile" until, "finding themselves unsupported on either right or left [they] were checked and finally driven back." Meade subsequently commanded the Army of the Potomac longer than any other officer. (Gary Gallagher)

explosions. The atmosphere was so perfectly calm and still that the smoke rose vertically in great pillars for several hundred feet before spreading outward in black sheets … the dark blue masses of over 100,000 infantry in compact columns, and numberless parks of white-topped wagons and ambulances massed in orderly ranks, all awaited the completion of the bridges. The earth shook with the thunder of the guns, and, high above all, a thousand feet in the air, hung two immense balloons. The scene gave impressive ideas of the disciplined power of a great army, and of the vast resources of the nation which had sent it forth.

Union troops held the city by evening and sacked it the next day.

Burnside's final plan called for a flanking movement that would cut the Army of Northern Virginia off from the direct routes to Richmond. The Federal army had been organized into three Grand Divisions of two corps each, commanded by William Buel Franklin (the left), Joseph Hooker (the center), and Edwin V. Sumner (the right). On December 13, Hooker would hold Lee's attention in front of Fredericksburg while Franklin worked his way around the enemy's right near Hamilton's Crossing.

Lee did not complete his defensive dispositions until the morning of the 13th, when the last of Jackson's corps reached the field from down the Rappahannock. The 75,000 men of the Army of Northern Virginia stretched nearly 7 miles (11km), their left anchored on high ground overlooking the Rappahannock and their right near Hamilton's Crossing. Longstreet's corps held the left, accounting for 5 miles (8km) of the front, and Jackson's corps presented a defense in depth along the rightmost 2 miles (3.2km) of the Southern front. Longstreet's men occupied several hills, most notably Marye's

Federal shelling of Fredericksburg on December 11 damaged a number of buildings and left many streets littered with rubble. In this regard, the old colonial city at the falls of the Rappahannock River anticipated the fate of many other southern communities. Confederates deplored the shelling of civilian neighborhoods in Fredericksburg, to which Federals responded that Lee's army should not have fought from the cover of private residences. (Gary Gallagher)

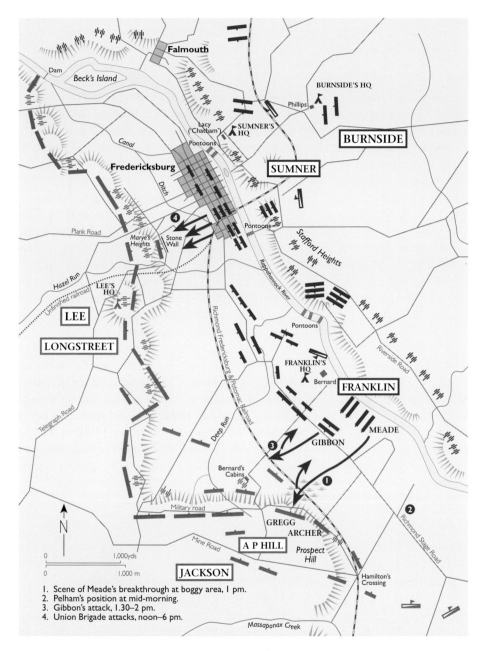

Battle of Fredericksburg,
December 13, 1862.

1. Scene of Meade's breakthrough at boggy area, 1 pm.
2. Pelham's position at mid-morning.
3. Gibbon's attack, 1.30–2 pm.
4. Union Brigade attacks, noon–6 pm.

Heights west of the city. Jackson's infantry and artillery enjoyed less commanding ground. Moreover, Jackson's final line suffered from a 600-yard (550m) gap that ran through a boggy area – a weakness the general had noticed. In 1864, D. H. Hill described a ride that he and Jackson had taken on the morning of the 13th: "As we passed by a flat boggy piece of ground the General said, 'the enemy will attack at this point.'"

The battle opened on the Confederate right. A mid-morning artillery duel included a daring set of maneuvers by the youthful Confederate Major John Pelham, whose brilliant use of two guns held up George Gordon Meade's division of Union infantry for an hour. About 1.00pm, Meade's Pennsylvanians advanced across an open plain against A. P. Hill's division. Some of the Federals struck the gap in the Confederate line, surging up a wooded hill to a second line of infantry. A confused South Carolina brigadier mistakenly thought the Federals to be Confederates and ordered his men not to fire. He fell mortally wounded, but two of Jackson's divisions quickly stopped Meade's progress. When Grand Division commander Franklin failed to provide supports for Meade's hard-pressed units, the Federals glumly withdrew. A pair of Confederate brigades pursued their retreating foe until savaged by Northern artillery. Lee witnessed this counterattack from his headquarters on Telegraph Hill. A nearby staff officer heard the commanding general say to James Longstreet in low tones, "It is well this is so terrible! We should grow too fond of it!"

John Gibbon's Union division also attacked Jackson's line, only to suffer the same fate as Meade's. This commitment of just a fraction of his Grand Division seemed to satisfy Franklin. He suspended active operations, having failed utterly to execute Burnside's instructions to turn the Confederate right.

The focus soon shifted to a series of Union frontal assaults against Longstreet's troops on Marye's Heights. The defenders occupied a splendid position. Infantrymen crowded behind a stone wall in a sunken road at the foot of the hill. Other brigades rested within easy supporting distance to their right and left. Artillery crowned the high ground above them. Longstreet exhibited the easy confidence of a soldier convinced his enemy could do him no serious harm. Other Confederates shared his outlook. One artillerist assured Longstreet just before the battle that Southern guns covered the approaches so thoroughly that "a chicken could not live on that field when we open on it."

Those words proved to be prophetic. Between noon and 6.00pm, several waves of attackers deployed west of Fredericksburg and marched up the gentle rise toward Marye's Heights. Temperatures climbed into the mid-50s Fahrenheit (about 13°C) on an unseasonably warm winter afternoon. The nature of the ground prevented deployment of more than one brigade at a time, which resulted in the sickening spectacle of successive units matching grit and courage against an unforgiving wall of Confederate musketry and cannon fire. None of the attackers received more attention from later writers than the famed Irish Brigade of Winfield Scott Hancock's division, which lost more than 500 men in its attack. But others absorbed far more punishment, including John C. Caldwell's brigade, which followed the Irishmen into the maelstrom and suffered 900 casualties.

One of Longstreet's soldiers in the sunken road described the action four days after the battle. "We waited until they got within about 200 yards of us," he observed, "& rose to our feet & poured volley after volley into their ranks which told a most deadening effect … another column & another & still another came to their support. But our well aimed shots were more than they could stand so about night they were compelled to give up the field covered with their dead." A Northern soldier described the harrowing passage back down the hill toward Fredericksburg: "All the way down the slope to the edge of the town I saw my fellow-soldiers dropping on every side, in their effort to get out of the reach of the murderous fire from the Confederate infantry securely entrenched behind the long stone wall and the batteries on the heights." A Union general observed simply that the area in front of Marye's Heights "was a great slaughter pen."

The Army of the Potomac remained in Fredericksburg and exchanged desultory fire with the Confederates for two more days. On the night of December 15, Burnside ordered a retreat across the river. A disappointed Lee, who had chafed at his inability to launch a counterattack because of Union batteries posted on high ground east of the Rappahannock, expressed disbelief that the enemy had given up the field without further struggle. The one-day battle had produced 12,650 Union casualties, most of whom had fallen in front of Marye's Heights. Most of the 5,300 Confederates who fell had been hit defending Jackson's position.

Burnside took full responsibility for the debacle and received fearful criticism from soldiers and civilians alike. Many in the North also assailed

Robert E. Lee and a group of staff officers and subordinates watch the Battle of Fredericksburg from atop Telegraph Hill (later called "Lee's Hill"). In this postwar engraving by Alfred A. Waud, James Longstreet is the fourth figure from the left. A witness on the hill described Longstreet, whom Lee had called "the staff in my right hand" after the Seven Days, as "about six feet, two inches high, a strong, round frame, portly and fleshy, but not corpulent or too fat." (Gary Gallagher)

Lincoln as a failed war leader. The seemingly pointless, unimaginative nature of the attacks at Fredericksburg triggered especially bitter reactions. When first informed of what had happened on December 13, Lincoln told a friend, "If there is a worse place than Hell, I am in it."

Confederates took heart from the easy victory. Their faith in Lee and his army deepened, prompting the general to worry lest they fall into the trap of believing the war was about to end. The enemy had "suffered heavily as far as the battle went," noted Lee, "but it did not go far enough to satisfy me… The contest will have now to be renewed, but on what field I cannot say."

Fighting in Virginia had ended for 1862, but Burnside's problems continued. An indifferent administrator, he presided over a dark period in his army's history. Morale plummeted and desertions increased. An attempted flanking movement around Lee's left, the infamous "Mud March," ground to an ignominious halt amid a spell of wet weather in January 1863. Many of Burnside's senior subordinates sought his removal. Although unhappy with several of Burnside's critics in the army, Lincoln decided a change was needed. On January 26, Burnside relinquished command of the Army of the Potomac to Joseph Hooker, who became the army's third helmsman in just five months.

Another West Pointer with extensive experience during the war with Mexico, Hooker had left the army in the 1850s to live on the Pacific coast. He reentered the army shortly after the firing on Fort Sumter and proved to be a hard fighter. A press report from the Peninsula headed "Fighting – Joe Hooker" had mistakenly appeared in print as "Fighting Joe Hooker," thus bestowing a nickname that the General loathed. Hooker harbored enormous ambition and had lobbied behind the scenes to replace Burnside. A handsome 48-year-old bachelor when he took command of the army, he set up a convivial headquarters that offended many observers. Charles Francis Adams, Jr, the grandson of one president and great-grandson of another, scathingly described Hooker as a "noisy, low-toned intriguer under whose influence army headquarters became a place to which no self-respecting man liked to go and no decent woman could go. It was a combination [of] barroom and brothel." Lincoln knew about Hooker's machinations against Burnside as well as his intemperate comment that the nation might need a dictator to win the war. In a remarkable letter dated January 26, 1863, Lincoln listed Hooker's strengths and weaknesses as a man and officer. "Only those generals who gain successes, can set up dictators," stated Lincoln pointedly. "What I now ask of you is military success, and I will risk the dictatorship."

Hooker rapidly restored morale in the army. The quality of food and sanitation improved, desertions fell off, and Hooker instituted a system of corps badges that soon became prized symbols engendering pride in belonging to a particular corps. Hooker also scrapped Burnside's Grand Divisions, preferring to work with individual corps commanders (seven Union corps would participate in the upcoming campaign). By the end of April, the Army of the Potomac represented a formidable military instrument. Its 134,000 well-equipped and supplied soldiers anticipated success. One Ohioan, impressed with the power of the army after a major review, remarked: "Such a great army! Thunder and lightning! The Johnnies could never whip this army!" Hooker described his force as "the finest army on the planet." A leading Confederate artillerist later agreed, writing of "Hooker's great army – the greatest this country had ever seen."

The Army of Northern Virginia lacked its opponent's size and material bounty, but fully matched its confidence. A difficult winter had compelled Lee to disperse much of his cavalry to secure food for the horses. James Longstreet and two of his four infantry divisions had been detached to southeast Virginia, where they foraged on a grand scale and stood guard against possible Federal incursions from Norfolk and North Carolina. Scarcely more than 60,000 Confederates of all arms prepared to defend the Rappahannock River lines. Yet most Confederates expected victory. They enjoyed superior generalship in the team of Lee and Jackson, who had forged remarkable bonds with their men and had an impressive record of victory. Dashing James Ewell Brown ("Jeb") Stuart supplied equally able leadership to the cavalry. The Army of Northern Virginia had often overcome intimidating odds to win victories, and its men believed their commanders would enable them to do so again. Stephen Dodson Ramseur, a youthful brigadier-general in Jackson's corps, reflected the army's confidence. The "vandal hordes of the Northern Tyrant are struck down with terror arising from their past experience," he stated. "They have learned to their sorrow that this army is made up of veterans equal to those of the 'Old Guard' of Napoleon."

Few incidents in the war exceeded in boldness Lee's decision to send Jackson's corps on a flanking march around Hooker's right. One of Jackson's staff officers described the scene on the night of May 1 when the two generals plotted their strategy (depicted in this painting). "I found him [Jackson] seated on a cracker box with his back against a tree while opposite to him Gen. Lee sat on another box with his back against a tree. They were engaged in conversation." (© Osprey Publishing)

Battle of Chancellorsville

The strategic initiative rested with Hooker, who developed an impressive plan. He proposed holding Lee's attention at Fredericksburg with about 40,000 men under John Sedgwick, while several corps made a rapid march up the Rappahannock to turn the Rebel left and get in Lee's rear. Most of the army's cavalry would ride toward Richmond, cutting Lee's lines of communication with the Confederate capital. The turning column would have to move through an area south of the Rappahannock and Rapidan Rivers known as the Wilderness of Spotsylvania, approximately 70 square miles (180 square kilometers) of scrub woods and tangled undergrowth that would retard effective deployment of Hooker's superior manpower and artillery. Once in Lee's rear, a fast march toward Fredericksburg would take the Federals out of the Wilderness into open ground, where their numbers would tell. If all went well, Lee's army would be trapped between the flanking column and Sedgwick's force at Fredericksburg.

The campaign began brilliantly for the Federals. On April 27, 1863, Hooker's turning column swung up the Rappahannock, negotiated fords over that river and the Rapidan, and by early afternoon on the 30th reached the crossroads of Chancellorsville some 10 miles (16km) west of Fredericksburg.

George G. Meade, who led the Union V Corps on the flanking maneuver, expressed unabashed enthusiasm at what Hooker had accomplished. "This is splendid," he said, "hurrah for old Joe; we are on Lee's flank, and he does not know it." A march of 2 or 3 miles (about 5km) would take the Federals from Chancellorsville, which lay in the Wilderness, to clear ground farther east. But Hooker ordered the troops to remain at Chancellorsville, where he joined them that evening. The Federal commander announced to his army that "our enemy must either ingloriously fly, or come out from behind his defenses and give us battle on our own ground, where certain destruction awaits him." Lee reacted boldly to Hooker's maneuver. He divided his small army, leaving Jubal A. Early and about 10,000 men to watch Sedgwick at Fredericksburg and marching the other 50,000 to deal with the Federals at Chancellorsville. The critical moment of the campaign occurred on the morning of May 1. Hooker's advancing infantry clashed with Confederates 3½ miles (5.6km) east of Chancellorsville near Zoan Church, whereupon the Union commander ordered a withdrawal. Some of Hooker's subordinates argued vehemently for maintaining the offensive. A retreat into the gloomy Wilderness, they insisted, would negate all that had been accomplished over the past several days. But all offensive thoughts had left Hooker's mind, as he ordered his troops to concentrate and dig in near Chancellorsville. Darius N. Couch, leader of the Federal II Corps, bitterly concluded that, "my commanding general was a whipped man."

Lee eagerly took the initiative. On the night of May 1, he and Jackson discussed how best to attack Hooker. The Federal left occupied strong ground and rested near the Rappahannock. A frontal assault against Chancellorsville would be too costly. The best course seemed to be turning the Union right, which ran west from Chancellorsville along the Orange Plank Road and Orange Turnpike (the two main east–west arteries through the Wilderness). Lee decided to divide his army again, sending Jackson's Second Corps on a flank march along narrow country roads. Lee would keep the 14,000 men of Richard H. Anderson's and Lafayette McLaws's divisions of Longstreet's corps to occupy Hooker's attention.

Jackson conducted the war's most celebrated flanking maneuver on May 2, launching a powerful attack at about 5.15pm that crushed Oliver O. Howard's Union XI Corps. Many of Howard's troops were Germans, and critics later accused the "damned Dutchmen" of fleeing without putting up a fight. In fact, no Union corps could have stood when Jackson's divisions swept out of the woods, shrieking the unnerving "Rebel Yell" and easily overlapping every potential defensive position. Half the regimental commanders and a quarter of the soldiers in Howard's corps fell during the fighting – evidence that they offered considerable resistance.

Darkness and confusion arising from the movement of large bodies of men through heavily wooded terrain slowed down the Confederate attack by about 7.00pm. Jackson hoped to reform and renew the attacks later that night. Riding to the front with the goal of finding a way to cut Hooker off from the Rappahannock fords, he rode into the path of a volley from a North Carolina regiment. Wounded in three places, he had his left arm amputated later that evening.

Despite Jackson's impressive attack, Lee's troops at Chancellorsville remained separated by Hooker's much larger force. Extremely hard fighting on the morning of May 3 enabled the Confederates to reunite their wings at Chancellorsville and push Hooker, who had been stunned when a Southern artillery shell struck a pillar against which he was leaning, back closer to the Rappahannock. While a groggy Hooker sought to form a new defensive line, Lee guided Traveller, his sturdy gray warhorse, through thousands of Confederate infantrymen in a clearing near Chancellorsville. Emotions flowed freely as the soldiers, nearly 9,000 of whose comrades had fallen in the morning's fighting, shouted their devotion. Lee acknowledged their cheers by removing his hat. Seldom has the bond between a successful commander and his troops achieved more dramatic display. Colonel Charles Marshall of Lee's staff later wrote that Lee basked in "the full realization of all that soldiers dream of – triumph," adding: "As I looked upon him in the complete fruition of the success which his genius, courage, and confidence in his army had won, I thought that it must have been from such a scene that men in ancient days rose to the dignity of gods."

Within minutes Lee learned that Sedgwick had broken Early's line at Fredericksburg and was moving toward Chancellorsville. He divided his army for a third time, deploying about half his troops to block this new threat. A sharp action on May 4 at Salem Church, located some 4 miles (6.4km) west of Fredericksburg, stopped Sedgwick. That night Hooker decided to retreat, and by the morning of the 6th the Army of the Potomac had returned to the left bank of the Rappahannock.

Chancellorsville marked the apogee of Lee's career as a soldier and cemented the reciprocal trust between him and his men that made the Army of Northern Virginia so formidable. That trust radiated outward to civilians in the Confederacy, who looked to Lee and his soldiers as their primary national rallying point from late 1862 onward. Jefferson Davis gratefully thanked Lee "in the name of the people ... for this addition to the unprecedented series of great victories which your army has achieved."

Oliver Otis Howard, a flag tucked under the stump of his right arm (he lost the limb at the Battle of Seven Pines), tries to rally his corps in the face of Jackson's flank attack. Having ignored warnings of an impending rebel attack, Howard exhibited courage on the field. He readily conceded that his lines collapsed "more quickly than it could be told." Two months later, his corps would be driven from the field again during the first day's fighting at Gettysburg. (© Osprey Publishing)

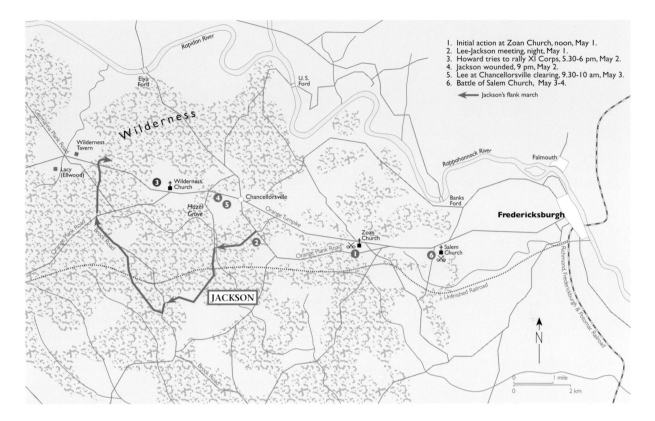

1. Initial action at Zoan Church, noon, May 1.
2. Lee-Jackson meeting, night, May 1.
3. Howard tries to rally XI Corps, 5.30-6 pm, May 2.
4. Jackson wounded, 9 pm, May 2.
5. Lee at Chancellorsville clearing, 9.30-10 am, May 3.
6. Battle of Salem Church, May 3-4.

← Jackson's flank march

The success had come at terrible cost. Among the 12,674 Confederate casualties was Stonewall Jackson, whose death on May 10 cast a pall over the Confederacy. Lee would never find an adequate replacement for the gifted lieutenant whom he called his "right arm."

On the Union side, Chancellorsville dealt a telling blow to hopes for victory. Once again a Northern army superior in numbers and equipment had suffered agonizing defeat. Once again a Federal commander had failed to commit all his troops to battle (two of the Union corps had lost fewer than 1,000 men). The Northern butcher's bill totaled 17,287. News of the defeat rocked Lincoln, who, while pacing back and forth, moaned, "My God! My God! What will the country say? What will the country say?" *New York Tribune* editor Horace Greeley rendered a common verdict: "It is horrible – horrible; and to think of it, 130,000 magnificent soldiers so cut to pieces by less than 60,000 half-starved ragamuffins!"

Chancellorsville exacerbated deep divisions in the North. A recently passed National Conscription Act, Lincoln's final Emancipation Proclamation (which had taken effect on January 1, 1863) and other issues fueled acrimonious debate. Hooker's failure increased unhappiness among Northerners already disposed to criticize the Lincoln administration's conduct of the war. Even loyal Republicans wondered whether the Rebels could be suppressed.

Area of operations for the Chancellorsville campaign, April–May, 1863.

Lee at the Chancellorsville clearing on the morning of May 3, where he and his soldiers experienced an epiphany. The men believed victory would come whenever he led them, and he believed they could do whatever he asked. (Gary Gallagher)

PORTRAIT OF A SOLDIER: ROBERT AUGUSTUS MOORE

Robert Augustus Moore participated in most of the Virginia campaigns during the first two years of the war. Born into a prosperous farming family near Holly Springs, Mississippi, on July 2, 1838, he enlisted as a private in an infantry company called the Confederate Guards shortly after Fort Sumter fell. The Guards subsequently became Company G of the 17th Mississippi Infantry Regiment. Mustered into service at Holly Springs, the 17th spent the last part of May and early June 1861 in Corinth before moving on to Virginia. As part of brigades commanded by D. R. Jones, Nathan G. ("Shanks") Evans, and William Barksdale between June 1861 and May 1863, the 17th fought at First Manassas, Ball's Bluff, Seven Pines, the Seven Days, Second Manassas, Antietam, Fredericksburg, and Chancellorsville. Moore kept a pocket diary throughout his Confederate service that sheds light on his motivation for fighting, his opinions about important issues and his experiences in camp, on the march, and in battle.

Like many common soldiers North and South, Moore expressed a strong religious faith. He frequently attended church, seemingly unconcerned with denomination and able to draw strength from a variety of messages from the pulpit. "This is Thanksgiving day all over the Southern Confederacy," he wrote on November 15, 1861. "Our Chaplain held services in camp this evening notwithstanding the inclemency of the weather. I think all should join in praise to Him who has been with us in every engagement we have had with the enemy." On a rainy Sunday in Fredericksburg in February 1863, he attended services twice. "The church is quite commodious," he noted approvingly, "& is always crowded to overflowing with attentive hearers." The next day he observed that "Our chaplain is now carrying on a protracted meeting. Everything bids fair for the outpouring of God's spirit." He later affirmed that he could "recommend the atoning blood of Christ to all. All seems bright to me. I hope to walk so as never to bring reproach on the cause of Christ."

Moore's piety did not prevent his indulging in small vices. In October 1861, he welcomed a windfall of 30 bottles of whiskey, recording that he and his fellow soldiers "had a fine time drinking it." He often mentioned incidents when soldiers imbibed too much. "Lieut. Jackson came in this evening very tipsy," he wrote on November 8, 1861. "Was sent out as Lieut. of the pickets. The provo marshall was also drunk." Unused to the cold weather in Virginia, he considered an occasional drink essential. "This being a rainy & cold day, we all received a little toddy," he complained on one occasion. "I think the drams are a little too small for the weather & that they do not come around often enough to one in camp."

Private Robert Augustus Moore, who wrote his diary in three 5 x 3in (12.7 x 7.6cm) leather-bound volumes. (Gary Gallagher)

Moore's early life in the Deep South had not prepared him for Virginia's winters. During his first summer in Virginia, he betrayed a slightly scornful attitude toward residents who complained about the heat. "The weather is very hot for this climate, the people here think extremely hot," he recorded, "but it is not near so warm as in Miss." Cold was another matter. "Bad weather for ill-clad Rebels," he wrote on December 5, 1862, adding that the "Rebels are shivering around their log fires as the Yanks would say." Two days later the weather had got worse, producing "as cold a day as I have ever felt in Va." After a brief warming trend during the next week (when the Battle of Fredericksburg was fought), the mercury plunged downward again. "This has been one of the most disagreeable days that I have ever experienced in camp," groused Moore. "The wind has blown very cold from the North & one could barely live for the smoke from burning green juice wood. Cold – cold, indeed."

Unlike soldiers who resented every moment spent on drill, Moore understood that such labor paid off in discipline on the battlefield. He lamented his regiment's shortage of trained officers early in the war. "Went out this evening on battalion drill," he wrote in June 1861, "made a very bad show, many of the companies need drill in the school of the soldiers & need some better officers." Leaders who lacked apparent zeal for the war angered Moore, who in November 1861 applauded when "Orders were read out this evening on dress parade informing officers that they could not resign & go home, or that their resignations would not be accepted unless recommended by the Surgeon. This, I think, is right as a great number are resigning for no other purpose than to get home." Shortly thereafter he grumbled that "the majority of the men of our Regt. are becoming very wild & contracting many bad habits."

Moore seems to have remained steadfastly in the ranks except when ill. In a typical pattern, contagious diseases swept through the 17th Mississippi during the war's first summer. Moore and many others in his company endured a bout with measles in June 1861 that sent them to hospitals in Culpeper. Although he recovered in time to fight at First Manassas, a fever landed him back in the hospital at the end of July. Other physical problems plagued Moore and his comrades in the 17th, including sore feet when on the move. On March 12, 1862, the regiment "marched but six miles" and had "a large number of lame men … who had to be hauled. Nearly all complain of their feet. The Pike is bad marching as the rocks are so rough." Here as in many other campaigns, most notably Lee's invasion of Maryland in 1862, roads with crushed stone surfaces wreaked havoc on poorly shod or barefoot soldiers.

Old and new loyalties sometimes clashed in Moore's ruminations. On January 8, 1862, his thoughts turned to an earlier war when all Americans had celebrated Andrew Jackson's victory over the British in the Battle of New Orleans. "This is the anniversary of the Battle of New Orleans," he wrote somewhat wistfully, "but we are so situated that we cannot celebrate it. Think we will have others more closely connected with the present generation to celebrate in the future, yet we should never forget the immortal hero of New Orleans."

As a Southerner and slaveholder, Jackson represented a thoroughly acceptable hero for Moore. Although he never specifically mentioned slavery in his diary, Moore obviously believed the institution formed an essential element of Southern society. He often labeled all Northerners abolitionists, as when he mentioned receiving troubling news from Mississippi in February 1862: "Have received a letter from home. The Abolitionists have committed many acts of vandalism." Earlier in the conflict, he lauded white Southern women willing to sacrifice their sons for the Confederacy. "When such sentiments are felt & expressed by the matrons and men of our country," he commented, "I should like to know how the Abolitionists of the North can expect to conquer the South."

Moore consistently demonstrated a strong allegiance to the nascent Confederate republic. On New Year's Day in 1862, he rejoiced at Southern "success in driving from our soil the ruthless invader who is seeking to reduce us to abject slavery." He predicted that a year hence "the North will have been taught a lesson not to be forgotten. We have already achieved many brilliant victories. May this prove a happy year to our country and to all mankind." Later that winter he affirmed his belief that "after much hard fighting" Confederates would "succeed in establishing our independence." He voluntarily reenlisted for three years in February 1862 (the Confederate Conscription Act passed shortly thereafter would have kept him in the army anyway), taking care to explain his motivation: "I joined after long consideration, believing that in that way I could best serve my country. It seems to be sacrificing much, but what should we not be willing to sacrifice, even life itself, for the liberty of our country." White Southerners who betrayed the Confederacy understandably upset him. "Have some very discouraging news from our homes in Miss.," he noted in December 1862. "Some are buying up & selling cotton to the abolitionists. Hope none of my friends or relatives are falling off so badly."

The change of years from 1862 to 1863 put Moore in a mood to reflect on his nation's future. The Confederacy had passed an eventful year in 1862, believed Moore, during which the North, "by the strength of numbers," more than once seemed likely to overrun the South. But by "heroic endurance, hard fighting & the favor of a just God," Confederates had resisted "every attempt at subjugation." Although Moore hated war, which he called the "greatest curse that can befall a land," he determined to fight on to victory. "We trust for success for our cause in the God of Battles," he averred. "We have had evidences that He is on our side & I hope for more signal display of His power in our behalf."

Promoted to corporal in April 1863, Moore anticipated a new season of campaigning. He had first experienced combat at First Manassas. He had fought the Union engineers who laid the pontoon bridges at Fredericksburg on December 11, 1862, and later heard "the groans of the wounded" after the slaughter of Burnside's attackers below Marye's Heights. During the Chancellorsville campaign, he and the 17th Mississippi fought under Jubal Early, delaying John Sedgwick's Union column at Fredericksburg while Lee and Jackson confronted Joseph Hooker in the Wilderness. Word of Jackson's death hit Moore very hard. "We to-day received the sad intelligence of the death of Lieut. Gen. Jackson who expired at Guinea' Station at 3 1/4 o'clock P.M. yesterday," he wrote in his diary. "No words can describe the sorrow with which this intelligence will be received from the Potomac to the Rio Grande."

Yet Jackson's death did not undermine Moore's morale or that of his comrades. "The opinion seems to prevail with us that hostilities will be resumed with us in a few weeks," he wrote on May 12, 1863. "The army, as far as I have seen is in excellent spirits." Moore marched into Pennsylvania with the army in June 1863. Surviving the Battle of Gettysburg, he traveled to northern Georgia with James Longstreet's

Soldiers of William Barksdale's Mississippi Brigade fire at Union pontoon bridge-builders on December 11, 1862. Moore recorded that the fighting began about 9.00am. The Union bombardment of Fredericksburg commenced shortly thereafter and continued until about 4.30pm, "when we were forced to retire down the river bank but held [the] Yanks out of the city until 8.00 p.m. when we retired & left the city in the hands of the Abolitionists."

corps in September. By that time he had been promoted to lieutenant. He was killed in action at the Battle of Chickamauga on September 20, 1863, along with 11 other members of the 17th Mississippi Infantry.

THE WORLD AROUND WAR

Although armies and battles often dominated the headlines, the war also touched the lives of millions of people behind the lines. Those in the Confederacy generally experienced the conflict more directly. The armies campaigned almost exclusively on Southern soil, disrupting the Confederate economy and social structure to a far greater degree than was the case in the North. Yet both societies coped with a range of changes and tensions as they prosecuted a war while also addressing day-to-day needs.

The Northern home front

The Northern economy proved fully capable of producing ample war-related materials and consumer goods. Farmers grew record crops of wheat in 1862 and 1863 despite the absence of about a third of the agricultural workforce. The widespread use of machinery, including reapers and mowers, and the labor of women and children allowed production to increase. One observer in 1863 noted a "great revolution which machinery is making in production." "At the present time," he continued, "so perfect is machinery that men seem to be of less necessity… We have seen, within the past few weeks, a stout matron whose sons are in the army, with her team cutting hay at seventy-five cents per acre, and she cut seven acres with ease in a day, riding leisurely upon her cutter." As it fed soldiers numbering in the hundreds of thousands, the North managed also to exceed prewar exports of beef, pork, corn, and wheat. Much of this bounty went to Great Britain, which imported a significant percentage of its grain from the North.

The United States government became a major purchaser of manufactured products and food, collecting goods for distribution to men in the ranks on a scale that anticipated patterns in two twentieth-century world wars. Several industries used antebellum technological advances to meet increased demand. In response to military contracts, production of canned foods, including condensed milk, shot up. Clothing manufacturers employed workers using sewing machines to churn out ready-made garments in standard sizes, and shoe factories delivered the nation's first mass-produced footwear differentiating between right and left feet. Shoulder weapons and pistols emerged from the assembly lines at arms companies in New England and elsewhere. Military-related businesses understandably benefited most from the war. Union soldiers wore wool uniforms, which helped double woolen production. Cotton textile firms, in contrast, felt acutely the loss of Southern cotton. Northern railroads doubled their traffic and improved their tracks, engines, and rolling stock.

Although the Northern economy presented a generally bright appearance, darker elements marred the overall picture. Wages lagged behind inflation, and strikes broke out in a number of industries. Anthracite coal miners in Pennsylvania accused the Lincoln administration of colluding with owners to keep wages low and break workers' resistance in the name of maintaining production vital to the national interest. Middle-class women entered the nursing profession in large numbers for the first time and filled some secretarial and clerical positions previously reserved mainly for men, but poorer women fared less well. They held roughly a third of the manufacturing jobs (up from about a quarter in 1860, and concentrated, as before the war, in such industries as textiles and shoe-making), receiving wages that increased at less than half the rate of men's. In the garment industry, for example, the piece rate declined from 17.5 cents to 8 cents per shirt during the first three years of the conflict. Women on single-family farms often struggled to plant and harvest crops and look after animals in the absence of husbands away at war. The widow of a poor soldier – whether he had been a farmer on marginal land or a laborer – often found herself literally cast into the streets. In 1863, despite a robust overall economy, women accounted for more than two-thirds of Philadelphia's vagrants.

An 1863 cartoon from *Harper's Weekly* shows a trio of Democrats, their heads atop the bodies of copperhead snakes, closing in to strike at a beleaguered female representation of the Union. (Gary Gallagher)

Profiteers and speculators inevitably emerged. *Harper's Monthly* noted the rise of speculation as early as July 1861, quoting an "eminent financier" who allegedly remarked that the "battle of Bull Run makes the fortune of every man in Wall street who is not a natural idiot." Most loyal citizens resented those who profited unduly from the national crisis. Poorer Northerners voiced especially venomous complaints about new fortunes built without honest labor. About midway through the war, the *New York Herald*, which reached a less affluent and educated audience than most of the major New York papers, undoubtedly touched a responsive chord among its wide readership with an unrestrained attack on the "dash, parade and magnificence of the new Northern shoddy aristocracy." "They are shoddy brokers in Wall Street," insisted the paper, "or shoddy manufacturers of shoddy goods, or shoddy contractors for shoddy articles for a shoddy government. Six days in a week they are shoddy business men. On the seventh day they are shoddy Christians."

The North financed the war with loans, paper money, and taxes. War bonds generated about two-thirds of the required revenues. Marketed to individuals as well as to institutions, the bonds yoked people to the war effort and set a precedent that the great bond drives of the First and Second World Wars would emulate. In response to a shortage of hard money in early 1862, Congress passed the Legal Tender Act, which authorized issuance of $150 million in Treasury notes (nearly $457 million of these "greenbacks" were eventually printed). Made legal tender and printed at a time when Union armies seemed about to win the war, this paper money held its value well. Taxes accounted for roughly a fifth of Union revenues and included an income tax of 3–10 percent as well as various excise taxes. Without government-imposed rationing or price controls, inflation peaked at about 80 percent (in the Second World War, with controls, it reached 72 percent). The Northern economy proved fully up to the task of producing guns and butter for the Union armies and Northern civilians.

Political battles during the first half of the war revealed deep divisions in the Northern populace. Much of the disagreement focused on war aims and emancipation. Within the Republican Party, the radicals argued from the outset that freedom for slaves should stand alongside restoration of the Union as a major goal. Hoping to appease slaveholding Border States and attract the broadest possible support from Democrats, Lincoln and other moderate Republicans preferred to keep Union paramount. Democrats almost universally hated the idea of forcing emancipation on slaveholders, insisting that they would fight for the Union but not for black freedom.

As the war unfolded in 1861 and 1862, the Republican-controlled Congress ended slavery in the Federal territories and the District of Columbia, declared slaves owned by Confederates subject to confiscation, and guaranteed the freedom of thousands of slaves who had escaped to areas controlled by Northern armies. By mid-July 1862, Lincoln had decided emancipation was necessary for Northern victory, but he held off issuing a preliminary proclamation until Lee's retreat from Antietam. His final proclamation of January 1, 1863 signaled to the world that Union victory would strike the shackles from all slaves in the Confederacy (the proclamation did not apply to the loyal Border states). Frederick Douglass, a frequent critic of Lincoln, approvingly commented that the proclamation would give "a new direction to the councils of the Cabinet, and to the conduct of the national arms."

Most Northern Democrats railed against this apparent shift in war aims. Working-class Northerners feared economic competition from freed black people, with no group more vocal in this regard than recent Irish immigrants. Democratic newspaper editors and politicians prophesied that various evils would follow Lincoln's proclamation. Thousands of soldiers bluntly stated their opposition to fighting for emancipation. "I don't want to fire another shot for the negroes," wrote a German-born artillerist, "and I wish all the abolitionists were in hell."

Unhappy with the course of the war, a sizable portion of the Democratic Party called for an armistice to be followed by peace negotiations. Called Copperheads by their opponents after the venomous copperhead snake, these Democrats used the Emancipation Proclamation, the Conscription Act passed in the spring of 1863, claims of other Republican transgressions against civil liberties, and the Federal military disasters at Fredericksburg and Chancellorsville to build formidable support. Growing war weariness and the drumbeat of opposition from Copperheads made the spring and early summer of 1863 one of the gravest periods of the war for Lincoln and his supporters.

Still, the absence of Southern Democrats from Congress enabled the Republicans to pass much of their legislative agenda in 1862–63. The National Bank Act of February 1863 sought to replace a plethora of state banknotes with a national currency that would promote economic development. The Homestead Act, which carried through on the old Free Soil idea of making western land available to free white settlers, passed in 1862, as did the Land-Grant College Act, designed to foster practical education in the mechanical and agricultural arts. The Pacific Railroad Bill of July 1862 offered substantial government support for the construction of the first transcontinental railroad. With all of this legislation, Republicans sought to construct a modern capitalist colossus.

The Southern home front

In many ways, the Confederate home front presented a stark contrast to the North. With its capital heavily invested in land and slaves and lacking a sophisticated financial infrastructure, the Confederacy struggled to meet the demands of a massive war. Like the North, it resorted to three options to pay for the conflict. Congress enacted a series of national taxes, beginning with a modest direct property tax in the summer of 1861 and eventually adding others on personal income, consumer goods, and wholesalers' profits. As a group, these taxes yielded only about 5 percent of the government's needs. An array of bonds provided another 35 percent of revenues. Treasury notes accounted for the remaining 60 percent and, as with paper money during the American War of Independence, proved to be a disaster. Inflation began almost immediately and quickly grew worse. The Northern blockade, loss of agricultural areas to advancing Union armies and disruption of the Southern transportation network (due to military activity and the absence of an industrial base able to replace worn-out tracks, engines, and rolling stock) caused shortages of crucial goods. These shortages combined with ever-larger issues of paper money to fuel inflation.

A clerk in the Confederate War Department named John Beauchamp Jones kept a diary that charted increasing financial hardships. In November 1861, he noted that "dry goods have risen more than a hundred percent since spring, and rents and boarding are advancing in the same ration." Ten months later, "blankets, that used to sell for $6, are now $25 per pair; and sheets are selling for $15 per pair, which might have been had a year ago for $4." Wood cost $16 per cord and coal $9 per load, provoking Jones to ask rhetorically, "How can we live here, unless our salaries are increased?" By the end of March 1863, the prices for wood and coal had reached $30 and $20.50 respectively, meat had "almost disappeared from the market, and none but the opulent can afford to pay $3.50 per pound for butter."

News of the bread riot spread quickly to the North, where this cartoon conveyed a very negative impression of the women in Richmond. Many middle- and upper-class Confederates also commented dismissively about the rioters, among them a Richmonder who called them "a heterogeneous crowd of Dutch, Irish, and free negros" bent on looting businesses at random. (Gary Gallagher)

Many Confederates attributed shortages and soaring prices to hoarding by ruthless speculators. A group of women took to the streets in Richmond on April 2, 1863, to protest against prices and scarcities, smashing windows and looting stores in a "bread riot." Jones called it "a frightful spectacle, and perhaps an ominous one, if the government does not remove some of the quartermasters who have contributed very much to bring about the evil of scarcity. I mean those who have allowed transportation to forestallers and extortioners." Another diarist, much disturbed by news of the riot, remarked: "I fear that the poor suffer very much; meal was selling to-day at $16 per bushel. It has been bought up by speculators. Oh that these hard-hearted creatures could be made to suffer! Strange that men with human hearts can, in these dreadful times, thus grind the poor."

Working-class and poorer farming families suffered most. Real wages declined by nearly two-thirds from their late-antebellum levels. Soldiers earned only $11 per month (Congress increased the sum to $18 in 1864), which left them virtually powerless to respond to pleas from home for economic help. As in the North, wives on small farms assumed greater burdens – but they did so in the midst of far more pernicious inflation. Many Confederates coped with spiraling prices by adopting a barter system and simply doing without items previously taken for granted. In the spring of 1863, Congress levied a 10 percent tax-in-kind on corn, wheat, potatoes, fodder, and other agricultural products, provoking outraged complaints and hitting smaller farmers especially hard.

Although formal parties never developed in the Confederacy, the nation divided politically over issues relating to the central government's efforts to wage an expensive war. The Richmond government not only taxed its citizens (there had been no direct taxes on citizens of the United States for many years prior to 1861), but also impressed supplies in return for paper currency, imposed martial law in some areas, and, most ominously for those who feared a strong central power, conscripted men into the army from the spring of 1862 onward. Jefferson Davis and other Confederate nationalists argued for the need to mobilize manpower, food, and other resources by whatever means necessary. A vocal minority that included Vice-President Alexander H. Stephens disagreed, accusing Davis of trampling on sacred state and individual rights. The President became a lightning rod for sometimes intemperate criticism. An extreme example of anti-Davis vitriol written in 1863 called the President a "miserable, stupid, one-eyed dyspeptic, arrogant tyrant who … boasts of the future grandeur of the country which he has ruined, the soil which he has made wet with the tears of widows and orphans and the land which he has bathed in the blood of a people once free, but now enslaved. Oh, let me see him damned and sunk into the lowest hell."

Few images give a better sense of the war's displacement of Confederate civilians than this photograph of a family of refugees, their belongings tied down in a wagon, preparing to leave their home. Some refugees lacked the time even to gather belongings before departing. (Library of Congress)

Unlike their Northern counterparts, most black and white Southerners saw at least some direct evidence of the war. The appearance of Union armies created two kinds of refugee. Thousands of slaves made their way from Southern farms and plantations to Northern lines. In late May 1861, General Benjamin F. Butler, who commanded a Union enclave at Fort Monroe at the tip of Virginia's peninsula, refused to return some fugitive slaves to their masters. Butler called them "contraband of war" and remarked that loss of their labor would hurt the Confederacy (several of the men had been constructing Southern fortifications). The term "contrabands" for escaped slaves soon caught on.

Over the next two years, as Union armies campaigned across the Confederacy, thousands of slaves left Southern farms and plantations. They did so at great risk and, for the first 15 months of the conflict, with no guarantee of freedom. Placed in camps and often assigned to menial jobs with the army, their presence behind Union lines helped force the government to define the status of contrabands. In March 1862, Congress forbade the return of fugitives to Confederate owners, and the Second Confiscation Act of July 1862 declared slaves of Rebel masters free. Lincoln's Emancipation Proclamation extended freedom to all slaves in the Confederacy, regardless of the owner's loyalty.

Slaves who remained at home also experienced change. With so many white men away in the army and old routines otherwise disrupted by the war, the bonds of slavery loosened somewhat. There were no slave uprisings in the Confederacy, but both white and black Southerners understood that some of the rules no longer applied. Typical was Fannie Christian of Nelson County, Virginia, who wrote to the Secretary of War in June 1862 about her difficulties in running a farm and supervising slaves (her husband had been the overseer on this farm, whose 60-year-old owner was bedridden). Returning from a brief walk with a neighbor, explained Christian, she found that "one of the negroes had gone in the house and pull[ed] off her shoes and star[t]ed up[stairs], what to do I can not say." "I could do nothing but tell her to go out," continued the woman: "I have no one to correct them when they do [wrong]." She hoped her husband could be discharged from the army to look after things at home. "Im just surrounded with a gang of negroes," she stated, "I am afraid about [*sic*] to get a breath." A woman in Winchester expressed similar concerns about two months later, reporting "a very annoying affair" with a slave who "took offense at some imagined grievance, and took up her baby and walked off." The slave soon returned to work, but her mistress pronounced herself prepared "at any moment to find she has gone off in earnest."

White families fleeing from advancing Union armies represented the second type of Southern refugee. Among the first Confederate refugees was Mrs Robert E. Lee, who left her ancestral home at Arlington in May 1861 never to return. Thousands of displaced people congregated in Richmond, helping swell the city's population from about 40,000 in 1860 to more than 100,000 during the war. A diarist from northern Virginia recorded thoughts about abandoning her home: "I cannot get over my disappointment – I am not to return home!… It makes my blood boil when I remember that our private rooms, our chambers, our very sanctums, are thrown open to a ruthless soldiery."

Thousands of other Confederates lived in areas either occupied by Federal forces or subject to frequent incursions. A woman in Warrenton, Virginia, described the impact of a single Union foray in April 1862. A party of Federals "came down to [a friend's] house and took every thing in the way of eating from him, his sugar, meat, and corn… They went to Mr Hunton's near Broad Run and stole all his *horses, hay, and corn – turkeys chickens, meat*, and in fact all the man had to live on." This woman believed that residents of towns fared better than those in rural areas: "The country people suffer much more … for parties go out as foraging parties and plunder and steal all they can lay their hands on."

Armies left indelible marks on the Southern landscape. Battles scarred the areas around Manassas Junction, Fredericksburg, and Richmond, but armies did not have to fight to have a devastating impact. A British visitor traveling through Virginia's Piedmont in June 1863 left a graphic description of a region that had seen no important military clashes. "The country is really magnificent," he wrote, "but as it has supported two large armies for two years, it is now completely cleaned out. It is almost uncultivated, and no animals are grazing where there used to be hundreds." Fences had disappeared, buildings had been burned and chimneys had been left as silent sentinels. "It is difficult to depict and impossible to exaggerate," this witness concluded, "the sufferings which this part of Virginia has undergone."

As in the North, Confederate women played a more prominent part in the workforce. They filled in for their husbands on farms, served as full-time or occasional nurses, wrapped cartridges in ordnance facilities, and signed bond certificates or performed other clerical duties for the government. Their labors could prove to be not only exhausting but also dangerous. In March 1863, an explosion in an ordnance lab on Brown's Island in Richmond injured 69 women, at least 34 of whom died.

Between the beginning of the war and early summer 1863, Confederate civilians adjusted to a society thrown into considerable disarray. They coped with more shortages and relatively higher prices than Northern civilians, endured the uncertainty and fear that Union armies inspired, and sometimes faced the cruel choice of whether to become refugees. Black Southerners similarly encountered war-related problems, as well as opportunities, that affected them and their families. In sum, the South knew war in ways that were typical of other times and other nations, but that generally spared the people of the North.

PORTRAIT OF A CIVILIAN: ELIZABETH HERNDON MAURY

The war came early to Elizabeth Herndon Maury. Born into a leading Virginia family in 1835, she was the daughter of famous oceanographer Matthew Fontaine Maury, and his wife, Anne Hull Herndon. She married a cousin named William A. Maury, and the couple were living in Washington, DC, with their young daughter when war erupted in 1861. Like Mrs Robert E. Lee, Betty and Will Maury became refugees almost immediately. Their staunch Southern sympathies and loyalty to Virginia dictated that they move south. Over the next two years, Betty spent most of her time with relatives and friends in Fredericksburg, Richmond, and other places between those two cities. A diary for the period June 1861 to March 1863 details her thoughts and movements and illuminates several facets of civilian life in the Confederacy.

Betty made no apologies for her support of Virginia's decision to secede. When a gentleman from New York voiced regret at her father's resignation from the United States navy, Betty immediately defended the action. "He speaks ... of Pa's resignation ... as if he were dead," she wrote on June 3, 1861. "I told him that I was proud of my father before, but I was a hundred times prouder of him now." Northerners had always honored her father "far more than those at the South, but he could not take sides against his own people, against his native State and against the right." Betty bore no good will toward Virginians who failed to support the Confederacy. Learning of Winfield Scott's decision to retire as general-in-chief of the Union armies in November 1861, she penned a scathing reaction: "Lincoln and his Cabinet called upon the old humbug to express their regret and thank him for his services to his country and his adherence to the Union," she wrote. "The old crocodile was effected to tears and wishes that he was able to assist in crushing the rebellion. And he is a Virginian."

Elizabeth Herndon Maury, whose diary was published privately by her daughter in 1938. The edition ran to just 25 copies, making it one of the scarcest and most desirable Civil War diaries. (Collection of Fredericksburg and Spotsylvania National Military Park)

The precipitate departure from Washington had left Betty without most of her possessions – a common experience for Confederate refugees. She had lived a comfortable life, and she missed her things. A sense of longing and unpredictability accompanied a diary entry written in Fredericksburg in the summer of 1861: "It is strange how one can become accustomed to almost any mode of life. Here we are now *almost* as happy as in our best days and we cannot look into the future of this world at all. Cannot form an idea as to where or in what condition we may be one month hence."

Betty paid considerable attention to the problems of inflation and shortages of goods. Less than five months into the war, she noted that, "every thing in the South in the way of dry goods and groceries are very high and continue to increase in price." The cost of sugar, tea, and coffee had escalated significantly, though meat and vegetables remained more affordable. "We can do without tea and coffee," she remarked, "until we whip the Yankees." By early April 1862, "goods of every kind" had become scarce, a spool of cotton had increased threefold in price, butter was unobtainable, and many shops had closed. Maury claimed that she and other Confederates did not mind the hardship "if we can only whip the Yankees and conquer a peace." Two months later the Federal army had occupied Fredericksburg, and "Yankee citizens and Yankee Dutchmen" had "opened all the stores on Main street." This brought a confusion of currencies that must have been typical of Confederate areas controlled by Union forces: "A pair of boots are worth so much in specie, so much more in Yankee money, and double their real value in Virginia money."

Civilians on both sides avidly followed news from the military fronts, relying on newspapers, letters from family members or friends, and rumors to shape their understanding of events. Betty Maury often commented about campaigns, battles, and generals. "More good news!" she exclaimed on July 22, 1861, upon learning of the Confederate victory at First Manassas. "The battle yesterday was more extensive than we thought. It extended along our whole line. The enemy are routed and we are in hot pursuit. Thank God, thank God, I hope it is all true. What would I not give to hear that they are now on Arlington Heights." Her enthusiasm abated the next day when it became clear that the Confederates had not hounded their beaten foe to Washington: "Am disappointed that our troops only pursued the enemy to Centreville. I had hoped they were now in Arlington."

The dreary procession of Southern defeats in the Western Theater during the first half of 1862 upset her, but failed to break her resolve. "The news from the West is disastrous," she observed in mid-February 1862. "The enemy have penetrated into North Alabama as far as Florence. The coils of the 'Great Anaconda' seem to be tightening around us. That is the name the Yankees have given their plan to crush us simultaneously from all points. God help us." The surrender of New Orleans in late April 1862 elicited a defiant response from Betty: "The enemy has advanced with mighty strides in the last few months, but hope is strong with us yet."

Stonewall Jackson's exploits in the Shenandoah Valley and McClellan's retreat from Richmond after the Seven Days thrilled Maury. On April 23, 1862, she lamented the absence of a great Confederate commander, predicting that, "If we succeed in this struggle it will be in spite of our Generals. The man for the times has not yet been developed." Jackson soon emerged as Betty's ideal type of leader. With reports of his final successes in the valley in hand, she proclaimed, "Jackson is doing great things. He has whipped three of the Yankee Generals on three successive days… He is somewhere between Winchester and Staunton." She mistakenly credited Stonewall with playing a major role in Lee's victory over McClellan in the Seven Days battles. "This has been a most anxious and exciting week and even now I am afraid to boast of the great deeds that have been done, and the fields that have been won by our brave soldiers in the past ten days," she wrote on July 5. "Jackson came down from the valley with a portion of his forces and got in McClellan's rear. We commenced the attack on Wednesday at Mechanicsville and God has blessed us with a series of glorious victories since then."

Living in Fredericksburg placed Betty near Virginia's military frontier for much of 1862 and early 1863. She worried ceaselessly about whether Union soldiers would appear and if she would have to move again. She also fretted about the well-being of relatives in Confederate service, including her brother Richard Launcelot, an officer with the 24th Virginia Infantry who suffered a serious wound at Seven Pines. The arrival of Federal troops opposite Fredericksburg in April 1862 proved to be almost anticlimactic. "One can scarcely realize that the enemy are so near and that we are in their hands," wrote Betty. "Every thing is so quiet. The stores have been closed for the last three days and the streets are deserted except by the negroes." A Union band's playing "Yankee Doodle" and "The Star Spangled Banner" on the night of April 20 spurred thoughts of Betty's earlier loyalties. "The old tunes brought back recollections of the old love for them," she wrote. "It was a sad and painful feeling."

Part of the pain derived from Betty's loss of her privileged prewar economic circumstances. As a member of the South's slaveholding class, she had wanted for little and shouldered no burden of work. Her mother commented in March 1862 about missing "the old Union sometimes. We never felt any of the evils of it and the advantages of being an independent nation will not be felt in our life time." Betty reflected on her mother's statements in her diary entry for that day: "I know what the answer is – that it is very plain we should have felt the evils in a short time very severely – that we are fighting for the good of posterity, that we may prevent a servile war, etc." Having listed the usual arguments in favor of secession and founding a new slaveholding republic, she admitted to "being unpatriotic enough to feel a little selfish sometimes and regret our peace and comfort in the old Union."

Refugees from the Battle of Fredericksburg huddle around a fire in this 1865 painting by David English Henderson. Betty Maury undoubtedly knew many of the people who fled the city as Burnside's army massed across the Rappahannock River in late November 1862. Robert E. Lee helped some of the civilians leave their homes. "I was moving out the women & children all last night & today," he wrote to his wife on November 22. "It was a piteous sight." (Gettysburg National Military Park, National Park Service)

Betty's antebellum society had rested on a system of slavery that underwent enormous change in the midst of war. White Southerners lost a measure of control over their slaves as Union military forces drew near, and thousands of black people in Virginia fled to Union lines. In mid-March 1862, as rumors of Union advances swirled through Fredericksburg, Betty noted that "seventeen of Mr Mason's servants have run off. They stole all of cousin Nanny's dresses but three, and took both cloak and shawl. One party of them went off in a wagon and carried their feather beds."

In late April, after Federal troops had reached Fredericksburg, Maury wrote that the "negroes are going off in great numbers, and are beginning to be very independent and impudent. We hear that our three are going soon." The reality of war mocked the notion, so often trumpeted by white Southerners, that slaves were happy with their lot. Indeed, the specter of slaves wreaking vengeance on their old masters haunted Confederates such as Betty Maury. "I am afraid of the lawless Yankee soldiers," she wrote, "but that is nothing to my fear of the negroes if they should rise against us."

Betty had moved to Richmond by the time of the Battle of Fredericksburg. She celebrated Lee's victory over Burnside, but lamented the destruction of much of the city. In the neighborhood where she had lived, reports indicted that "almost every house has six or eight shells through it, the doors are wide open, the locks and windows broken and the shutters torn down." Two blocks of buildings had been burned, and "our house was a hospital."

She soon faced a more personal challenge. Pregnant with a second child in the spring of 1863, Betty learned that cousins from whom she rented rooms in Richmond meant to turn her out. "No one will be willing to take us," she wrote, "when told that I expect to be confined in a month or two. It is most unchristian and uncharitable treatment." An aunt in central Virginia declined to provide a place for Betty and her daughter, after which the pair endured a difficult trip to Charlottesville, where the new child was born on June 7. Betty Maury lived another 40 years, having experienced in full measure the traumatic events of the Civil War era.

HOW THE PERIOD ENDED: AN UNCERTAIN FUTURE

Two years of war in the Eastern Theater had not produced a decisive resolution on the battlefield. The armies had waged six major campaigns, testing each other's mettle twice on the plains of Manassas, in the fetid lowlands outside Richmond, amid the rolling Maryland countryside near Sharpsburg, on the banks of the Rappahannock River at Fredericksburg, and at Chancellorsville in the dreary thickets of the Wilderness. More than 150,000 men had fallen on these fields, mocking the widespread belief in 1861 that the conflict would be settled on a single battlefield. Dramatic fluctuations of military fortunes had taught perceptive observers not to expect Cannae-type victories.

Most people North and South, weary of the war's butchery and general disruption of normal patterns of life, hoped for peace but saw no end in sight. Voicing a sentiment prevalent in both armies, one of Lee's soldiers wrote after Chancellorsville: "I have never felt as tired of the army since I have been in it as I am now… I'm hoping for a time when the filth, lice, scurvy, and slavery of war shall be a thing of the past – and then – I close my eyes and am off to the dim and dusky future peopling it with dreams which I know are too bright ever to be realized."

Only the South had succeeded in the search for competent military leadership. With Lee's emergence during the Seven Days, Confederates had found the general whose talent and achievements would place him at the center of their quest for nationhood. Stonewall Jackson had been Lee's peerless lieutenant, the pair forming a seemingly unbeatable team. Jackson's death plunged the Confederacy into mourning. "He was the nation's idol," wrote one woman, "not a breath even from a foe has ever been breathed against his fame. His very enemies reverenced him. God has taken him from us that we may

Stonewall Jackson in front of the Confederate battle lines on the evening of May 2, 1863, just before being wounded by a volley from his own soldiers. This postwar engraving by Confederate veteran Allen C. Redwood mistakenly shows Jackson on the Plank Road. The general and his small party were on the Mountain Road, a smaller track that paralleled the Plank Road a few dozen yards to the north. (Gary Gallagher)

lean more upon *Him*, feel that He can raise up to himself instruments to work His Divine Will." An officer in the Army of Northern Virginia commented that, "No man in the Confederacy would have been more missed and more deeply lamented, except Lee perhaps." Many who mourned Jackson's loss tried to put on a brave face, as when Richmond's diarist J. B. Jones wrote that "there are other Jacksons in the army, who will win victories – no one doubts it."

Although most Confederates looked with confidence to Lee and his army, they harbored few illusions about how quickly the war would end. A Richmond paper observed in mid-May 1863 that the "Yankees have now made up their minds that this is to be a long war, and they are determined to fight it out to the end. Of course, we shall beat them in every battle, but they can afford to lose five men for the sake of destroying *one* of us." The paper grimly concluded that the Confederates fought "at fearful disadvantage with terrible loss, in spite of our superiority in pluck and in generalship, and the state of things may well continue twenty years longer, for these mean Yankees cannot afford to acknowledge our independence."

The Army of the Potomac's high command had endured enormous turmoil during two years of fighting, and few in the North believed in Joseph Hooker. A staff officer in the VI Corps captured the frustration of several failed campaigns in a single sentence: "I hope we shall not have to cross this river again," he wrote from camp near the Rappahannock on May 12, 1863, "for it is not the way to Richmond but I am afraid we shall have to try it over again and that very soon." Elizabeth Blair Lee, whose husband Samuel Phillips Lee served as a Union admiral, took heart from rumors that George G. Meade, John Sedgwick, and other subordinates had told Hooker they "would never willingly go in battle under him again." Although Lee's information was faulty, her sentiment underscored the lack of trust in Hooker.

The North could take heart from the fact that Great Britain and France had backed away from recognizing the Confederacy. In mid-September 1862, with Lee's victories at the Seven Days and Second Manassas in mind, Prime Minister Viscount Palmerston and Foreign Secretary Lord John Russell had concluded that the Confederacy was winning the war. If Lee triumphed again while in Maryland, suggested Palmerston, Britain and France should offer "an arrangement upon the basis of separation" between the United States and the Confederacy.

The Union soldiers who fought at Antietam helped change the picture radically. Following Lee's retreat and Lincoln's issuance of the preliminary proclamation of emancipation, Palmerston decided that the "whole matter is full of difficulty, and can only be cleared up by some more decided events between the contending armies." In late October, the British Cabinet rejected a French proposal for a six-month armistice and suspension of the Union blockade. Because emancipation had been added to the Northern agenda, it would take a spectacular series of Confederate victories to bring European intervention.

Each side girded for another round of campaigning in late spring 1863. During the lull after Chancellorsville, events in the Western Theater contended for primacy. "Affairs in the South West now engage all our attention," stated Catherine Edmondston on May 23. For two years, Union forces had fought to gain control of the Mississippi River, and the Confederacy retained just two bastions on that mighty waterway – at Vicksburg, Mississippi, and Port Hudson, Louisiana. But whatever happened west of the Appalachians and along the Mississippi, no one doubted that future confrontations between the Army of the Potomac and the Army of Northern Virginia would do much to shape the destinies of the two North American republics.

CHAPTER 2

THE WAR IN THE WEST 1861–JULY 1863

THE FIGHTING: STRUGGLE FOR THE HEARTLAND

The Western Theater, delineated by the Appalachian Mountains in the east and the Mississippi River in the west, also included the states of Missouri and Arkansas. The states that were most perplexed about how to proceed at the outbreak of war included Kentucky, Tennessee, and Missouri. The fact that the Ohio and Mississippi Rivers, as well as two significant tributaries, the Cumberland and the Tennessee, flowed through this region made it all the more significant as a war zone. "Whatever Nation gets … control of the Ohio, Mississippi, and Missouri Rivers," concluded Union General William T. Sherman, "will control the continent."

This region was settled largely by Southerners, but it was tied geographically and economically to the Ohio and Mississippi River valleys. This meant that economic exchanges with Northern markets were commonplace and thus a shared regional identity took shape in the pre-Civil War decades. Nowhere were loyalties more divided and the term a "brother's war" more applicable than in the west. John L. Crittenden, the Kentucky politician who had proposed the Crittenden Compromise months before, would have two sons who fought on opposite sides.[*]

[*] The Crittenden Compromise was an unsuccessful proposal which aimed to address the grievances of the slave states which led to the secession crisis of 1860–61. The Compromise would have guaranteed the permanent existence of slavery in the slave states.

As mentioned in the first chapter, volunteers came from all over the United States and filled the ranks of both armies as soon as the war broke out. Some 700,000 men mustered into the Northern armies during the initial months of the war. Most enlisted for three years' service. Out of approximately one million white males of military age, the Confederate Congress called on 500,000 men to enlist, which inspired hundreds of thousands to muster into service. Roughly 50 percent signed up for three years and the other half enlisted for 12 months.

As armies began to take shape, so did military strategy. Reunion of Northerners and Southerners was the principal goal of Northern political and military leaders. Preservation of the Union was paramount to Union war aims, and politicians and commanders planned to fight a limited war for limited goals. By pledging to protect noncombatants and by respecting their constitutional guarantees (a strategy intended to attract Southerners back to the Union), the Union army could concentrate on fighting the Confederate army. But between 1861 and 1863, the means for obtaining reunion changed dramatically. The experience of fighting in the west brought about fundamental political and military changes that shifted and broadened Union war aims. Over time, winning the war became more important than winning the peace.

Because slavery and states' rights were central to Southern life, the Confederate war effort struggled with building a nation founded on these beliefs while attempting to fight a war that did not necessarily serve these interests. To wage a war that did not deliberately protect slavery and preserve

states' rights would diminish popular support for the conflict. Confederate political and military leaders therefore sought to wage a defensive war. Protection of the South and its institutions from invading armies became the overall strategy for the war in the west.

The Union occupies Missouri

When Kentucky declared neutrality at the outbreak of the conflict, both Lincoln and Davis ordered military commanders to respect the state's dubious position. This meant that Northern penetration in the west would have to skirt Kentucky, and thus Northern armies would be forced to traverse the Appalachian Mountains to the east and the Mississippi River to the west, neither of which seemed feasible in the spring of 1861. Southerners feared that a neutral Kentucky might soon fall prey to the Union. Kentucky was indeed important. "I think to lose Kentucky," remarked Lincoln with obvious concern, "is nearly to lose the whole game." "Kentucky gone, we can not hold Missouri, nor, as I think, Maryland. These all against us, and the job on our hands is too large for us."

Whatever Kentucky's importance, while it remained neutral, little could be done in the Bluegrass State. Missouri then became all the more important for the Confederacy, as its border was just across the river from Kentucky. Missourians rejected secession in March and remained in the Union, but considering the heavy pro-South contingent in the southern part of the state and along the river, war came early to the western state. After rejecting

The Western Theater of War.

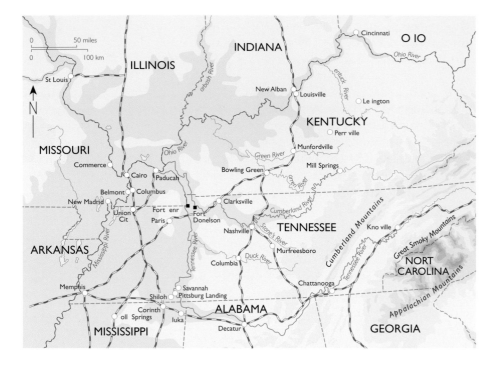

Lincoln's call for volunteers in April, secessionist Governor Claiborne Jackson, with the support of the pro-secessionist legislature, attempted to seize the federal arsenal and federal subtreasury in St Louis. On May 10 the rival factions came to blows at Camp Jackson, near St Louis, where Jackson's militia encamped. Federal Captain Nathaniel Lyon, a fiery, antislavery veteran of the earlier skirmishes in Kansas, captured the Confederate force and marched them through the streets of St Louis back to the arsenal. An angry pro-South mob gathered and triggered a riot that left at least 28 dead and dozens more wounded.

Days later, Lyon and Jackson met to discuss the future of Missouri in the hope of avoiding more bloodshed. The meeting ended when Lyon refused to concede to the governor's demands. "Rather [than] concede to the State of Missouri for one instant the right to dictate to my Government in any matter," he defiantly remarked, "I would see you … and every man, woman, and child in the State, dead and buried. *This means war*."

Ironically, the move to suppress Confederate sympathy had in fact fueled war. In the weeks that followed, Union forces managed to push Jackson's militia toward the southwestern part of Missouri, capturing in the process the state capital at Jefferson City on June 15. Lyon and Colonel Franz Sigel, a prominent German-American leader, pursued with about 5,500 men and occupied the town of Springfield. But Lyon's soldiers were at the end of a weak supply line with no promise of reinforcements. Soon the 8,000 secessionist militia led by Major-General Sterling Price were joined by 5,000 Confederate troops under

Major-General Benjamin McCulloch. Lyon nevertheless refused to retreat and, learning that the Rebels would soon launch an offensive, decided to attack first.

On August 10 the Union forces struck the Southerners at Wilson's Creek or Oak Hills, 10 miles (16km) south of Springfield. Lyon's attack was risky, but came close to success. The Rebel troops were poorly trained and equipped, and Lyon managed to achieve surprise with a daring two-pronged attack. A confused savage battle ensued along the banks of Wilson's Creek. Lyon's men managed to hold their ground, in the face of nearly three-to-one odds, until Lyon was fatally wounded. The combination of Lyon's death and depleted ammunition forced the Federals to retreat. Eventually they fell back over 100 miles (160km) to Rolla, a railroad town that linked them to St Louis.

Union and Confederate forces both suffered roughly 1,300 casualties in this battle. In the weeks that followed, Confederates marched into the Missouri River valley, and they captured Lexington, Missouri, in mid-September. Thus, for a few months, Price's militia controlled half the state. The Confederate commander, however, soon discovered that he lacked the manpower to hold

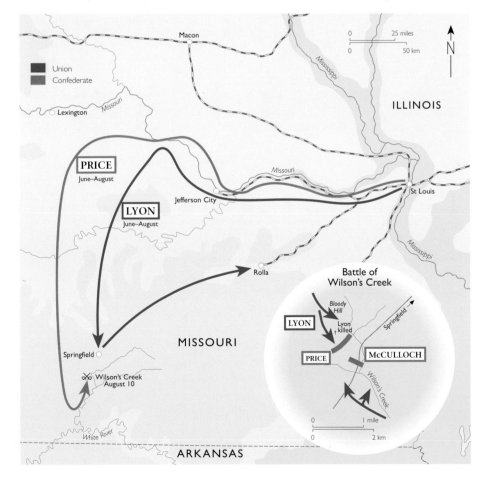

Missouri, 1861 and Wilson's Creek.

GEN: F. SIEGEL AND LATE GEN: N. LYON.

THE HEROES OF MISSOURI

Published by L. PRANG & Cº. 34 Merchants Row Boston.

Designed & drawn with Pen on Stone by E. ACKERMANN.

Printed by L. PRANG & Cº Boston.

such a vast region, and in October he withdrew again to the southwest corner of Missouri. Although they had lost the key battle, the Federals ironically managed to hold on to Missouri, although their grip was tenuous and remained so until the next year. Throughout the war, Missouri was the battleground for continual and vicious guerrilla warfare.

Had the Union authorities only confronted organized armies in Missouri, they would probably have eliminated the threat in 1863. But longstanding tensions, ideological differences over slavery, and the conduct of Union troops stirred up a hornets' nest of trouble from guerrilla bands. Although many Rebel guerrillas there had strong ties to slavery, quite a few others exhibited a passion for violence and destruction that may have been pathological. Helping to ignite this tinderbox were Kansans who combined fervent abolitionism with a passion for plundering.

During the Missouri campaign of 1861, there were pockets of fighting in which neither side gave quarter. Yet raids from Kansas fueled the violence when they extended from confiscation of slaves and livestock to arson, robbery, and murder. These Kansans insisted they were merely retaliating for the slaughter of seven of their people by guerrillas a few days earlier, but acts of savagery begat more acts of savagery, and soon the entire region was ablaze in deeds of violence or brutal reprisals.

Union advances in Kentucky

Meanwhile, in Kentucky, while both presidents attempted to steer armies around the state, secessionist Governor Beriah Magoffin also repudiated Lincoln's request for troops. Still, he allowed the Unionist legislature to exercise a degree of power throughout the summer. Nonetheless, recruiting for both sides went on in the state until Confederate fears over possible Union occupation of the region along the Mississippi River forced the Confederates to seize Columbus, Kentucky. Major-General Leonidas Polk ordered a force under Gideon Pillow to seize the strategic town, positioned on a high bluff overlooking the Mississippi River, which he did on September 3. Although he was prompted to strike because of the town's military importance, the political consequences were monumental. Declaring that the Confederacy had invaded the Bluegrass State, Kentucky's Union authorities pledged their support for the Union and forced Magoffin to resign. Federal forces under Major-General Ulysses S. Grant immediately occupied Paducah, Kentucky, near the mouth of the Tennessee River and connected to Columbus by railroad. Although the Union held only a thin strip of Kentucky's border, its strategic significance far outweighed its small size.

As in Missouri, Union and Confederate authorities moved quickly to shore up strategic points in the state. Federal forces immediately took Louisville, the largest city, and Frankfurt, the Kentucky capital. Major-General Robert Anderson commanded Louisville until he was replaced in September by Major-General William T. Sherman. As Union politicians contemplated how

OPPOSITE PAGE:
This lithograph shows Franz Sigel, the leader of German-Americans in the war, who served under Nathaniel Lyon during the Missouri campaign, being inspired by Lyon, who was killed during the Battle of Wilson's Creek. (Anne S. K. Brown Military Collection, Brown University Library)

A close prewar friend of McClellan, who shared his superior's limited-war beliefs, Don Carlos Buell became commander of the Department of Ohio and played an instrumental role in bringing about success in the west. (Ann Ronan Picture Library)

Henry Halleck was known in the regular army before the Civil War as "Old Brains" for his impressive intellect. McClellan appointed him commander of the Department of Missouri in November 1861 and his leadership in the western campaigns so impressed Lincoln that he became the President's chief of staff. (Massachusetts Commandery Military Order of the Loyal Legion and the US Army Military History Institute)

In 1861, Albert Sidney Johnston was regarded as one of the nation's finest military commanders, but his Civil War career was one of the great disappointments of the Confederacy. He was wounded at the Battle of Shiloh and bled to death while his staff physician was attending to wounded Southern and Northern soldiers. (Ann Ronan Picture Library)

best to occupy the region they now held militarily, significant changes were occurring in military personnel.

In early November, Major-General George B. McClellan replaced General Winfield Scott as general-in-chief of the Union armies. McClellan moved quickly to stabilize the political and military situation in the west and he appointed like-minded commanders for the war's most important commands.

McClellan replaced John C. Fremont, who had issued an unauthorized emancipation proclamation in Missouri, with Major-General Henry Wager Halleck.* At 46, Halleck, a West Point graduate, had already demonstrated brilliance as a writer of military theory. When the war broke out, he was perhaps the most sought-after Union commander. He would be sent to St Louis to

---

* The Republican Party candidate for president in 1856, Major-General John C. Fremont had declared martial law in St Louis in August 1861, proclaimed the death penalty for all guerrillas, and freed all slaves of Confederate supporters. Having irritated his commander-in-chief and many others with this action, Fremont needed a victory to restore his reputation. He accumulated a large force, some 38,000, and began a pursuit of Price. An order relieving Fremont reached him before he caught up with Price.

bring some semblance of order to the chaos. As a result of the reorganization of military departments in the west, Halleck would be responsible for the area that stretched westward from the Cumberland River through Missouri.

Major-General Don Carlos Buell commanded the newly organized Department of the Ohio, which comprised the region stretching from the Appalachian Mountains to the Cumberland River, but included all of Kentucky. Since his graduation from West Point in 1841, Buell was one of the few regular army officers in the western command and was a staunch advocate of limited war. He had acquired eight slaves through his prewar marriage and was a conservative Democrat, like McClellan and Halleck. McClellan thought that sending him to Kentucky might placate Kentuckians. Although its command in the west was divided, the Union had twice the number of troops as the Confederates with which to conduct affairs in the respective departments, which stretched some 500 miles (800km).

The Confederates meanwhile sought to unify the command of the western region under the leadership of Major-General Albert Sidney Johnston. A charismatic Texan, with outstanding credentials, having graduated from West Point eighth in his class and having served in the Black Hawk War, the Mexican War, and the Mormon War of 1858, Johnston was an excellent choice.

Kentucky and Tennessee, winter and spring 1862.

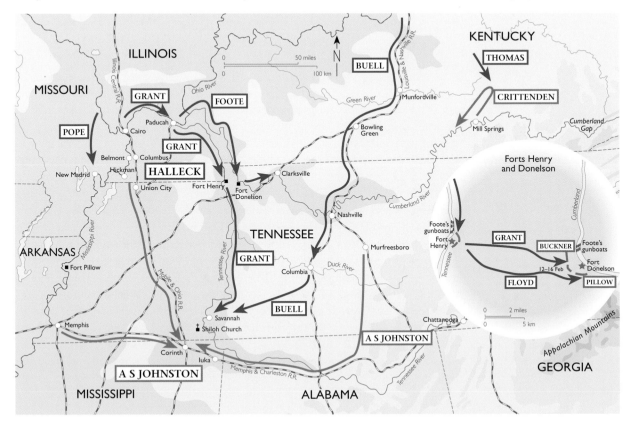

Moreover, he was a good friend of President Davis. On his shoulders would fall the responsibility of defending the 500-mile (800km) line that stretched from the Appalachians to the Ozarks in the west across the Mississippi River. He constructed a defensive cordon that ran from Columbus on the Mississippi to Cumberland Gap in the Appalachians.

Besides the daunting task of defending such a vast line, Johnston was also strapped with the liability of having a core of subordinates whose authority exceeded their abilities. Polk, the commander of the western stronghold at Columbus, was also a West Point graduate, but left the military to become an Episcopal bishop before the war. On the extreme of the Confederate defensive line was Brigadier-General Felix Zollicoffer, a prewar journalist who advanced his Southern forces into eastern Kentucky. To block a Union invasion from Louisville, the Confederates occupied Bowling Green in the center of the state and command of the forces there went to Simon Bolivar Buckner. To assist in holding the front, Johnston had two political generals, Gideon Pillow and John B. Floyd, who proved wholly incompetent as military commanders.

Trying to defend a huge expanse of territory with inept leadership, Johnston's task was further handicapped by a lack of resources – a problem that would plague the Confederacy throughout the war. East of the Mississippi River, Johnston could concentrate at any one place only about 45,000 men, and west of the river, perhaps 15,000 soldiers. Still, once they occupied Kentucky, the Confederates enjoyed excellent railroad connections that gave them the distinct advantage of interior lines. They could reinforce any one region quickly by moving troops through these interior lines and a maze of tiny installations. To buoy this strength, Johnston's troops had built two forts on the Cumberland and Tennessee Rivers just below the Kentucky–Tennessee line. Fort Henry on the Tennessee River and Fort Donelson on the Cumberland River were designed to inhibit Federal navigation on these rivers.

While the newly-appointed Halleck and Buell considered the best avenue by which to penetrate the South, Grant decided to head down the Mississippi River from Cairo, Illinois. On November 7, some 3,000 troops were ferried downriver to Belmont, Missouri, opposite the bluffs of Columbus, Kentucky. Although Grant's troops moved swiftly to capture the tiny river hamlet, driving the defenders away, General Polk sent reinforcements across the river and soon forced Grant's troops to retreat. Aside from the casualties, which cost Confederates and Federals about 600 men each, Grant came to appreciate the strength of Columbus and the viability of using the Mississippi as an avenue of invasion south. Another route would have to open up.

The campaign in Kentucky and Tennessee, 1861–62

As winter approached, the prospects of campaigning were dismal and the difficulty of moving men in the winter brought the Federal offensive to a halt. Both Union and Confederate armies went into winter quarters expecting little military activity, but commanders began to exploit the natural advantages afforded them by the rivers. In the months that followed, the Union's edge on the water helped it recover from the defeat at First Manassas, Wilson's Creek, and Belmont. Union commanders pondered the best avenues of invasion. They could move down the Mississippi River against Columbus, which had proven to be impregnable; they could move by railroad from Louisville to Bowling Green into central Kentucky, which the Confederates could easily stall; or they could move up either the Tennessee or Cumberland River or both toward the river forts.

Whatever the case, the western commanders would first have to agree on the same avenue and, secondly, be willing to commit significant numbers of troops to hold on to supply areas as they moved south, which would reduce the number of troops for combat. A seemingly logical solution at the time, the divided departments would come to plague Union operations in the west, as neither Halleck nor Buell, cautious by nature and sensitive about administering their departments, could agree on the same route of invasion. Thus, the better part of the winter of 1861–62 was spent campaigning with a map. They convinced themselves that because the Confederates had the advantage of interior lines, any Union assault would have a distinct disadvantage. Consequently, an impatient Northern public and a frustrated president, tired of the inactivity, demanded an end to procrastination and the beginning of some movement in the west.

It was the subordinates of Halleck and Buell who, disheartened by the inactivity of camp life, convinced their superiors to allow them to take the initiative. The war began to move in the west in early January when Halleck ordered Grant to send a small expeditionary force up the Tennessee River to test the defenses at Fort Henry. This diversionary trip, Halleck thought, might also force Johnston to consider his options as to where he might concentrate his force.

At the other end of the Confederate defensive line, major-generals George B. Crittenden and George H. Thomas engaged and defeated Confederate forces under Brigadier-General Felix Zollicoffer at the Battle of Mill Springs or Logan's Cross Roads, Kentucky. The battle, on January 19, 1862, revealed the weakness

Ulysses S. Grant seized Fort Donelson and with it considerable fame. When he was asked for terms after defeating a Confederate breakout attempt, his reply earned him the nickname "Unconditional Surrender" Grant. (Ann Ronan Picture Library)

The *St Louis* was one of the earliest ironclad gunboats constructed. It saw action against Confederate batteries at Columbus, Kentucky, Fort Henry, Fort Donelson, and Memphis. In October 1862, its name changed to *Baron de Kalb* and it participated in river action against Vicksburg in 1862–63. A Confederate torpedo sank the ironclad on July 12, 1863, in the Yazoo River. (Ann Ronan Picture Library)

in Johnston's line and advanced the Union cause in the eastern portion of the Bluegrass State and in eastern Tennessee.

Meanwhile, Grant had finally convinced Halleck that Fort Henry could easily be taken. In early February about 15,000 troops boarded transports and steamed up the Tennessee. To cooperate with the Union troops, Grant ordered a flotilla of gunboats commanded by Flag Officer Andrew H. Foote to accompany the expedition. On February 6, while Grant disembarked his troops, the flotilla continued upriver and at 11.00am opened fire on the fort. Realizing that the Union forces were closing in by land and river, Brigadier-General Lloyd Tilghman decided to send the 2,500-man garrison out of the fort to Fort Donelson some 12 miles (19km) east. The winter rains had forced the Tennessee out of its banks and the fort had succumbed to nearly 6ft (2m) of water. Within three hours, the gunboats had reduced the fort and forced Tilghman to surrender before Grant's infantrymen even arrived on the scene. "Fort Henry is ours," read the news as it made its way east. "The flag of the Union is reestablished on the soil of Tennessee," asserted Halleck.

The Federals had correctly pinpointed the weakness in the Confederate defensive line: the Cumberland and Tennessee Rivers. Thinking that the Confederates would reinforce Fort Donelson on the Cumberland River, Grant destroyed the railroad over the Tennessee, sent gunboats south toward northern Alabama, and prepared to move eastward toward the river stronghold. Brigadier-General John B. Floyd commanded the Confederates at Fort Donelson, and Johnston decided to strengthen his line by sending some reinforcements, withdrawing part of the garrison at Columbus and abandoning Bowling Green. Confederate authorities had faced the crucial dilemma that would plague them for the rest of the war: how and where to defend the several-hundred-mile line with insufficient forces at their disposal.

Although reinforcing the fort seemed the strategic thing to do, it ultimately proved to be a colossal mistake. On February 13, Grant's army of 23,000 men made it to Fort Donelson and encircled it. The following day, Foote's gunboats arrived and began shelling the fort from the river, expecting to force its surrender. After several hours of heavy shelling, however, the fort's well-positioned artillery forced the gunboats to retire. The cold and blustery day ended and the two disheartened armies prepared to do battle the next day. During the night, the Confederate command, convinced that Grant had completely invested the fort by now, determined to attempt a breakout and head south. The next day, February 15, General Pillow, aided by some of General Buckner's men, broke through the Federal line after a brutal fight. When nothing was done to break the entire army out of the fort, Floyd ordered his army to return to their fortifications.

That evening the Confederates held a council of war and determined to surrender. Floyd and Pillow abdicated their responsibility as the highest-ranking commanders and left the job to General Buckner, a prewar friend of Grant's. When Buckner requested terms of surrender on February 16, Grant replied,

"No terms except unconditional and immediate surrender can be accepted." The words that forever immortalized him as "Unconditional Surrender" Grant gave the Union its first real victory of the entire war.

Strategically, the loss of the river forts was catastrophic to the Confederacy, but equally significant was the fact that Grant also captured the reinforcements sent to support the garrison. Some 12,500 soldiers and 40 guns were surrendered. The next day, the Northern press printed a sensational story of the Donelson campaign, made Grant an unsuspecting hero, but gave Halleck credit for planning the entire invasion. Frustrated by the news that "All was quiet along the Potomac," all winter, Lincoln was elated by the news along the Tennessee and Cumberland Rivers and instantly rewarded the nation's new hero with a promotion to major-general of volunteers.

The Union invasion along the rivers forced the Confederates to retreat south all the way to the Tennessee–Mississippi and Alabama border. Northern gunboats now threatened Southern river towns as far south as Clarksville and Nashville. Columbus, a Confederate stronghold on the Mississippi, also succumbed to the Federals, as did a significant portion of Middle Tennessee. Tennessee Governor Isham Harris prepared to abandon Nashville and move the government with him to Memphis. Significantly, the rivers, the great market highways that had provided a regional unity at harvest times, had now become the axis of military invasion and the great weakness of the Confederacy during the winter.

On the heels of the defeats in the west, there was a somber mood in Richmond on February 22, the day Jefferson Davis was inaugurated President of the Confederacy. As the rain poured, the Confederate President claimed that, "The tyranny of the unbridled majority, the most odious and least responsible form of despotism, has denied us both the right and the remedy. Therefore we are in arms to renew such sacrifices as our fathers made to the holy cause of constitutional liberty." While he was speaking, the citizens and soldiers of Nashville were evacuating the city. By the 25th, the Tennessee capital had surrendered to Union commander Don Carlos Buell. Wanting to move quickly to restore civilian government to the occupied region, Lincoln had named Andrew Johnson military governor of the state.

West of the Mississippi River, Major-General John Pope assumed command of the Army of the Mississippi at Commerce, Missouri. He ordered his troops to move against New Madrid, Missouri, in an attempt to dislodge the Confederate stronghold at Island No. 10 near the Kentucky–Tennessee border. By the time the Confederates had evacuated Columbus, Kentucky, Federal troops under Brigadier-General Samuel R. Curtis had pushed the Confederates under Major-General Sterling Price south out of Missouri and into the northwestern portion of Arkansas. At Fayetteville, Confederate General Earl Van Dorn joined Price in an effort to stop the Federal advance, and on March 7–8 they counterattacked at the Battle of Pea Ridge. The Union victory allowed Halleck to concentrate his energies east of the Mississippi.

Having assumed command of the entire west, Halleck ordered his armies south to occupy Corinth, Mississippi, an important railroad junction on the Memphis and Charleston line, or the "Vertebrae of the Confederacy," as the Confederate Secretary of War, Leroy P. Walker, characterized it. The Mobile and Ohio line bisected the Memphis and Charleston line at Corinth, and Halleck came to believe that after Richmond, occupation of this tiny railway junction might bring the rebellion to a close.

Halleck ordered Grant to Savannah, Tennessee, to wait for Buell to reinforce him before heading south. Confident that the Confederates would not attack, Grant assembled his army at Pittsburg Landing, a well-known landing for river transports. It was about 25 miles (40km) north of Corinth, and above the river bluffs the land was relatively flat, which made the landing a suitable choice to land a large number of troops. Still, it was on the west side of the Tennessee River and Halleck had ordered Grant to await reinforcements from Buell's army before heading south toward Corinth. Buell had departed Nashville with 36,000 men and was expected to meet up with Grant before he crossed his army over the river.

The Battle of Shiloh

After a bleak winter that had proved tremendously unsettling to the Southern cause, spring 1862 brought hope that the Confederates in the west might redeem their losses. Johnston concentrated his defeated forces near Corinth, for an offensive into Tennessee. He had pleaded all winter for reinforcements, but none were forthcoming until March, when he was able to muster some 40,000 troops to engage the enemy. Realizing that the Federals possessed superior numerical strength, he knew that the Confederates would have to pull off a stunning surprise and run Grant's army into the river before Buell arrived if they were to be successful. The concentration of forces brought together a colorful group of commanders, including major-generals Braxton Bragg and Pierre G. T. Beauregard, the hero of the Battle of First Manassas. Johnston assumed overall command.

The largely unseasoned Confederate Army of the Mississippi left Corinth on April 3. Muddy roads and the inhospitable terrain, however, stalled the advance for two days, forcing Beauregard to conclude that the element of surprise had been lost. Nonsense, Johnston remarked on the evening of April 5, "I would fight them if they were a million." The same evening Buell had made it to Savannah, a few miles downriver from Pittsburg Landing. The countryside around Pittsburg Landing was cut by ravines, blanketed by heavy underbrush and blossoming peach trees, and crossed by a maze of small creeks and old wagon trails that bisected one another. The only distinguishing landmark was a small Methodist church that stood near the main road to Corinth. The church was known as Shiloh, which in Hebrew means "Place of Peace."

It was early on Palm Sunday, April 6, when a Union patrol ventured out toward the woods and detected a wave of Confederates, who fired an enormous

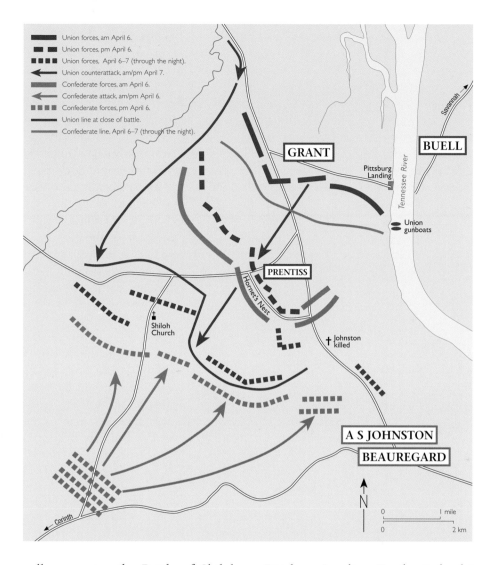

Union forces, am April 6.
Union forces, pm April 6.
Union forces, April 6–7 (through the night).
Union counterattack, am/pm April 7.
Confederate forces, am April 6.
Confederate attack, am/pm April 6.
Confederate forces, pm April 6.
Union line at close of battle.
Confederate line, April 6–7 (through the night).

GRANT

BUELL

Pittsburg Landing

Tennessee River

Savannah

Union gunboats

PRENTISS

Hornet's Nest

Shiloh Church

Johnston killed

A S JOHNSTON

BEAUREGARD

Corinth

N

0   1 mile
0   2 km

The Battle of Shiloh, April 6–7, 1862.

volley, opening the Battle of Shiloh, or Pittsburg Landing. To the Federals' surprise, the Confederates had struck at dawn. Major-General William T. Sherman, who had insisted that the enemy was no closer than Corinth, commanded the Federals near the church and was forced to form a line to hold off the Confederate wave. The Confederates thrust forward throughout the early morning hours, pushing the panic-stricken soldiers back toward the river. Although somewhat oddly formed and badly intermingled in its deployment, the Confederate offensive was nonetheless so successful that by noon thousands of the disorganized Federals had simply run for cover, some cowering beneath the river bluff, others swimming across the river for safety. Still, most of the Federal troops remained steadfast and throughout the morning both sides engaged in a horrific slaughter.

In Hebrew, Shiloh translates as "Place of Peace." It is an ironic name given to a church near Pittsburg Landing, Tennessee, the scene of the most fiercely contested battle of the war in the Western Theater. Shiloh Church was located in the middle of the Battle of Shiloh. It proved the inspiration for the noted author Herman Melville to compose an elegiac memorial to those who perished beside the humble country church. In "Shiloh: A Requiem," Melville attempted with poetic words to return Shiloh church to the quiet refuge it had once been. (*Harper's Weekly*)

When Grant arrived on the grisly scene it was about 8.30am. He pulled stragglers together to form a defensive line and left word at Savannah for Buell to get his troops across the river. In the meantime, Grant had to hold on. As the Confederates continued to push the Federals back, they ran into a stubborn resistance in the center. Brigadier-General Benjamin Prentiss's division was located in a densely wooded area with open fields on both sides and an old sunken wagon trail in its front that provided an entrenchment. Grant ordered Prentiss to hold his position at all costs – an order that he obeyed throughout the day. Because of the intensity of the fight in this location, soldiers later dubbed this portion of the battlefield the "Hornet's Nest."

All day long, Johnston's Confederates tried in vain to envelop and dislodge the Federals. Although the Federals were running low on ammunition, they still repulsed wave after wave of Confederate assaults. At one point Johnston himself led one of the charges and was mortally wounded. He bled to death while his personal physician was helping to care for captured wounded Federals. After several futile and suicidal bayonet charges, the Confederates positioned over 60 cannon in a semicircle to rain down several hundred shells on the Union stronghold. Practically surrounded, Prentiss reluctantly surrendered at 5.30pm to save the 2,200 men left in his division. During the remaining hour of daylight, Grant struggled to reposition his artillery to hold off the anticipated final Confederate thrust. As darkness came, so did the rains, and the merciless fighting ended.

SHILOAH MEETING HOUSE.

Now in command of the victorious Confederate forces, Beauregard concluded that the Federals would retreat during the night, so he did not position his scattered and disorganized forces to receive an offensive. Instead, he waited for Van Dorn to arrive from Arkansas. Buell was reportedly too far away to reinforce Grant. But the night rains and darkness favored the Union army. Although both sides were exhausted, Buell had, in fact, arrived and the four divisions that crossed the river numbered some 28,000 men, who were anxious to fight. Although it had been a tough day, Grant had been significantly reinforced and he would assume the offensive the following morning. As he walked the lines during the night, he came across a fatigued General Sherman, who had been in the thick of the fighting all day. Sherman suggested that it had been a horrific fight; Grant agreed, but remarked, "Whip 'em tomorrow, though."

Early the following morning, the Federals stunned the unsuspecting Confederates with an overwhelming counteroffensive. Throughout the morning and early afternoon, the soldiers fought over the same terrain, scattered with wounded and dead soldiers and horses, and half-submerged artillery pieces sunken by the rain. Like the previous day, the combat was severe and bloody. From the river, Union gunboats lobbed scores of shells down on the Southern combatants. When Beauregard realized that Van Dorn was not coming, and that his troops were nearly out of ammunition and completely exhausted, he ordered a withdrawal to Corinth. Grant decided not to pursue because his soldiers were just as exhausted and disorganized as the retreating troops.

These riverboats provided much needed assistance for the Union army at the Battle of Shiloh in April 1862. Grant made his headquarters aboard the *Tigress*, the middle vessel of the three. It was aboard this steamer that Buell and Grant met briefly to discuss the strategy that brought ultimate victory on the second day of the battle. (Review of Reviews Company)

Although the Union won the battle, both sides lost overwhelming numbers of casualties. Union casualties totaled over 13,000, while the Confederates lost over 10,000. Never before was the American populace confronted by such staggering news as the losses at Shiloh. Northerners came to believe that the human toll far exceeded the strategic gains in the west and that something must have gone seriously wrong. Although the Federals had extinguished Confederate hopes for reclaiming West Tennessee and stalling the Union penetration of significant cotton-producing regions in Mississippi and Alabama, Northern politicians were pressed for answers about the high casualty rate. As rumors passed through the Federal camps that the Confederates had surprised Grant, that he had been drinking, and that he had not even been on the field when the battle opened, Lincoln and Halleck were forced to justify the commander. At one point, frustrated about the failures and inactivity in the east, Lincoln supposedly defended Grant, arguing that although he might be the cause of the losses at Shiloh, "I can't spare this man; he fights."

The same day that Grant and Buell defeated Beauregard, General Pope captured Island No. 10, which opened the Mississippi River all the way to Memphis, Tennessee. In the following weeks, the Union Navy steamed down

Confederate gunboats burning at New Orleans on the approach of the Federal fleets. (Public domain)

the Mississippi toward Memphis, and Halleck came to Pittsburg Landing to direct the combined Federal armies of Grant and Buell against Corinth.

Perhaps even more stunning than the Union victory at Shiloh was Flag Officer David G. Farragut's capture of New Orleans, Louisiana, three weeks later. His wooden frigates and gunboats, carrying Brigadier-General Benjamin Butler's 15,000 soldiers, approached the forts protecting the mouth of the Mississippi River. After a week of bombarding the strongholds, Farragut's mortars failed to reduce the forts, so the determined sailor decided to run his flotilla by the forts. Before daybreak on April 24, Farragut slipped his 17 vessels past the forts and moved upriver, though the Confederates managed to disable three smaller vessels. Only a few days later, Farragut's sailors and marines captured New Orleans without resistance as Brigadier-General Mansfield Lovell sent his forces away from the city. Simultaneously, General Butler forced the surrender of the river forts and then sent his men to occupy New Orleans.

Not only had the Federals captured the Confederacy's largest city and leading port, but also the capture came on the heels of the defeat at Shiloh. Again the Confederates suffered the consequences of a lack of manpower to cover the vast western terrain. Confederate authorities believed that the main

OPPOSITE PAGE:
This engraving of William T. Sherman conveys the image of the Union general as described by a contemporary, who wrote that Sherman was "the most American looking man I ever saw, tall and lank, not very erect, with hair like thatch." (Anne S. K. Brown Military Collection, Brown University Library)

Union offensive was to come from upriver, so they ordered most of the soldiers and several gunboats north, leaving New Orleans vulnerable to attack.

The cumulative effect of these disasters was devastating to the Confederacy. The loss of Forts Henry and Donelson, the bloody defeat at Shiloh, and the capture of two of the Confederacy's most prominent cities, Nashville and New Orleans, cast a dark shadow over the war effort. The loss of these strategic places and manpower, coupled with the fact that McClellan had besieged Yorktown, Virginia, and was preparing to advance against Richmond with the largest force ever assembled on the North American continent, forced the Confederate government to consider desperate measures. On April 16, the Confederate Congress approved the first National Conscription Act in the nation's history. Although some Confederates bitterly opposed this Act, arguing that it was an infringement of their liberties, others argued that the Confederacy with its limited manpower must raise troops and that states' rights would have to succumb to the Confederate cause. All white males between 18 and 35 years of age would be subjected to three years' military service.

As the victory bells rang throughout the North in celebration of the accomplishments in the west, Southerners had no such expression. In fact, in stark contrast, church bells and plantation bells in the South were being melted down to be used in the war effort. At one point, Beauregard wrote to Father James Mullen of St Patrick's church in New Orleans that although "our wives and children have been accustomed to the call, and would miss the tones of the 'Church-going bells,' … there is no alternative we must make the sacrifice…" As much as he wanted to spare the necessity of depriving the South's plantations and churches of their bells, he simply could not. The war was heating up and Beauregard needed every available resource to carry on his operations to restore the Confederacy in the west.

Union advances into Mississippi and Tennessee

After Shiloh and the capture of New Orleans, the pace of Union success slowed, but Federal armies were still on the move. By the end of May 1862, Halleck's enormous army of over 100,000 troops had cautiously inched its way to Corinth, Mississippi, thinking that the Confederates had regrouped and would give battle. Beauregard, however, was in no position to fight Halleck and deceptively evacuated the small rail town during the night of May 29, heading south to Tupelo, Mississippi, some 80 miles (130km) away. In one of the great ruses of the war, the entire operation was carried out so skillfully that Halleck and his commanders were oblivious.

When Halleck rode into Corinth on the afternoon of May 30, he found an empty town. At one point he noticed a blue uniform stuffed with straw hanging by the neck from a scrubby tree limb. Nearby a pine board was nailed fast, and on it was written "Halleck outwitted – what will old Abe say?" Nonetheless, Halleck claimed that the capture of Corinth the following day was as "brilliant and important a victory as any recorded in history." Lincoln was impressed.

The Union's capture of Corinth broke the Memphis and Charleston Railroad and disabled the Confederates' east–west link. Memphis was now vulnerable to Union gunboats on the river and foot soldiers from the east, who pushed their way toward the city. As thousands of people lined the river bluffs early on the morning of June 6 to witness what they believed would be the final river fight, Commodore Charles Davis steamed downriver and opened the fight. After two hours of furious gunboat warfare, the fighting ended at 7.30am. The Federals had completely destroyed the Confederates and a few hours later the mayor surrendered the city. With Memphis in Union hands, the Federals could use it as a supply base as they moved downriver. The Mississippi was now open all the way to Vicksburg, Mississippi, considered by Confederates to be the "Gibraltar of the West."

By June 1862, no commander in either army could boast of successes like Halleck's in the Western Theater of war. With Kentucky, Missouri, Tennessee, and much of Arkansas in Federal hands, "Old Brains," as Halleck was commonly known before the war (an inference due to the size of his forehead and his intellect), had become the architect of success. Northern hopes for an end to the war escalated. But as the rivers began to shrink due to the summer heat, so too did Union activity in the west begin to decelerate.

Waging a limited war for limited goals, at a time when Union armies were now poised to strike at the South's vital slavery districts in the west, proved cumbersome for Union commanders whose armies occupied a region about the size of France. Fighting in battle constituted one brand of warfare, but attempting to maintain supremacy in the occupied regions while respecting the constitutional rights of Southern civilians, including their right to own slaves, would soon demoralize soldiers and Northern civilians alike. Thus the summer of 1862 was a defining period not so much in combat, but rather in how far Union authorities and the Union populace would go in continuing to support Lincoln's desire to fight a war that made ultimate peace and reunion possible.

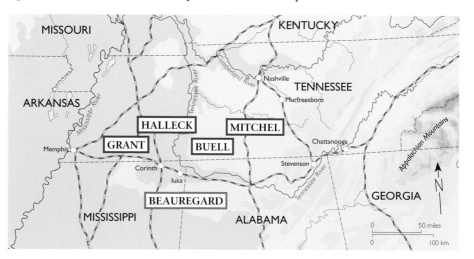

Situation after the fall of Corinth, May 30, 1862.

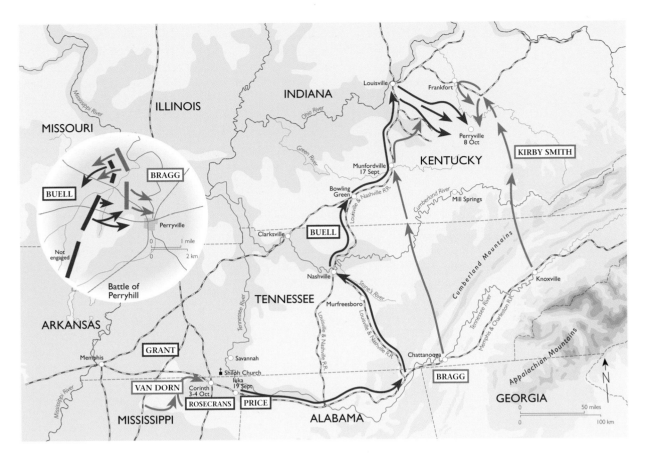

The Western Theater of War, summer–fall, 1862.

By mid-June, with the rivers no longer at his disposal, Halleck had dispersed his large army overland and turned his sights to securing the fruits of his army's labors. He ordered Buell and his 31,000 soldiers east toward Chattanooga, an important Tennessee city on the edge of the Appalachians, through which passed the Memphis and Charleston Railroad and the Tennessee River. Because his army would be marching in the same direction as the railroad, Halleck considered the use of the iron horse to be an asset to Buell's campaign. But the railroad in this case proved to be a curse, and Buell's army would have serious difficulty in moving east. In the meantime, Halleck used Grant and Sherman to police West Tennessee with the 67,000 soldiers left in his grand army. The string of victories ceased.

By mid-July, after Grant's promotion to general-in-chief, Lincoln had made Halleck his chief-of-staff, which left Grant the command in West Tennessee and Buell the command of his soldiers stalled in northern Alabama. Because of the disposition of their forces, neither commander was prepared to continue the momentum of offensive warfare. The recalcitrant temper of the Southern populace, guerrilla activity, and the frustration of protecting long and vulnerable supply lines and railroads all combined to stall operations.

Confederate General Braxton Bragg had a distinguished prewar career. After serving in the Seminole War, Bragg won three brevets in the Mexican War. He was ordered to command in the west in early 1862 and participated in the battles of Shiloh, Perryville, Stone's River, Chickamauga, and Chattanooga. He was constantly in dispute with several top commanders, which considerably weakened his command. (Ann Ronan Picture Library)

The Confederate counteroffensive

During the summer of 1862, in the absence of offensive Union strikes, the Confederates seized the opportunity to take the war back into the Upper South states of Tennessee and Kentucky. Besides, the Federals had held the upper hand long enough in those states that civilians might desire Confederate redemption, particularly in light of the fact that Northern authorities were directing their armies to strike at the institution of slavery. About the same time that Halleck left the west, so too did Beauregard. Major-General Braxton Bragg was his successor.

A West Point graduate and Mexican War veteran, Bragg enjoyed a prominent reputation. He was bright, industrious, and an able administrator, but his argumentative manner often invited criticism and alienated him from others. Still, once he assumed command of the Confederate army in the west, he was determined to redeem the Confederacy's lost fortunes. Having been driven from the Confederate heartland, Bragg devised a scheme that would reverse the war in the west.

Bragg's Kentucky invasion began after the Confederates retreated south to Tupelo in June. From there he would move his 22,500-man army by rail to Mobile and then to Chattanooga before Buell reached the city. In mid-July, he left Van Dorn at Tupelo and set out on a circuitous journey that would take several weeks, finally reaching Chattanooga by the end of August. From there he and Major-General Edmund Kirby Smith, already at Lexington, Kentucky, with 10,000 soldiers, would bypass Nashville and head north to Louisville. Along the way he was disappointed to find that Kentuckians showed little interest in enlisting in his Confederate ranks, as he had hoped. Nearing Louisville, Bragg's forces captured Munfordville on September 17 after convincing the Federal commander there, Colonel John T. Wilder, that he was greatly outnumbered. Residents of Louisville and across the Ohio River were panic-stricken that Bragg's army would soon arrive and advance across the river into Indiana.

Bragg's raid into Kentucky forced Buell to abandon northern Alabama and return to Louisville to protect the city. Consequently, he forfeited much of the region that his army had fought hard to conquer earlier in the year. Though it was a demoralizing march, to its credit his army moved swiftly north, some days marching nearly 30 miles (48km), and by the end of September had made it to Louisville.

In early October, Buell's 60,000 men engaged Bragg's force of less than half that size at the Battle of Perryville. The battle opened on the 8th when soldiers from both armies, searching for water, blundered into one another. The fight developed chaotically, as neither commander fully understood the strength or exact whereabouts of the other commander's entire army. In Buell's case, peculiar atmospheric conditions prevented him from realizing the seriousness of the engagement until the afternoon. By 2.00pm the battle was raging furiously, although Buell was unable to commit his entire army to the fight. By nightfall, the uncoordinated character of the battle yielded little of immediate significance, except that the Federals had lost roughly 4,200 casualties and the Confederates about 3,400 men.

Though both commanders interpreted the fight to be a victory on their part, Bragg recognized during the night that Buell outnumbered him and would make short work of the Confederates unless he abandoned the battlefield and retreated south. His invasion of Kentucky was over and in the days following the battle he crossed back into Tennessee and encamped at Murfreesboro. When Buell made excuses for not pursuing Bragg, Lincoln lost his patience with the overly cautious commander and eliminated him from command.

The initial Confederate late-summer thrusts to counter the Union spring offensive ended in October. By the time Bragg and Buell finally met at Perryville, other battles had taken place in northern Mississippi. At Iuka, just a few miles southeast of Corinth, General Grant sent Major-General William S. Rosecrans with 15,000 soldiers to dislodge Sterling Price's Confederates. On September 19, Rosecrans succeeded in driving Price away before he could be reinforced by Earl Van Dorn at Tupelo and move into West Tennessee. In the weeks that followed, however, Van Dorn arrived to reinforce Price. Together the Confederates advanced to Corinth and battled Rosecrans for two days, on October 3–4, but failed to defeat him. Fresh from victory, Rosecrans replaced Buell.

With Price and Van Dorn checked by Grant's forces in northern Mississippi, and now with Bragg retiring back to Tennessee, the Confederates would never again be poised to redeem either Kentucky or Tennessee. The Southern populace would have more to worry about than the sacrifice of their plantations and church bells. The Union army was bearing down on the South's wealthiest cotton and agricultural regions, where slaves were most numerous.

The Vicksburg campaign

A politician turned general, John A. McClernand, had received authority from Lincoln to raise a command to capture the Mississippi River citadel of Vicksburg, located 300 miles (480km) south of Memphis on a hairpin turn high above the river. However, Grant, who knew McClernand well, had serious doubts about McClernand's ability and temperament to lead such an expedition, judging him "unmanageable and incompetent." Having survived the Confederate attack at Corinth, and at the urging of Halleck, Grant decided to preempt McClernand's Vicksburg campaign by attempting it himself.

The city's small size, however, belied its military importance. Not only was it a prosperous and strategically significant city linked by rail; it was also the link between the Confederate forces east and west of the river. If Vicksburg were captured, the Confederacy would have no chance to coordinate operations in the region or move supplies from Texas to the east. Throughout the spring

and summer the Union had failed to capture the city. But with renewed vigor, Grant decided to direct a more concerted effort to achieve that objective.

In November 1862, Grant's army, now designated the Army of the Tennessee, set out overland south on a 250-mile (400km) journey. It would require quartermasters to perform herculean labors to keep his 40,000 soldiers fed by using the north–south Mississippi Central Railroad. The inhospitable geography of the Yazoo Delta country, characterized by swamps and vast stretches of woodlands without roads, made for frustrating campaigning. Grant had concluded that the only feasible way to reduce the risk to his army and to be in a position to capture the city once the army arrived would be to move slowly, but steadily.

Lieutenant-General John C. Pemberton was the Confederate commander assigned to defend Vicksburg. As Grant advanced south, Pemberton retreated in the face of numerical superiority all the way to Grenada, Mississippi. To strengthen his chances, Grant divided his army into two movements on Vicksburg in early December. He ordered Sherman to return to Memphis with a division, collect enough troops to give him more than 20,000 men, and move down the Mississippi River with Admiral David Dixon Porter's gunboats. The amphibious expedition was designed to strike at Vicksburg from one direction while Grant advanced from central Mississippi, hoping to paralyze Pemberton.

This sketch by an artist of *Frank Leslie's Illustrated Newspaper* depicts the Battle of Stone's River. On Friday January 2, 1863, at about 4.00pm, General Rosecrans ordered a final charge of General James Negley's Union division across Stone's River. Here the 18th Ohio Infantry, followed close behind by the 19th Illinois and the 21st Ohio, made their way across the river. The artist of this sketch reported that, "the scene was grand in the extreme. It was indeed a momentous battle on a miniature scale." (Ann Ronan Picture Library)

Grant advanced all the way to Oxford, Mississippi, and Sherman had made it to Vicksburg by the time Nathan Bedford Forrest's Confederate cavalrymen had destroyed numerous stretches of the railroad. Meanwhile, on December 20 Earl Van Dorn raided Grant's supply base at Holly Springs, Mississippi, capturing 1,500 Federals and destroying $1,500,000 worth of supplies. With his communications severed and his principal supply depot wrecked, Grant pulled back, enabling Pemberton to swing a portion of his army at Sherman. On December 29, the Confederates managed to repel both Union forces.

Forced to live off the countryside in mid-December, Federal troops stripped the landscape bare of livestock, grain, and forage. When the inhabitants begged for enough to live on through the winter, Grant sternly ordered them to move further south. It was a dismal winter, although the Federals managed to suffer less than the Southerners.

The Battle of Stone's River

Some 300 miles (480km) northeast of Vicksburg, Rosecrans replaced Buell in late October 1862. The army became known once again as the Army of the Cumberland. Rosecrans's nickname, "Old Rosy," was an accurate characterization of his temper. Red-cheeked, affable, and energetic, Rosecrans was a favorite among the soldiers. Slovenliness infuriated him and he impressed soldiers by

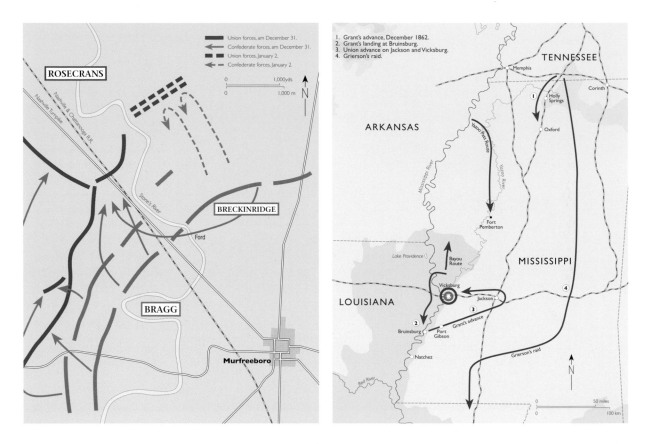

Union forces, am December 31.
Confederate forces, am December 31.
Union forces, January 2.
Confederate forces, January 2.

0   1,000yds
0   1,000 m

ROSECRANS

BRECKINRIDGE

Ford

BRAGG

Murfreeboro

1. Grant's advance, December 1862.
2. Grant's landing at Bruinsburg.
3. Union advance on Jackson and Vicksburg.
4. Grierson's raid.

TENNESSEE

Memphis   Corinth

ARKANSAS   Holly Springs

Oxford

Fort Pemberton

Lake Providence   Bayou Route   MISSISSIPPI

Vicksburg

LOUISIANA   Jackson

Bruinsburg   Port Gibson   Grant's advance

Natchez   Grierson's raid

Red River

0   50 miles
0   100 km

ABOVE LEFT:
The Battle of Stone's River,
December 31, 1862–January 2,
1863.

ABOVE RIGHT:
The Vicksburg campaign,
December 1862–May 1863.

purging his command of incompetents. "Everything for the service, nothing for individuals," was his motto. Still, he was cautious and wavered at the critical hour.

When he inherited the army it was in Nashville, where he spent nearly two months preparing to move against Bragg's 38,000-man army, encamped at Murfreesboro along a swollen Stone's River. On December 26, he set out with his 47,000 men to hit Bragg. Having been abused by the press and feeling political pressure for abandoning Kentucky, Bragg was determined not to be defeated. To the east of Stone's River he positioned Major-General John C. Breckinridge, and to the west of the river Bragg deployed his main force. By December 29, Rosecrans's army had arrived in the vicinity of Murfreesboro, and during the night he positioned his men along the Nashville Turnpike several hundred yards from the Confederate line.

Ironically, both Rosecrans and Bragg had determined to attack the enemy's left flank, which meant that whoever attacked first would be advantaged. Bragg awaited an attack throughout the day on December 30, but none was forthcoming. Bragg then struck the first blow on the following day by marching Major-General William Hardee's corps around the Federal right flank. At dawn, Hardee's men surprised the Federals and drove them back toward the Murfreesboro–Nashville Turnpike and pinned them against Stone's River. The

Union General William S. Rosecrans was sent west at his own request and served under John Pope during the advance on Corinth, Mississippi, in May 1862. He fought successfully at the Battle of Corinth in October, and replaced Don Carlos Buell in November. Well liked by his men and a brilliant strategist, Rosecrans was known for his heavy drinking, profuse language, and hot temper, and his soldiers dubbed him "Old Rosy." (Anne S. K. Brown Military Collection, Brown University Library)

Confederates threw brigade after brigade at the Federal line, but failed to break it as both generals George H. Thomas and Philip H. Sheridan resisted stubbornly.

As the early sunset, the last of 1862, closed the day's fighting, Bragg believed he had won a major victory. Indeed, he had redeemed his army's fortunes. "God has granted us a Happy New Year," he telegraphed Richmond. That night

Rosecrans held a council of war and questioned his corps commanders as to the feasibility of a retreat. "Hell," Thomas replied, "this army can't retreat." Impressed by the resolve of his subordinates, Rosecrans decided to stay and fight.

The new year opened quietly and ominously. It was cold and the soldiers were tense with anticipation. They had recovered from the previous day's fight and were expecting any minute to commence fighting again. But the fighting never came. Rosecrans redeployed his troops to strengthen his lines, while Confederate scouts concluded that this was a ruse to mask the Federal retreat. On January 2, 1863, Bragg was dumbfounded to find that Rosecrans had not left. When the Confederate commander ordered Breckinridge to dislodge what he thought remained of the enemy force east of Stone's River late in the afternoon, the Federals initially fell back. As the Confederates advanced to the river, they found to their tremendous surprise that the Federals had prepared to counter the charge. Nearly 60 Federal cannon unleashed a thunderous barrage, and a counter of infantrymen followed that retired the Confederates in short order.

With his army exhausted and convinced that Rosecrans had been reinforced, Bragg reluctantly left the battlefield that night. He fell back to Tullahoma, Tennessee, thus conceding the battlefield and the victory to Rosecrans, whose soldiers had stood their ground. The Battle of Stone's River was a stalemate that cost the Union some 13,000 casualties and the Confederates roughly 10,200 casualties, or in both cases roughly 30 percent of their forces. In proportion to men engaged and men lost, this battle ranked as the bloodiest of all battles.

The Union campaign on the Mississippi

Southern hopes of redeeming the western losses had been significantly dashed by the new year. The Union army was now poised to move against Chattanooga. One demoralized Confederate remarked, "I am sick and tired of this war, and I can see no prospects of having peace for a long time to come, I don't think it ever will be stopped by fighting, the Yankees can't whip us and we can never whip them." Lincoln was so impressed by the victory that he later confided to Rosecrans, "you gave us a hard earned victory which, had there been a defeat instead, the nation could hardly have lived over."

The Civil War had not begun with Union authorities arguing that points of occupation were more important than defeating Confederate armies. By 1863, however, it certainly appeared that this was the case in the Western Theater. The war in this region was about occupation of significant Southern ports, railroad junctions, cities, loyalist pockets, and plantation districts. Although this meant supplying armies over long distances and protecting the vital transportation arteries, the Union held firm to a belief that occupying strategic points would ultimately bring about the demise of the Confederacy. It was how to conduct affairs as proprietors of Southern domain rather than how to combat soldiers that consumed the attention of Union authorities. The resolve of Southern soldiers and civilians alike convinced many commanders that the war

would not end until popular support ended. Consequently, the limited-war attitude gave way to total war – the seizure and destruction of personal property as part of subjugating the enemy, irrespective of their presumed loyalty.

The Union campaigns of 1863, therefore, would be at a distinct advantage over those of the previous year. Commanders were able to exercise more liberality in foraging, confiscating contraband, and dealing with Southern civilians. Still, the objects remained the same. Control of the Mississippi River was paramount to the Union's strategic plan in the west. Although Confederates considered the Memphis and Charleston the backbone of their nation, Federals came to believe that the great spinal cord of the Confederacy

A Confederate siege-gun mounted in the river fortifications at Port Hudson, Louisiana. The Confederates blasted 20 of these pieces with deadly precision at David Farragut's fleet throughout the night of March 14, 1863. (Review of Reviews Company)

was the Mississippi. The Confederates still held two vital points on the river: Port Hudson, Louisiana, 25 miles (40km) north of Baton Rouge, and Vicksburg, near the mouth of the Yazoo River. But because they never managed to develop sufficient naval strength, Confederates were unable to control the river that they claimed for the Confederacy. Meanwhile, because of the river campaigns of early 1862, Union authorities had invested in new boats specifically designed for river warfare.

However, the new year had brought a blend of headaches and hope for Grant and Sherman. On January 2, 1863, McClernand arrived by transport north of Vicksburg with his newly created army. Commissioned a major-general of volunteers that ranked him above Sherman, McClernand took command of all forces there. They had no prospects of capturing Vicksburg from below Chickasaw Bluffs. Sherman, therefore, proposed a joint army–navy operation against Fort Hindman, often called Arkansas Post, on the Arkansas River, from which Confederates had launched raids against Federal transit along the Mississippi River. McClernand endorsed the concept so warmly that he eventually claimed the idea as his, while Admiral David Dixon Porter needed coaxing from Sherman. Porter had all the confidence in the world in Sherman and none in McClernand, and as a result he extracted a promise from McClernand that Sherman would run the operation. On January 9, the Federal expedition reached the vicinity of Arkansas Post, and within two days, Porter's bombardment had compelled the defenders to raise up the white flag. Nearly 5,000 prisoners fell into Union hands.

Grant, meanwhile, had resolved some important questions in his own mind about the upcoming Vicksburg campaign. Since McClernand lacked the fitness to command, he would direct operations personally. McClernand, Sherman, and a Grant protégé named James B. McPherson, a personable engineer officer who graduated first in the West Point class of 1853, would command corps in the forthcoming campaign.

Winter storms inhibited further military operations in January. On February 2, in broad winter daylight, the Union ram *Queen of the West* steamed past the Vicksburg batteries. Although it was struck 12 times, its commander, Colonel Charles R. Ellet, made it past and then struck three Confederate vessels, destroying the supplies on board. Ellet was under orders to continue south all the way to the Red River near the Mississippi–Louisiana state line, disrupting Confederate shipping as he went.

By February, Grant's army had taken up winter camp at Milliken's Bend, a few miles north of Vicksburg, where he devised a series of plans to take the river fortress. The difficulty of getting his army into a position to successfully attack the city remained his nemesis. Throughout the winter and early spring, he attempted a number of schemes. He put his soldiers to work constructing a complex makeshift waterway by connecting creeks, old river channels, and bayous, through which he could send Union vessels south around Vicksburg. Once the waterway was completed, Grant thought he would simply march his

army down the river and the vessels could then ferry troops across to the eastern bank. But after several long weeks of arduous labor, he abandoned the operation. Then he put his army to work digging an alternative channel bypassing the city, through which they could redirect the river waters and float vessels south. Again, the operation failed. Next, he ordered an expedition to cut a waterway through Yazoo Pass via a bayou. When that failed, Grant put his men to work creating a waterway that ran down from Yazoo Pass at the northern end of the delta, but it was blocked by the Confederates when they constructed Fort Pemberton in its path. After weeks of monotonous laboring for nothing, one soldier called this winter "the Valley Forge of the War."

Although Grant's futile attempts to get at the river fortress did little to satisfy an anxious and demanding Northern public, by mid-April the commander had settled on a plan that would work. It would ultimately prove so successful that it would immortalize Grant as the great victor of Vicksburg. He would move his troops below the city, head to Jackson and cut the railroads, and then move west toward Vicksburg and seize the high ground in the rear of the city.

As Grant moved his forces from Milliken's Bend to below Vicksburg, Admiral David Dixon Porter, the naval commander accompanying the land expedition, sent his fleet of 12 vessels past the city on the night of April 16. In dramatic fashion, all but one vessel managed to run past Confederate batteries and they grouped together near Hard Times on the west bank of the Mississippi, where Grant's troops were concentrated. Five nights later, six Federal transports and 12 barges loaded with supplies attempted to run past the city. Although Confederate batteries sank one transport and six barges, the operation was a success. Grant could now get his men across the river to the eastern shore.

Fifty miles (80km) south of Vicksburg, Bruinsburg, Mississippi, provided Grant with the ideal place to ferry his army across the river. Although the Confederates frustrated the initial crossing, on April 30 Grant had his army back in Mississippi poised to strike. To divert attention from his main force and to destroy Confederate supplies, Grant would need some help. Rosecrans kept Bragg sufficiently busy in Tennessee, so he could not send reinforcements to Pemberton's aid. "Old Rosy" accomplished this by setting out on what became the Tullahoma campaign. Sherman was ordered to demonstrate against the high bluffs north of Vicksburg and would then catch up to the main force. Grant also ordered raids against the Confederates' logistics bases. One of the most successful raids was undertaken by Colonel Benjamin H. Grierson, a professional bandmaster before the war. Beginning on April 17, Grierson's 1,700 cavalrymen started from La Grange, Mississippi, and in a few short weeks wreaked havoc all the way south to Baton Rouge, Louisiana.

Jackson, the state capital of Mississippi, was more important to Grant because four railroads intersected the city, the most important of which went to Vicksburg. Jackson provided the lifeline to the river fortress and to destroy it meant that Vicksburg would wither on the vine. Still, Pemberton commanded 52,000 soldiers and if Grant attempted to supply his 41,000-man army from Bruinsburg 40 miles (64km) away, the Confederates could easily put up a stern defense while possibly cutting the Union supply. Grant concluded then to live off the land. After all, his army had done this before in Mississippi during the winter. Now, with the growing season about to provide Southern farms with bountiful crops, there would be plenty for his troops to feed on. In addition to forage for the animals, Mississippi farms yielded corn, hogs, cattle, sheep, and poultry. Many planters had reduced the cultivation of cotton in favor of food staples.

By the second week of May, Grant's army had started east for Jackson. Resupplied and eager to move, his three corps commanded by Sherman, McPherson, and McClernand moved along the Black River, a natural boundary that flowed north–south and east of Vicksburg and that favored his advance. On May 12, the Federals met resistance at Raymond, 15 miles (24km) south of Jackson. After several hours of fighting, the Confederates pulled back to the capital. The following day, Confederate General Joseph E. Johnston, recently sent to take command of all the troops in besieged Mississippi, pulled together 12,000 troops to protect Jackson. On May 14, in a severe rainstorm, Sherman's and McPherson's corps drove the Confederates through the city and captured it by mid-afternoon. Outnumbered nearly five to one, Johnston headed north.

While Sherman's corps destroyed the city of Jackson, burning manufacturing installations, Grant ordered McPherson's corps to head west toward Vicksburg and threaten the enemy's communications. Pemberton responded to an order to join Johnston and strike a counteroffensive against Grant's army while it remained at Jackson. The Confederate commander moved a portion of his army out of Vicksburg and placed it on the railroad east of the Black River. The two Confederate forces were only miles apart.

On May 16, just before noon, a division of Grant's army attacked Pemberton's 20,000 Confederates at Champion's Hill, a commanding ridge east of the Black River, driving them back on the left. The Confederates, however, countered and a full-scale battle ensued. McPherson's men were called up to support the Union right flank, bringing the effective Union strength to 29,000 men, and late in the day, the Federals managed to take the ridge. Pemberton fell back to the Black River, and eventually all the way to Vicksburg. After another successful Union battle the previous day, on May 18, the triumphant Federals crossed the Black River and seized the bluffs around the town. Now, having taken the high ground that skirted the town, Grant dug in.

The siege of Vicksburg

While Johnston was being reinforced by troops from Tennessee and South Carolina, Grant collected his troops and, thanks to Halleck in Washington, also received reinforcements. Pemberton, meanwhile, was contemplating a way out of Vicksburg. Realizing that attempting to evacuate the city would not only be futile, but also give the Federals complete control of the Mississippi, Pemberton chose to stay and try to outlast the siege. Anxious to capitalize on his string of

OVERLEAF:
The capture of Vicksburg and Port Hudson cut the Confederacy in half and opened the entire Mississippi River to Union gunboats and transports. Lincoln remarked at the time that the "Father of Waters goes unvexed to the sea." (Hulton Getty)

successful operations and capture the entire force and the town, Grant launched a series of quick assaults on May 19. Within minutes the Confederates shattered the Union wave, causing about 1,000 casualties. Three days later, a determined Grant made another attempt on the town using his entire 45,000-man force, but it produced the same bloody result. Grant resolved not to assault the town again, and instead began the siege in earnest, using not only land forces but also his gunboats. "The enemy are undoubtedly in our grasp," wrote Grant on May 24. "The fall of Vicksburg and the capture of most of the garrison can only be a question of time."

Elsewhere, Federals were on the move and shoring up their strongholds. On May 21, Major-General Nathaniel Banks moved from Baton Rouge toward Port Hudson, below Vicksburg on the Mississippi River. On May 27, Banks launched an uncoordinated assault. Among the participants were two black regiments, the 1st and 3rd Louisiana Native Guards. Charging well-defended fortifications, and part of the way through floodwater, the black infantrymen exhibited courage, even in the face of severe losses. After these initial assaults were repulsed, his 13,000 Federals besieged the 4,500-man garrison under the command of Major-General Franklin Gardner. Banks maneuvered his troops around the Confederate defenses, taking a horseshoe-shaped position, with the ends stretching to the riverbank. Banks attacked again on June 11 but was repulsed. On June 14, Banks ordered the garrison to surrender, and when they refused he stormed the fort, but the Confederates held strong. The siege continued. Meanwhile, on June 23, Rosecrans moved south from Murfreesboro against Bragg's Confederates at Tullahoma. By outflanking Bragg, the Federal commander had forced him to retreat across the Tennessee River by the end of the month.

As the siege of Vicksburg progressed, Grant attempted to break through the Confederate defenses by mining under them and blowing them up. On June 25, Federal engineers detonated 2,200lb of powder in a tunnel that had been run under the Third Louisiana Redan. Two Union regiments stormed into the gap, but Confederates had ordered a second defensive line slightly to the rear in case the Federals broke through, and they repelled the advancing Yankees.

By late June, Grant's communications along the Mississippi, safeguarded by gunboats, were secure and the Federal command simply waited for the Confederates to capitulate out of starvation. Day after day, artillery shells poured down on the trembling town. Trapped against the river and forced to abandon the town for the immediate countryside, the residents flocked to the nearby caves in the hills. Federals and Confederates alike wondered how long the siege would continue. Hundreds of wounded Southern soldiers were forced to remain in the Vicksburg hospitals, many of which were makeshift operations and converted abandoned homes. As the shelling continued, so too did the starvation of soldiers and citizens, many forced to eat mule meat, rats, and dogs. Most serious was the lack of fresh drinking water.

Finally, after 47 days the siege came to an end. Pemberton decided he must surrender on July 4, 1863. Grant and Pemberton had served in the same

division during part of the Mexican War and the two men greeted one another as old acquaintances. When Pemberton asked for terms, Grant responded that "the useless effusion of blood you propose stopping by this course can be ended at any time you may choose, by the unconditional surrender of the city and the garrison." As the fatigued and disheartened Southern soldiers marched out of the city, the Federals quietly lowered the Confederate flag and raised the Stars and Stripes in its place. River vessels blew their whistles and the Union bands struck up the "Battle Cry of Freedom." From a distance residents watched with

Soldiers and residents alike dug into the hillsides around Vicksburg during the siege on the city. The bombproof shelters in this picture were carved out by the soldiers of the 45th Illinois. (Hulton Getty)

tears in their eyes as the jubilant Yankees went wild. Grant recalled years after the war that the capture of Vicksburg "gave new spirit to the loyal people of the North." Embittered Vicksburg residents did not celebrate the 4th of July again until the Second World War inspired a renewed patriotic enthusiasm and devotion for the United States.

The siege cost the Federals nearly 5,000 casualties, while the Confederates suffered significantly fewer casualties resulting from combat. The cumulative effect of the capitulation, however, handed over 29,000 soldiers to the Federal army. More important was the loss of the Confederacy's final fortress itself and the heavy equipment and small arms.

The capitulation was hailed all over the North with exuberance, especially when just a few days later Port Hudson succumbed to siege and surrendered. Capturing Port Hudson, however, had cost nearly 10,000 Union soldiers, while the Confederates had lost 871 men. The Union had reclaimed the river. "The Father of Waters again goes unvexed to the sea," remarked Lincoln. Not only had Lincoln been given the "Gibraltar of the West," but also he had found in Grant a general unlike any he had in the Eastern Theater. "He doesn't worry and bother me," remarked Lincoln. "He isn't shrieking for reinforcements all the time. He takes what troops we can safely give him … and does the best he can with what he has got. And if Grant only does this thing right down there … why, Grant is my man and I am his the rest of the war."

The summer of 1863 was a defining period in the Civil War. The campaigns in the Western Theater went a long way in determining whether or not the Confederacy would win its independence. The Union victories in the West had shaped the contours of the conflict. Much fighting had been done, but the conflict was hardly nearing an end. Equally important to the Union overall scheme in the west, Chattanooga remained in Confederate hands. Since the opening of the conflict, possession of the strategic railroad nexus and river city had been the desire of Lincoln. Positioned in the heart of East Tennessee, Chattanooga in Union hands would open the way for Union armies in the west to penetrate further into the Southern heartland. Although the Union armies were positioned to further dominate the Western Theater, it was still too soon to tell whether or not those who had fallen in the battles in the previous two and a half years had died in vain for their cause.

COMMON SOLDIERS: BILLY YANK AND JOHNNY REB AT WAR

Three million men served in the Union and Confederate armies, the majority of whom enlisted during the first two years of the war. They hailed from widely disparate backgrounds. Muster rolls reveal more than 100 prewar

In a typical regimental portrait, these soldiers of the 125th Ohio Volunteers reflect the worn yet determined character of the men who fought the war between the Appalachian Mountains and the Mississippi River. (Massachusetts Commandery Military Order of the Loyal Legion and the US Army Military History Institute)

occupations for Confederate soldiers and more than 300 for their Northern counterparts. The 19th Virginia Infantry, for example, counted among its original members 302 farmers, 80 laborers, 56 machinists, 24 students, 14 teachers, ten lawyers, three blacksmiths, two artists, a distiller, a well-digger, a janitor, a dentist, and a quartet of men who identified themselves as gentlemen (the entire roster of occupations is too long to enumerate). Most Northern regiments would have been even more diverse, though about half of the North's volunteers were farmers.

The typical soldier on each side was unmarried, white, native born, Protestant and between 18 and 24 years old. But many men younger then 18 served (some 10–14-year-olds as drummer boys or in other capacities), as did thousands of men in their thirties and forties (a few volunteered in their fifties, sixties, and even seventies). First- or second-generation immigrants, mostly Germans or Irish, accounted for about a quarter of the Union's soldiers. Foreign-born men made up just 9 percent of the Confederate forces. Although more than 175,000 black soldiers served in the Union armies before the end of the war, virtually none fought in the Eastern Theater between First Manassas and the Chancellorsville campaign.

The Civil War was a conflict fought mainly between foot soldiers. Nearly 80 percent of Union fighting men were infantrymen, with 14 percent serving as cavalry and the remaining 6 percent serving in the artillery. Seventy-five percent of the soldiers in the Confederacy were infantrymen, 20 percent served in the cavalry, and 5 percent served with artillery units.

Motivation for war

It is difficult to generalize about what motivated such a large body of men to enlist and fight. One of the reasons that the war was so fiercely contested was because soldiers of both armies came to believe they were fighting for a common cause: personal liberties, constitutional guarantees, democratic principles, and republican ideals. Still, some 630,000 soldiers lost their lives over conflicting means of achieving the same ends.

Ideology certainly played a major role. Federals and Confederates used many of the same words to explain their actions, though the words could have different meanings. Many Union men spoke of liberty and the republican ideals for which the Revolutionary War generation had waged its struggle for independence. "Our Fathers made this country," an Ohio soldier remarked, "we, their children are to save it... Without Union & peace our freedom is worthless." Untold other Northerners fought to defend the sanctity of a Union they saw as a priceless democratic example. "I do feel that the liberty of the world is placed in our hands to defend," averred a Massachusetts private in 1862, "and if we are overcome then farewell to freedom." Confederates also mentioned their Revolutionary forebears, as when a North Carolinian urged his father to "compare our situation and cause to those of our illustrious ancestors who achieved the liberties we have ever enjoyed and for which we are now contending."

Pride in country and state induced men to volunteer, and Union soldiers often expressed their devotion to the cause by using patriotic rhetoric. "The cause for which the majority of men now in the army have enlisted to defend is sacred," wrote an Illinoisan. "I consider that we should do what we can for the cause for which we enlisted and strive on until it is accomplished." A Louisianian concluded, "I had rather fall in this cause than to see my country dismantled of its glory and independence – for of its honor it cannot be deprived." Thousands of Southern soldiers, whether slaveholders or yeomen farmers, battled to defend their homes and the right to order their society as they saw fit. Just before the Battle of Chancellorsville, a member of the 44th Virginia Infantry described the conflict as "a struggle between Liberty on one side, and Tyranny on the other" and vowed to uphold the "holy cause of Southern freedom."

Beyond ideology or patriotism, men joined the army out of boredom or because of peer or community pressure. Others undoubtedly sought to participate in what they viewed as a great adventure or to pursue military glory that would impress their family and neighbors. Because many enlistees were unmarried, the adventure of traversing the countryside and the chance of potentially becoming a hero was an additional motivation. From the outset, some white volunteers in the North saw the war as a crusade against slavery. "Old John Brown Set this war in motion, and threw himself beneath … as the first martyr," declared Orrin Stebbins, "and it will never Stop until that dark Stane of African Slavery is wiped out so dry." The desire to maintain a robust masculine identity also figured in decisions to enlist. Mid-19th-century American culture taught that it was a man's responsibility to his nation and family to fight. More than one of these factors probably influenced most of the men.

Because the nation was in the midst of a depression when the war began, army pay was quite attractive. A Union private received $13 a month and a Confederate private received $11 a month, and both governments provided incentives in the way of bounties or bonuses to enlist for longer periods.

Army life

The new soldiers marched off to war under banners charged with meaning. Often sewn by women in their community and presented at a public ceremony, the regimental flag later served as a reminder of the tie between men in the ranks and those at home. Flags also stood as the most obvious symbols of allegiance to a cause, evoking images of nation and state as well as community. Because loss of a flag in battle brought disgrace to a unit, many soldiers went to extreme lengths to protect their colors. In the fight in Miller's cornfield at the Battle of Antietam, for example, a veteran of the Texas Brigade recorded: "As one flag-bearer [in the 1st Texas Infantry] would fall, another would seize the flag, until nine men had fallen beneath the colors."

Varied uniforms and equipment became a problem, and soon the governments enforced a standardized code in both armies. Because gray had been the popular color of militia and cadet uniforms in the prewar years, both

Regimental flags proved to be a morale booster to the men as they marched into battle. Shown here is the flag of the 2nd Wisconsin Infantry, a regiment in the Army of the Potomac's Iron Brigade, and the flag of the 1st Texas Infantry, a regiment in the Army of Northern Virginia's famed Texas Brigade. (Osprey Publishing)

sides initially marched off in variations of the same color. The Union would eventually adopt blue as the official uniform color, as that had been the color of uniforms in the professional army. Confederates would eventually adopt gray as their national color.

Several Northern units adopted the Zouave uniform worn by French troops. It consisted of a red turban with white band and orange tinsel, a short blue jacket with gold trimming, loose red trousers, and yellow buckskin leggings. The 11th Indiana Zouaves, known as the "Wallace Zouaves" in honor of their commander, Lew Wallace, wore a midwestern variation of the uniform. Still, whatever their specific unit identities, Northerners became known as "Billy Yanks," and Southerners became known as "Johnny Rebs."

Once in the service, volunteers confronted a strange new world. Few had previously traveled far from home. Most had an ingrained, democratic aversion to hierarchy and bridled at military discipline (especially when the officers giving orders had frequently been acquaintances in their local communities). In June 1862, one exasperated soldier vowed that "When this war is over I will whip the man that says 'fall in' to me." Early in the conflict, enlisted men often elected the lieutenants and captains in their company and sometimes even their regimental colonels, lieutenant-colonels, and majors. A Mississippian matter-of-factly described such an election in June 1861: "Held an election for field officers. W. S. Featherston was elected [colonel] on the first ballot against Rodgers. Lyles was elected on the second ballot for Major, against Foote & Kay. The election for Lieut.-Col. failed because no one of the candidates got a majority. There has [sic] been two ballots." Popularity often trumped military skill among these candidates, which prompted virtually all professional soldiers to declare the elections pernicious.

The core of military life, however, was discipline and uniformity, both of which caused problems for the typical soldier. Disrespect for authority was the first and most common offense committed by men of blue and gray. Although both governments attempted to nationalize their armies, Northerners proved more amenable to adherence to regulations and nationalism than did Southerners.

Because most soldiers marched through landscapes that were vastly different from their local communities, soldiers were initially awed by the grandeur of their surroundings. Camps were where soldiers spent the bulk of their time, and they became both homes and training grounds, filled with excitement at some times and endless monotony at others. The discipline of drill and training could prove the difference between life and death in combat, so soldiers spent hours each day drilling and preparing for the inevitable fight. Soldiers in the Western Theater typically slept in tents or huts, depending on the weather. The shelter tent or "dog tent," as it was commonly known for its small size, was the standard issue by 1862. During the winter of 1862–63, a Union soldier described a typical hut: "Three of us have, by digging about 4 feet into the ground and raising it 6 logs high, then using our shelter tent for roofing, made quite comfortable quarters."

Soldiers rose at 5.00am, assembled, drilled, ate breakfast, then went to their assigned duties. The bugle sounded lunch at noon, and regimental drill followed for two to three hours. Soldiers then returned to their quarters until dress parade at 6.00 pm, followed by dinner and free time until 9.00pm.

Soldiers spent their free time writing letters home, detailing their reactions to their new surroundings, politics, and emotions about missing home. When they were not writing, they were reading dime novels and newspapers from home or national newspapers, including the popular pictorial papers such as *Frank Leslie's Illustrated*, *Harper's Weekly*, and *Southern Illustrated News*. Soldiers frequently indulged in playing cards, horse racing, drinking, fist-fighting, story-telling, animal chasing, and other irreverent activities to escape the loneliness of army life. When time permitted, theatrical productions gave the men immense pleasure. *Bombasties Furioso*, a farce staged by the Confederate 9th Kentucky, was the hit of the 1862–63 season in the west. Sometimes men sought the company of prostitutes (venereal disease was a major problem in both armies). Pious men attended services conducted by chaplains and met in small prayer groups, while those less religiously inclined reveled in their freedom from old restraints. Shocked by the number of transgressions he detected among his comrades, one Virginian inelegantly described "some of the orneriest [orneriest: most stubborn] men here that I ever saw and the most swearing and card playing and fitin [fighting] and drunkenness that I ever saw at any place." A Federal put it more succinctly: "In our camps wickedness prevails to an almost unlimited extent."

Singing was as popular as letter writing, and soldiers were just as expressive in song as they were in writing. Soldiers voiced their longing for home, their patriotism to the cause, and their sentimental feeling for the fight. Billy Yank and Johnny Reb alike sang "Home, Sweet Home," "The Girl I Left Behind," and "When This Cruel War is Over." "The Bonnie Blue Flag" and "Dixie" were popular with Confederates and Federals enjoyed "Yankee Doodle" and "The Battle Hymn of the Republic." Northern soldiers passed the hours marching to the popular tune "John Brown's Body." At the beginning of the war, brass bands accompanied many units into service, and they were constant sources of entertainment throughout the conflict.

Food probably ranked first among a soldier's concerns. A member of the Army of the Potomac's Iron Brigade explained to his mother in January 1863 that, "a good soldier cares more for a good meal than for all the glory he can put

Allen C. Redwood's engraving shows a ragged Confederate soldier eating an ear of corn during the 1862 Maryland campaign. A civilian who visited the battlefield at Antietam spoke bluntly about the physical effects of such a diet: "We traced the position in which a rebel brigade had stood or bivouaced in line of battle for half a mile by the thickly strewn belt of green corn husks and cobs, and also, sit venia loquendi, by a ribbon of dysenteric stools just behind." (Stephen Engle)

in [a] bushel basket." Union soldiers tended to be somewhat better fed than their Confederate counterparts. Staples of Union rations included beef or pork (salted or freshly dressed), coffee and tea, sugar, and, quite frequently, some type of vegetables. The northern bread ration was hardtack, which one veteran accurately described as "about the same size as common soda crackers we buy at home and perhaps a little thicker and made of two ingredients only, viz. flour & water without salt, Saleratus [baking soda], or shortening, & baked as hard as a hot oven will bake them so you can imagine what kind of bread it is." Confederates received far more pork than beef, with cornbread as their staple bread.

Men on both sides complained bitterly about the quality and quantity of their rations. Foraging and packages of food from home helped supplement rations, but many men complained of hunger. Shortages proved especially vexing to armies on the march, as commissaries struggled to transport sufficient foodstuffs. The Army of Northern Virginia suffered acutely during the 1862 Maryland campaign. "We are hungry," wrote one of Lee's soldiers of his ordeal north of the Potomac, "for six days not a morsel of bread or meat had gone into our stomachs – and our menu consisted of apples and corn."

The novelty of camp life soon wore off, however, and during the long indistinguishable days of boring life, preachers and camp chaplains attempted to maintain morale among the ranks. Religion proved to be the link between the home front and the battlefront. When all else failed, faith in God provided hope that life might improve. Army chaplains on both sides received officer status and substantial pay – $100 per month in the Union and $80 in the Confederacy. Still, they were forced to live a spartan life and, as the war continued, both sides suffered chronic shortages of qualified chaplains. Nonetheless, whether they attended Sunday service or not, Civil War soldiers relied on scriptures and faith to get them through combat. Pennsylvanian Milton Ray expressed a typical sentiment to his sister: "I hope you may continue in earnest prayer for the preservation of my life if it is God's holy will that I should be spared… Pray that I may be a faithful soldier of the cross and of my country."

Death and disease

If the daily routine of harsh drilling and unrelenting discipline, the indistinguishable days of boredom, and the lack of good-quality, plentiful food that made up a soldier's camp life did not kill him, then disease or disability from a battle-inflicted wound often did. Of the 360,222 Union men who died in the war, over 250,000 deaths resulted from disease; nearly three-quarters of the Confederate casualties also perished to disease. Because camp sites were chosen for military and not health considerations, soldiers suffered tremendous depredations. Inadequate drainage, ignorance of sanitary practices, and the natural carelessness associated with army life characterized Union and Confederate camps and produced a contaminated atmosphere. "We have had an awful time drinking the meanest water not fit for a horse (indeed I could hardly get my horse to drink it)," remarked a Texas surgeon.

Working before the age of many important breakthroughs in treatment, physicians lacked the knowledge and medicines to help their patients. Measles, mumps, whooping cough, and chicken pox ravaged units in the early months of the war. Men from isolated rural backgrounds lacked the immunities of urban dwellers and suffered most cruelly. Diarrhea and dysentery ran rampant throughout the war. Malnutrition, filthy camps (soldiers often went for weeks without bathing), and tainted water from streams and ponds contributed to a woeful medical picture. So did poorly designed and located latrines. Many soldiers, avoiding the "sinks" because of foul odors and poor drainage, relieved

Because regimental surgeons had to perform frequent amputations of arms and legs, a kit specifically designed for amputations such as the one in this picture was standard issue for military doctors. (Image courtesy of the Military & Historical Image Bank, www. historicalimagebank.com)

themselves near sleeping areas – with results described by a Virginian in 1862: "On rolling up my bed this morning I found I had been lying in – I won't say what – something though that didn't smell like milk and peaches."

More than 1,700,000 cases of diarrhea were recorded by Federal doctors during the war, and 57,000 proved fatal. Because many soldiers were farm boys who had largely escaped a host of communicable diseases – such as measles, smallpox, typhoid, and maleria – these spread like epidemics in camp. Soldiers, uneducated about the importance of hygiene, exacerbated their problems by not bathing or changing their clothes. Army surgeons were few in number and their limited knowledge and medical supplies often combined to make the attempt to save a life as fatal as the attempt to take one. Amputations were common.

In early May 1862, Corinth highlighted the familiar consequences of war. After the bloody two-day battle at Shiloh, the Confederates attempted to recover from the devastating effects of the battle. Corinth, a small railroad junction in northern Mississippi, was in no way prepared to accommodate 20,000 sick and wounded Confederate soldiers. Residents used every building possible to accommodate the wounded men. However, more soldiers died during the seven-week stay at Corinth than had fallen in two days of battle. A Confederate nurse, Kate Cumming, was at the Tishomingo Hotel in Corinth, where she found scores of disabled soldiers, "mutilated in every imaginable way." She recalled that the wounded soldiers were lying on the bloody floors so close together that it was difficult to avoid stepping on them.

Houses, churches, barns, and other structures near large battles were converted into field hospitals. In early May 1863, wounded soldiers from the Battle of Chancellorsville poured into Salem Church. "The sight inside the building," wrote a Georgia soldier, "for horror, was, perhaps, never equalled within so limited a space, every available foot of space was crowded with wounded and bleeding soldiers. The floors, the benches, even the chancel and pulpit were all packed almost to suffocation with them. The amputated limbs were piled up in every corner almost as high as a man could reach; blood flowed in streams along aisles and out at the doors."

During the siege of Vicksburg in May–July 1863, countless Confederate soldiers and civilians fell victim to disease. Despite herculean attempts to administer to the wounded, the city and military hospitals, with cots arranged even outside on the grounds, could not take care of the flow of casualties from the trenches. Scarcely a woman at Vicksburg was not involved in ministering to the wounded.

Wounded soldiers confronted a range of problems. Often left on the field for hours (or even days), they were taken to makeshift hospitals where overworked surgeons sought to cope with overwhelming numbers of patients. The vast majority of wounds were inflicted by shoulder weapons, typically 58-caliber smoothbore or rifle muskets. Physicians could do almost nothing for men shot in the torso, concentrating instead on those struck in the limbs. Most field surgery consisted of amputations, and many veterans left graphic descriptions of the grisly results.

On the battlefield

More pathetic than the soldiers in hospitals suffering from disease were the soldiers who suffered on the battlefield. Before the fight soldiers wrestled with fear, often pinning their name and unit on their shirts. Even the most seasoned veteran was routinely shocked by the grisly aftermath. The Battle of Shiloh baptized the soldiers and the country in the vast number of ways men could be killed. Before the battle, one Tennessean penned in his diary, "I shall never forget how I felt that day … knowing that with the early tomorrow many of us most likely would pass away." In many respects, experiencing combat cured the anxious soldier's desire to "see the elephant," as fighting in battle was commonly known. The end of a battle often brought exhaustion and the realization that the soldier's unit had suffered tremendous losses.

Soldiers confronted their ultimate trial on the battlefield. Reared with heroic images of combat as depicted in woodcuts and paintings, they were ill prepared for the reality of noise, smoke, confusion, dismemberment, and death. Many green troops feared cowardice above all else, certain that word of faintheartedness in the face of the enemy would reach home. Men described a range of emotions and physical reactions as they braced for action. Some thought of loved ones; others experienced a surge of hatred toward their foe. Mouths grew dry, hearts pounded, arms and legs felt weak. Some men confessed to losing control of their bowels or involuntarily urinating. Most stood the test, though a good number inevitably ran or sought shelter.

Battle and its grisly aftermath set soldiers apart from civilians. During the Seven Days battles, a Texan who participated in the Confederate attacks at Gaines's Mill wrote, "I never had a clear conception of the horrors of war untill that night and the [next] morning. On going round on that battlefield

Brass bands accompanied many units into the Civil War and soldiers came to greatly appreciate them. Here the "Tiger Band" of the 125th Ohio Regiment poses for a picture. (Massachusetts Commandery Military Order of the Loyal Legion and the US Army Military History Institute)

with a candle searching for my friends I could hear on all sides the dreadful groans of the wounded and their heart piercing cries for water and assistance. Friends and foes all together." The "awful scene" made him wish never to "see any more such in life" and left him "heartily sick of soldiering." Many veterans developed a callousness readily apparent in their comments about scenes that would have horrified them earlier in the war. After the Battle of Antietam, one unusually hardened Federal affirmed that he did not "mind the sight of dead men no more than if they was dead Hogs." Another Union soldier groping to describe the carnage at Antietam revealed the inability of veterans to explain something civilians could never grasp. "No tongue can tell," he wrote, "no mind conceive, no pen portray the horrible sights I witnessed this morning."

Although desertion rates exceeded 10 percent in both armies and every unit had its share of malingerers and cowards, most common soldiers served honorably. They adjusted to their world of boredom in camp and terror on the battlefield, of capricious disease and the possibility of agonizing wounds. They forged a record that did credit to them and illuminated the degree to which they saw the conflict as a contest over important issues.

The common soldiers who fought the war were the unsung heroes of camp and combat. Americans who were otherwise ordinary became heroes in many ways, simply because they endured the ordeal and penned something of their experience. The war became central to their peacetime lives and to the lives of their children and grandchildren. "What an experience the last few years have been!" wrote a Wisconsin soldier. "I would not take any amount of money & have the events which have transpired in that length of time blotted out from my memory."

PORTRAIT OF A SOLDIER: JOHN BEATTY

In many ways, John Beatty typified the common soldier of the Union army, and his journal details army life in the Western Theater throughout the early years of the war. Beatty was born on December 16, 1828 near Sandusky in the western region of Ohio, a region known for its strong antislavery sentiments. At the outbreak of war, he raised a company of local volunteers, which joined the 3rd Ohio Volunteer Infantry Regiment. When the unit was mustered into service, Beatty, recently promoted to lieutenant-colonel, became the regiment's commander. In November 1861, however, his regiment was transferred to General Don Carlos Buell's Army of the Ohio in Kentucky. Throughout 1862 and 1863, he campaigned across the Bluegrass State, Tennessee, northern Mississippi, and northern Alabama, participating in many of the battles. At 33 years of age, Beatty was older than the typical soldier who mustered into the army in 1861, and at 5ft 11in, he was taller than most mid-19th-century Americans. He was thin, possessed dark hair, and wore a mustache, characteristic of Civil War soldiers.

Like most soldiers, Beatty typically began his journal entries with comments about the climate. "The weather has been delightful, warm as spring time. The nights are beautiful" is representative of the remarks he frequently made. The landscape was also a source of interest. "This is peculiar country," he remarked while in Louisville, "there are innumerable caverns, and every few rods places are found where the crust of the earth appears to have broken and sunk down hundreds of feet."

Beatty was also struck by the obvious and routine role that slavery played in the lives of the Southern people. Upon arriving in Louisville, Beatty came across a sign that read "Negroes Bought and Sold," and this struck a cord with the Ohioan. "We have known to be sure, that negroes were bought and sold, like cattle and tobacco, but it nevertheless, awakened new, and not by any means agreeable, sensations to see the humiliating fact announced on the broad side of a commercial house." To this he added, "These signs must come down."

Beatty found camp life both rewarding and a nuisance. It was rewarding to enjoy the weather of the South and to hear the pleasantries of music under moonlit nights. "The boys are in a happier mood, and a round, full voice comes to us from the tents with the words of an old Scotch song." Still, it was difficult to keep the men out of trouble. "The boys, out of pure devilment, set fire to the leaves, and to-night the forest was illuminated." In August 1862, he wrote, "I am weak, discouraged, and worn out with idleness." Excessive drinking often brought retribution and insubordination from the soldiers. When Beatty arrested a half-drunk soldier and strapped him to a tree for being insolent, the soldiers reacted scornfully. "It was a high-handed outrage upon the person of a volunteer soldier," Beatty observed, and the common soldiers never let their commanders forget they were volunteers.

There were also casualties beyond the battlefield for the soldiers of Beatty's regiment. When a soldier got a letter from home that his girlfriend

When Confederate General Braxton Bragg marched into Kentucky in the summer of 1862, Union General Don Carlos Buell was forced to pursue him and to build bridges across the rivers. In this picture, Buell's troops are crossing the Big Barren River. Here the 19th Michigan Engineers had to reconstruct the bridge by using pontoons located in the middle of the river. (Review of Reviews Company)

had married someone else, Beatty remarked that the news made this soldier "crazy as a loon." The poor soul "imagined that he was in hell, thought Dr Seyes the devil, and so violent did he become that they had to bind him." Worse yet was the disease of the soldiers, particularly during the winter months. "There is a great deal of sickness among the troops; many cases of colds, rheumatism, and fever, resulting from exposure," Beatty observed. "Passing through the company quarters of our regiment at midnight, I was alarmed by the constant and heavy coughing of the men. I fear the winter will send many more to the grave than the bullets of the enemy, for a year to come." It surely did.

Beatty also noted that the Union army had become a haven for runaway slaves. "We have much trouble with the escaped negroes … the colored folks get into our regimental lines, and in some mysterious way are so disposed of that their masters never hear of them again." Near Murfreesboro, he remarked: "We have in our camp a superabundance of negroes."

During spells of boredom, Beatty usually turned his thoughts "to the cottage home, to wife and children, to a time still further away when we had no children, when we were making the preliminary arrangements for starting the world together, when her cheeks were ruddier than now, when wealth and fame and happiness seemed lying just before me, ready to be gathered in, and farther away still, to a gentle, blue-eyed mother – now long gone – teaching her child to lisp his first prayer." Religion often found expression in music and was a way for the men to escape the boredom of camp life. "Surely nothing has the power to make us forget earth and its round of troubles as these sweet old church songs, familiar from earliest childhood," commented Beatty.

Beatty read the newspapers and was particularly interested in the politics of the war. In July 1862, the Ohioan commented on the Confiscation Act passed by the Congress. "I trust the new policy indicated by the confiscation act, just passed by Congress, will have a good effect." "It will, at least, enable us to weaken the enemy," he argued, "and strengthen ourselves, as we have hitherto not been able to do." "Slavery is the enemy's weak point, the key to his position. If we can tear down this institution, the rebels will lose all interest in the Confederacy, and be too glad to escape with their lives…"

He clearly viewed the institution of slavery as the cause of the war and the root of the evils of Southern society. By the end of 1862, the Emancipation Proclamation had changed the war. In February 1863, Beatty remarked that the "army is turning its attention to politics somewhat," particularly when it came to Lincoln's Proclamation. "Generals and colonels are ventilating their opinions through the press. I think their letters may have a good effect upon the people at home, and prevent them from discouraging the army and crippling the Administration."

Beatty also wrote about commanders. For the most part he liked his division commander, General Ormsby Mitchel. Mitchel was a professional and proper gentleman who "never drinks and never swears," and in Beatty's estimation was "indefatigable." But Beatty came to detest Don Carlos Buell for his slowness in campaigning and for his apparent sympathy with the Southern people during the summer of 1862. Buell "is inaugurating the dancing-master policy," which was Beatty's sarcastic expression for Buell's lethargy, which he declared was the policy of an "idiot."

Campaigning gave Beatty plenty of things to react to, not the least of which was the unexpected cheering of citizens for the Union soldiers. "We passed many fine houses, and extensive, well improved farms," he penned in 1862, "but few white people were seen. The negroes appeared to have entire possession." The sight of a pretty woman warmed his heart. While marching in Tennessee, Beatty came upon a scene where "a young and very pretty girl stood in the doorway of a handsome farm-house and waved the Union flag. Cheer after cheer arose along the line; officers saluted, soldiers waved their hats, and the bands played 'Yankee Doodle' and 'Dixie.'" "That loyal girl," he wrote, "captured a thousand hearts." Seeing his first cotton field was given space in his diary.

Murfreesboro was quite a place for Beatty. He remarked:

> Murfreesboro is an aristocratic town, many of the citizens have as fine carriages as are to be seen in Cincinnati or Washington. On pleasant week-day evenings they sometimes come out to witness the parades. The ladies, so far as I can judge by a glimpse through a carriage window, are richly and elegantly dressed. The poor whites are as poor as rot, and the rich are very rich. There is no substantial well-to-do middle class. The slaves are, in fact, the middle class here.

By April 1863, however, Murfreesboro had undergone a transformation. The fine houses and trees of the city had been "cut or trampled down and destroyed." "Many frame houses, and very good ones, too," he remarked, "have been torn down, and the lumber and timber used in the construction of hospitals." Even the air had changed: "There is a fearful stench in many places near here, arising from decaying horses and mules."

The Rutherford County courthouse in Murfreesboro, Tennessee. The courthouse reflects the aristocratic facade of the Tennessee town that so impressed soldiers like Ohio's John Beatty. The Battle of Stone's River was fought near the courthouse, which was converted into a hospital for Braxton Bragg's forces. (Review of Reviews Company)

John Beatty heard the band playing "Dixie" as he marched through Tennessee. The original version of this song was written in September 1859 by Dan D. Emmett. It soon gained popularity, particularly in the South. The version printed here was re-worked by Albert B. Pike and printed in *The Natchez Courier* on April 20, 1861 but the new words were only a temporary replacement for Emmett's original.

Southrons, hear your country call you!
Up, lest worse than death befall you!
To arms! To arms! To arms, in Dixie!
Lo! All the beacon-fires are lighted,
Let all hearts be now united!
To arms! To arms! To arms, in Dixie!

Fear no danger! Shun no labor!
Lift up rifle, pike and saber!
To arms! To arms! To arms, in Dixie!
Shoulder pressing close to shoulder,
Let the odds make each heart bolder!
To arms! To arms! To arms, in Dixie!

Advance the flag of Dixie
Hurrah! Hurrah!
For Dixie's land we take our stand,
And live or die for Dixie!
To arms! To arms!
And conquer peace for Dixie
To arms! To arms!
And conquer peace for Dixie

Advance the flag of Dixie
Hurrah! Hurrah!
For Dixie's land we take our stand,
And live or die for Dixie!
To arms! To arms!
And conquer peace for Dixie
To arms! To arms!
And conquer peace for Dixie

Hear the Northern thunders mutter!
Northern flags in South winds flutter!
To arms! To arms! To arms, in Dixie!
Send them back your fierce defiance!
Stamp upon the accursed alliance!
To arms! To arms! To arms, in Dixie!

Swear upon our country's altar
Never to submit or to falter,
To arms! To arms! To arms, in Dixie!
Till the spoilers are defeated,
Till the Lord's work is completed!
To arms! To arms! To arms, in Dixie!

Advance the flag of Dixie
Hurrah! Hurrah!
For Dixie's land we take our stand,
And live or die for Dixie!
To arms! To arms!
And conquer peace for Dixie
To arms! To arms!
And conquer peace for Dixie

Advance the flag of Dixie
Hurrah! Hurrah!
For Dixie's land we take our stand,
And live or die for Dixie!
To arms! To arms!
And conquer peace for Dixie
To arms! To arms!
And conquer peace for Dixie

Perhaps nothing caught Beatty's attention more than the ordeal of the battle. In February 1862, he wrote that although it was bitterly cold, "the conviction that a battle was imminent kept the men steady and prevented straggling." The evening before the Battle of Stone's River in December 1862,

Beatty wrote: "To-morrow, doubtless, the grand battle will be fought, when I trust the good Lord will grant us a glorious victory, and one that will make glad hearts of all loyal people on New-Year's Day." At one point during the battle, he glanced up to see a soldier who was heading to the back of the line struck in the back between the shoulders, killing him instantly.

After the battle he walked the battlefield and found the dead and wounded scattered for miles. As he walked across the terrain, he commented:

> we find men with their legs shot off; one with his brains scooped out with a cannon ball; another with half a face gone; another with entrails protruding … another boy lies with his hands clasped above his head, indicating that his last words were a prayer.
>
> How many poor men moaned through the cold nights in the thick woods, where the first day's battle occurred … calling in vain to man for help, and finally making their last solemn petition to God!

The fact that Beatty survived the Civil War was a testament to his fitness as an officer and to a significant degree the result of simple luck. When he resigned his commission in January 1864 and returned to Sandusky, the Civil War became central to his life. An everyday banker from Ohio who had witnessed the drama of the Civil War, Beatty was no longer an ordinary citizen.

PORTRAIT OF A CIVILIAN: KATE STONE

Kate Stone was 20 years old when the Civil War broke out. She was living with her widowed mother, five brothers, and younger sister at Brokenburn, a 1,200-acre (485ha) cotton plantation in northeast Louisiana, about 30 miles (48km) northwest of Vicksburg, Mississippi. The Stones owned 150 slaves and their antebellum plantation life imbued strong devotion to the Confederate cause in 1861. Kate began writing her diary in May 1861 and it chronicles the hardships she and her family endured until they were forced to leave Louisiana as a result of the Vicksburg campaign in the summer of 1863.

In 1861, Kate was coming of age and keenly aware of the significance of her times and of her own maturation as woman. The war threatened her family's affluence and social status, and her chances of marriage. She resented the fact that the Confederate army mobilized three out of four white males in the South, including her brother and uncle, leaving behind mostly women and slaves to conduct the affairs of economic and social life. Kate was dissatisfied with her isolation on the plantation. "When quietly our days are passing," she commiserated, "when the whole planet is in such a state of feverish excitement and everywhere there is the stir and mob of angry life – O! to see and be in it all." "I hate weary days of inaction," she remarked, "yet what can women do but wait and suffer?"

159

The inability of many slaveholders to provide their slaves with sufficient food and clothing helped undermine white authority. In this woodcut, four Confederate women accompanied by two slaves make their way to a Union commissary to request rations. (Gary Gallagher)

Although Kate recognized that life would be difficult for the soldiers, remarking that "They go to bear all hardships, to brave all dangers, and to face death in every form," she soon learned that the home front could be just as challenging as the battlefront. "We who stay behind," she wrote, "may find it harder than they who go. They will have new scenes and constant excitement to buoy them up and the consciousness of duty done." Still, the waiting and the monotony were exasperating. "No war news or any other kind. Oh, this inactive life when there is such a stir and excitement in the busy world outside. It is enough to run one wild. Oh! to be in the heat and turmoil of it all, to live, to live, not stagnate here."

For Kate, writing was a way to participate. But as the war closed in on her world, she came to feel the attack, the occupation, and the devastation of thousands of Southerners in the west. As early as May 1861, Kate commented that, "Times are already dreadfully hard."

The press made an impact on Kate, particularly because she came to believe that Northern papers had terribly misrepresented the South. "The Northern papers do make us mad!" she commented in May 1861. "Why will they tell such horrible stories about us?" One of the most significant changes on the plantation was the change in attitude among the slaves. "The runaways are numerous and bold." In June 1861, she wrote, "We live on a mine that the Negroes are suspected of an intention to spring on the fourth of next month."

Like thousands of Southern women, Kate found refuge in prayer groups and religion. In late June after an abundant rain, Kate remarked that the crops were thriving and that "The North cannot starve us, try as they may, and God will aid us in our righteous cause." "May I always be able to put my trust in God ... satisfied that He will order our future as is best... He has given us wise rulers, brave and successful generals, valiant and patriotic men, and a united people, self-sacrificing and with their trust in God."

As the war moved closer to northeast Louisiana, Kate's scorn for the Yankees increased. She reported on the sacrifices of Southern planters in late January 1862, commenting that Confederate General Leonidas Polk had called on all the planters along the Mississippi River to send their slaves to assist in fortifying Fort Pillow some 40 miles (64km) north of Memphis. "Separating the old family Negroes who have lived and worked together for so many years is a great grief to them and a distress to us," she observed. After reading a January letter from her brother, she came to the realization that, "The manner in which the North is moving her forces, now that she thinks us surrounded and can give us the annihilating blow, reminds me of a party of hunters crouched around the covert of the deer, and when the lines are drawn and there is no escape, they close in and kill."

Kate reported the fall of Forts Henry and Donelson, and the capture of significant points in Kentucky, Tennessee, and Missouri, which left Vicksburg open from the North. She abhorred the sight of Federal gunboats on the Mississippi River only a few miles from Brokenburn. She lamented the fact that the southern approach to Vicksburg was opened by the fall of New Orleans, Baton Rouge, and Natchez. She was concerned that the loss of the river cities would allow the Union army to "descend the Mississippi and get all the cotton they can steal." Benjamin Butler's occupation of New Orleans in April 1862 provoked a fierce reaction. "It made my blood boil to ... think of New Orleans completely in his power." Kate hoped such losses would inspire the populace. "All other tidings are gloomy but they have aroused the country with a trumpet call. There is the greatest excitement throughout the country. Almost everyone is going and going at once," she recorded. "The whole country is awake and on the watch – think and talk only of war."

By the summer of 1862, Kate's daily entries focused almost exclusively on military affairs. She was beginning to comprehend the significance of the Union victories of the spring. "The merchants are selling only for cash and that cash is hard to get, unless we can do as they seem to be doing in the towns – make it," she observed. She also wrote of the tension that conscription caused in the Confederacy:

> The conscription has caused a great commotion and great consternation among the shirking stay-at-homes... Around here many are deluding themselves with the belief that the call will not be enforced in Louisiana now that New Orleans has fallen and Vicksburg is threatened... We earnestly hope these coward souls will be made to go... Not a single man has joined for the last two months.

The surrender of Nashville and the river forts, and much of the Mississippi River, made Kate realize that, "fair Louisiana with her fertile fields of cane and cotton … lies powerless at the feet of the enemy." "Though the Yankees have gained the land, the people are determined they shall not have its wealth, and from every plantation rises the smoke of burning cotton." Her own family burned $20,000

H.O

worth in May 1862. Although the planters looked upon the burning of cotton as almost ruin to their fortunes, it must be done for the cause, she argued. As the Union soldiers pressed on to Corinth, Mississippi, Kate invoked the Almighty to produce Confederate success in the west, writing in her diary: "Grant a victory, Father, we pray."

Plagued by shortages of food, clothing, and medicines, Kate watched with scorn as the Union army threatened to close Vicksburg in the summer of 1862. "It seems hopeless to make a stand at Vicksburg," she wrote. "We only hope they may burn the city if they meet with any resistance." "How much better to burn our cities than let them fall into the enemy's hands." It seemed that God had answered her prayers as the Confederates blocked Federal attempts to lay siege to Vicksburg in the summer and fall of 1862.

While Kate was entertaining Confederate soldiers at Brokenburn on Christmas Eve 1862, General William T. Sherman with 30,000 men arrived at Milliken's Bend, only a few miles away. In the winter months, his troops swarmed the plantation, confiscating horses and supplies, seizing slaves to work on a new canal, and encouraging others to leave their masters. On January 26, 1863, "preparing to run from the Yankees," Kate tucked her diary away in the bottom of a packing box, "with only slight chance of seeing it again." After going for more than a month without writing an entry, she opened the diary and wrote of the chaos and violence around her. Such was the violence that she wrote in March, "For the last two days we have been in a quiver of anxiety for the Yankees every minute." When the Yankees came on March 22, she wrote that, "The life we are leading now is a miserable, frightened one – living in constant dread of great danger, not knowing what form it may take, and utterly helpless to protect ourselves."

While she was visiting a neighbor, an armed slave seized Kate, her little sister, and several other women, forced them into one room, and held them at gunpoint while other slaves looted the house. Though Union authorities forbade planters to leave, this incident convinced Kate's mother that the family must flee.

Grant depicted at the battle for Fort Donelson. The loss of the river forts gave the Union its first real victory of the war. (Anne S. K. Brown Military Collection, Brown University Library)

With only the clothes on their backs, the Stones left Brokenburn on a cold March night. When the family reached Delhi, Louisiana, they found the chaos of a fleeing countryside, "everybody and everything," Kate wrote, "trying to get on the cars, all fleeing from the Yankees or worse still, the Negroes." Despite the confusion, the Stones finally got on the train and reached Monroe, 80 miles (130km) inland from the Mississippi. There they spent seven weeks before they continued their trek to Texas. To add to Kate's despair, news came of the death of her brother Walter in Mississippi two months earlier. The family would spend the remainder of the war in Texas.

HOW THE PERIOD ENDED: THE PROMISE OF SUMMER

By the summer of 1863, the war in the Western Theater had produced significant changes. Thousands of soldiers had fought several major battles in the Upper South states, which ultimately kept Missouri and Kentucky in the Union. The North could boast of a series of military successes, including the fall of Forts Henry and Donelson, the victories at Shiloh, Perryville, Iuka, and Stone's River, and the capture and occupation of Nashville, Corinth, Memphis, New Orleans, Port Hudson, and Vicksburg. The cumulative effect of these victories brought tremendous economic hardships to many Confederates and transformed the character of the war.

The Confederate war effort in the west was trapped in a tumultuous cycle that only got worse as the war continued. To be successful against the Union armies in the west, the Confederate government had to resort to coercive measures that centralized its authority over the states. These measures, however, became counterproductive and increased discontent among Southerners, which eroded the morale and strength of the very armies that the controls were designed to benefit. Some soldiers began to feel that the danger in the rear was worse than the danger in the front. Southern soldiers, particularly those in the Army of Tennessee such as John Magee, were weary of the war.* "This news [Vicksburg] causes a depression of spirits in the whole army," wrote Magee in July.

The campaigns in the Western Theater in the first two years of the conflict proved invaluable for both armies. With tremendous military experience that few officers on either side could boast of, Albert Sidney Johnston emerged early as the savior of the west, a hero of the republic of Texas, the United States, and the Confederacy. Jefferson Davis referred to him as the "great pillar of the Confederacy." In many respects he had been a military idol, and his death at Shiloh left a significant void in the Confederate high command. Braxton Bragg said at the time that, "No one cause probably contributed so greatly to our loss of time, which was the loss of success, as the fall of the commanding general."

---

* The Union Army of the Tennessee (named after the river) should not be confused with the Confederate Army of Tennessee.

Whether the outcome of the battle would have been different had Johnston lived, his death was a turning point in the war in the west. "Death on the battlefield, after taking Grant by surprise made him a martyred genius in Southern eyes," argued one scholar; it "placed a halo around his head," complained Beauregard.

Thanks to an effective use of combined military operations, the Union held a distinct advantage in the Western Theater, and the experience of war produced an invaluable lesson for conducting the war. Not only had the Union combined army and naval operations successfully, but also it learned that conducting half-hearted campaigns designed to achieve a harmonious peace was losing them the war. At a time when policy makers were beginning to see the advantages of expanding the war, Lincoln and the North found in Grant the military hero they had been seeking to wage a more vigorous war. Though an "awesomely common man," as some characterized him, after Vicksburg the commander's star rose rapidly.

Grant also found in William T. Sherman a commander in whom he placed much confidence in carrying out the same kind of war. The two commanders had proven that they could learn from the experience of war, and they supported the total commitment to bringing defeat to the Confederacy. Both were now willing to have their men make war on the South, not just its armies. At a time when the Northern economy and leadership had harnessed the industrial and technological advances, they had military commanders who would utilize these resources and bring the war to a close.

By July 1863, the war seemed almost endless for Southern soldiers. Morale was rapidly plummeting in the Confederacy due to military setbacks. Grant had eliminated an entire army from further military action, yet had sustained fewer than 10,000 casualties himself. Such exploits caused Treasury Secretary Salmon P. Chase to remark to Massachusetts Governor William Sprague, "Our military prospects now look really bright." "The people all along the [Mississippi] River, and throughout the Western Mississippi are abjectly submissive." Although most Confederates were still committed to Southern independence, they increasingly turned against the Davis administration. The fall of Vicksburg eroded the solidarity of purpose between the civilian populace and Confederate authorities.

The Confederacy could win the war if they went on the offensive and frustrated the Union armies on the field. Victory in the west might turn the Northern populace away from the Lincoln administration and force political leaders to consider a negotiated peace. Though the Union held the upper hand in the west in the summer of 1863, only time would tell if they could sustain their domination in the occupied zones while fighting the Rebels on the field of battle.

CHAPTER 3

THE WAR IN THE EAST MAY 1863-1865

THE FIGHTING: THE WAR WITHOUT JACKSON TO LEE'S LAST STAND

The spring of 1863

A great, mournful cry went up all across the Confederacy as news spread in May 1863 of the death of General Thomas J. "Stonewall" Jackson, of wounds received at the Battle of Chancellorsville. A Georgia Confederate wrote dolefully on May 15 that, "all hopes of Peace and Independence have forever vanished." Another Confederate told his wife back in Alabama, with more earnestness than literary precision: "Stonewall Jackson was kild... I think this will have a gradeal to due with this war. I think the north will whip us soon." General Robert E. Lee faced the daunting task of reorganizing his army in Jackson's absence, and filling it with a sturdy spirit that could keep the "whip us soon" forecast from becoming a self-fulfilling prophecy.

Lee's stunning victory at Chancellorsville in early May, against daunting odds, had generated enough momentum to carry the Confederate Army of Northern Virginia northward on a new campaign. Before he could launch such an effort, though, Lee had to reorganize his army to fill the yawning chasm left by Jackson's demise. He decided to go from the two-corps system that had worked so long and well for managing his infantry to an organization in three

The Confederates counterattack at Brandy Station. (Painting by Don Troiani, www.historicalartprints.com)

corps. The veteran General James Longstreet, reliable if contentious, kept command of the First Corps. General Richard S. Ewell, returning after nine months of convalescing from a wound, assumed command in late May of Jackson's old Second Corps. General A. P. Hill won promotion to command a new Third Corps composed of pieces extracted from the other two, combined with a few new units drawn to Virginia from service elsewhere in the Confederacy. General J. E. B. Stuart remained in command of the army's capable cavalry arm. Lee's artillery benefited from an excellent new organization into battalions, and from an officer corps that included many brilliant young men; but at the same time it suffered from inferior weaponry and at times from woefully inadequate ammunition.

Across the lines, General Joseph Hooker's Army of the Potomac loomed in Lee's way. The seasoned Northerners in that army by now knew their business thoroughly well and stood ready to continue their role as bulwark of the Federal Union. What they wanted and needed was a competent commander. At Chancellorsville, Hooker had demonstrated beyond serious contention that he was not such a man. The Army of the Potomac would finally receive a leader who matched its mettle in late June, but as the 1863 campaign unfolded, Hooker's palsied hand remained at the helm. His veteran corps commanders offered reliable leadership at the next level below Hooker.

After two consecutive battles along the line of the Rappahannock River, both armies knew the countryside intimately. Lee had won both battles in resounding fashion, but had not been able to exploit the victories into overwhelming triumphs that destroyed his enemy. Now he proposed to move north across the Potomac and carry the war into the enemy's country. Political hyperbole (including President Lincoln's famous "Gettysburg Address") always insisted that the Confederates hoped to conquer the North and subjugate that much larger portion of the continent to some sort of serfdom. Such rodomontade, of course, reflected nothing of actual Southern aims.

Lee's move north must be recognized as a raid, not an invasion designed to conquer Pennsylvania or any other territory. He

OPPOSITE PAGE:
General Joseph Hooker. (Public domain)

General J. E. B. ("Jeb") Stuart led most of the Confederate cavalry on a long ride around the Federal army en route to Pennsylvania, thus depriving Lee of his "eyes and ears" as he maneuvered toward Gettysburg. (Public domain)

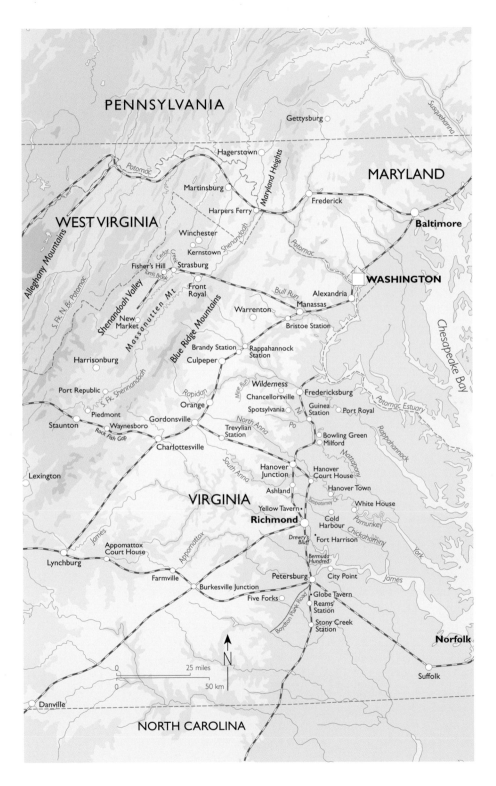

PENNSYLVANIA

Gettysburg

Hagerstown

Maryland Heights

MARYLAND

WEST VIRGINIA

Martinsburg

Frederick

Harpers Ferry

Baltimore

Winchester

Kernstown

Alleghany Mountains

Potomac

Shenandoah

Fisher's Hill

Strasburg

Front Royal

Cedar Creek

Tom's Brook

S. Fk. N. Br. Potomac

Shenandoah Valley

New Market

Massanutten Mt.

Bull Run

Alexandria

WASHINGTON

Manassas

Warrenton

Blue Ridge Mountains

Bristoe Station

Harrisonburg

Brandy Station

Rappahannock Station

Culpeper

Port Republic

Rapidan

S. Fk. Shennandoah

Wilderness

Chancellorsville

Fredericksburg

Piedmont

Orange

Spotsylvania

Guinea Station

Port Royal

Chesapeake Bay

Potomac Estuary

Staunton

Waynesboro

Gordonsville

North Anna

Po

Rappahannock

Rock Fish Gap

Trevylian Station

Bowling Green

Milford

Charlottesville

Mattapony

Lexington

South Anna

Hanover Junction

Hanover Court House

Hanover Town

White House

VIRGINIA

Ashland

Hanover Town

Pamunkey

James

Yellow Tavern

Richmond

Cold Harbour

Chickahominy

Totopotomoy Ck.

Appomattox

Drewry's Bluff

Fort Harrison

York

Appomattox Court House

Appomattox

Bermuda Hundred

Lynchburg

Farmville

Petersburg

City Point

James

Burkesville Junction

Five Forks

Globe Tavern

Reams' Station

Boydton Plank Road

Stony Creek Station

Norfolk

0   25 miles

N

0   50 km

Suffolk

Danville

NORTH CAROLINA

Susquehanna

Piedmont

OPPOSITE PAGE:
From June 1862 to May 1863, Confederate General Robert E. Lee had steadily defeated an array of opposing Federal generals. (Robert Krick)

The campaigns in the Virginia Theater, 1863–65.

sought to lift the heel of war from Virginia, not only for humanitarian reasons, but also to allow that home country to recover from hostile occupation so that it could sustain Lee's army in future months. The country north of the Potomac also offered a much wider field for maneuver, a military element in which Lee excelled. An ostensible threat to the Federal political capital in Washington also held out potential advantages: knowing that his enemy *must* keep the city covered foreshadowed in mirror image the 1864 campaign in which Richmond served as a similar focus and pivot for Lee on the defensive.

Lee moved away from Fredericksburg and the Rappahannock River line early in June 1863, and headed northwestward through piedmont Virginia toward the Shenandoah Valley. On June 9 his cavalry force fought one of the largest all-mounted engagements of the war around Brandy Station. Hooker had sent his own cavalry out with orders to "disperse and destroy" the Confederates they found, and the Northern troopers came close to doing that. They completely surprised the usually vigilant Southern mounted men early in the morning and drove them some distance. A rally on the low, rounded eminence of Fleetwood Hill saved the day for General Stuart's men. They inflicted about 1,000 casualties on the Northern attackers and suffered half that many themselves. Brandy Station ended as a tactical draw, but Union troopers who had been battered relentlessly for two years had finally stood up to their adversaries and now had a positive experience upon which to build.

The Battle of Gettysburg

"Jeb" Stuart's Southern cavalry again occupied center stage as the armies sidled northward and crossed the Potomac – or, more accurately, Stuart's cavalry exited stage right and became conspicuous by their absence. While Lee pushed north, into and through the Shenandoah Valley, Stuart embraced the chance to ride a raid entirely around the Union army. He had done just that twice before, in June and October 1862. This time the dashing maneuver backfired in deadly fashion. The cavalry detachment accompanying the main force in Stuart's absence had neither the men nor the leadership necessary to perform the essential function of screening Lee from enemy view, while simultaneously finding the enemy and tracking his progress and intentions. When Stuart finally rejoined Lee very tardily at Gettysburg, the commanding general said quietly, but in clear rebuke, "Well … you are here at last," and "I had hoped to see you before this." Stuart's ride became one of the most-disputed subjects among postwar Confederates, and remains controversial to this day.

While Stuart galloped fecklessly across northern Virginia and Maryland and Pennsylvania, Lee's infantry achieved notable success at Winchester, Virginia, on June 14–15. Ewell's energy and success there prompted Southerners to hope that he would emerge as a sort of reincarnation of Stonewall Jackson. On through Maryland and deep into Pennsylvania the Confederate columns pressed. Some of them reached Carlisle and York and the outskirts of the state's capital city, Harrisburg. Fighting at the crossroads town of Gettysburg that began on July 1 would draw all of them back south into the maw of the war's greatest battle. The long columns of blue-clad Union troops marching north through an arc surrounding Washington also wound up adjusting their route of march for that place. Gettysburg was a "meeting engagement" in every sense. No one picked the battle site. Roads drew small contending formations together and soon everyone else pitched in.

The battle of July 1, 1863, considered alone, must be adjudged one of the Army of Northern Virginia's greatest victories. Fighting opened that morning west of Gettysburg, a farming community of about 2,400 souls. Confederate skirmishers ran into Northern cavalry commanded by salty, unflappable General John Buford. A brigade of Southern infantry under President Jefferson Davis's nephew, General Joseph Davis, drove forward with marked success, but then the green brigadier clumsily allowed his men to be trapped in a deep cut of an unfinished railroad and lost most of them.

Confederate fortunes were abetted when a bullet killed Union General John F. Reynolds, a soldierly and much-admired officer commanding everything Federal on the field at that early hour. They benefited even more from the superb timing – the result of luck, not prescience – with which the fresh Southern division of General Robert E. Rodes dropped squarely onto the north flank of the Federal position. Intense fighting ensued on both sides of the road leading from Chambersburg to Gettysburg, with success perching first upon one banner then another, but the arrival of Rodes's division and other associated troops at a fortuitous point doomed Federal resistance. Eventually the whole Union line west of town collapsed and the Confederates enjoyed a field day chasing their fleeing foe into Gettysburg. Alexander Schimmelfennig, a Prussian-born general, eluded capture by hiding in a pigsty. Thousands of other men in blue became prisoners of war.

One of the battle's most-discussed turning points came as Confederates converged on Gettysburg from the north and west, and contemplated riding the crest of the tidal wave of momentum they had created. Lee characteristically left to the discretion of his new corps commander, General Ewell, the responsibility for continuing the advance. Possession of the crest of a long ridge that curled around Gettysburg and ran east to East Cemetery Hill and Culp's Hill would guarantee control of the military terrain for a considerable distance. Ewell equivocated, consulted, temporized – and never attacked. For the next two days, his troops would suffer mightily against the same two hills, by then

Confederate General James Longstreet's behavior on July 2 remains the most controversial aspect of the Battle of Gettysburg. (Public domain)

The Battle of Gettysburg, July 1–3, 1863.

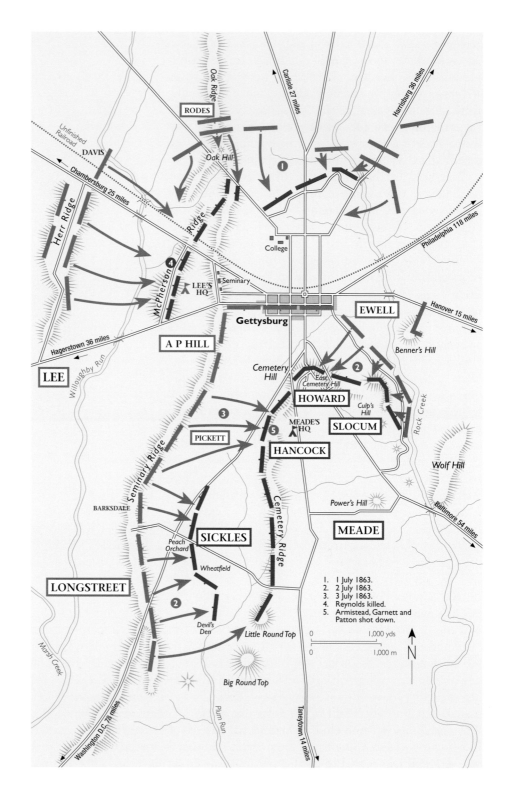

RODES

DAVIS

Oak Ridge

Oak Hill

Unfinished Railroad

Chambersburg 25 miles

Herr Ridge

Carlisle 27 miles

Harrisburg 36 miles

1

College

Philadelphia 118 miles

4

McPherson Ridge

LEE'S HQ

Seminary

Gettysburg

EWELL

Hanover 15 miles

A P HILL

Benner's Hill

Hagerstown 36 miles

Willoughby Run

LEE

Cemetery Hill

East Cemetery Hill

HOWARD

Culp's Hill

SLOCUM

Rock Creek

3

MEADE'S HQ

5

PICKETT

HANCOCK

Wolf Hill

Seminary Ridge

BARKSDALE

Cemetery Ridge

Power's Hill

MEADE

Baltimore 54 miles

SICKLES

Peach Orchard

Wheatfield

LONGSTREET

2

Devil's Den

Little Round Top

1. 1 July 1863.
2. 2 July 1863.
3. 3 July 1863.
4. Reynolds killed.
5. Armistead, Garnett and Patton shot down.

0   1,000 yds

0   1,000 m

N

Marsh Creek

Washington D.C. 78 miles

Plum Run

Big Round Top

Taneytown 14 miles

strongly occupied, attacking again and again where he had not chosen to fight under far better terms. On the evening of July 1, Ewell did nothing. His inaction remains highly controversial today. The counterfactual question, "What would Jackson have done had he been there?" is, of course, unanswerable. A North Carolina soldier who fought there thought he knew. "We missed the genius of Jackson," he wrote a few days later. "The simplest soldier in the ranks felt it."

Federals scrambling to get to Gettysburg to blunt Lee's burgeoning success faced far better prospects than they would have a few days earlier. A Federal turning point in the campaign, indeed in the entire war in Virginia, had come on June 27 when General Hooker submitted his resignation in a fit of pique over having his wishes ignored. President Lincoln delightedly accepted the resignation and on June 28 General George G. Meade reluctantly took command of the Army of the Potomac.

Three days later Meade was fighting the war's largest battle. No American officer, in any war or era, has ever had so much crucial responsibility thrust upon him with such short notice. Meade met the challenge masterfully, beyond any imaginable degree that could have been expected, and far more ably than Hooker could have done. He confronted Lee's army at the high tide of Southern success, positioned deep in Federal country, and with Confederate numerical strength at a peak. At Gettysburg, Meade reached the battlefield as Lee swept everything before him late on July 1. Against those odds the brand-new Federal commander won a pivotal battle.

Meade's challenge early on July 2 was to restore confidence in his army and place it carefully on the powerful position available to him. The Federal line around Gettysburg resembled a fishhook. The shank of the fishhook ran straight south from the town along Cemetery Ridge and ended on the massive anchor of two commanding hills, Big Round Top and Little Round Top. The hook curled around Gettysburg, turning east to another superb anchor at Culp's Hill. Meade's line enjoyed the obvious tactical advantage of high ground. Its hook also ensured the ability to exploit interior lines, with the invaluable privilege of reinforcing from one point to another directly and under cover. The sole tactical defect of the line was its vulnerability to artillery rounds pouring in from across a wide arc – the "converging fire" that is an artillerist's ideal. That defect never came into play. Confederate artillery, out-gunned and tacitly commanded by an ineffectual preacher-general, never levied converging fire against Meade's fishhook.

Although the great Confederate charge of July 3 garners the most attention, Gettysburg came to its decisive juncture on July 2 as Lee tried to exploit the advantages gained on the 1st. Meade resisted stoutly and to good effect, aided to some degree by Confederate failings. On the Federal right, Southern assaults against Culp's Hill faltered after much desperate bravery on both sides. The attack never came close to substantial success. At dusk, two brigades of Rebels pressed determinedly up the steep face of East Cemetery Hill – precisely where Ewell had feared to go the previous day under far more advantageous

General George E. Pickett, a foppish fellow of starkly limited capacity, became one of the most famous names in American military history because of the mighty charge on July 3, 1863. He and his division did little else during the war. (Public domain)

circumstances. Despite canister flung into their flanks, and Federal musketry in front, the Confederates reached the crest and held there for some time before Northern reinforcements flocked to the site in enough numbers to expel them. Meanwhile, the most portentous Confederate initiative during the Battle of Gettysburg had faltered far down on the Federal left, near the Round Tops.

At Chancellorsville, Lee had won a great victory by deploying to the point of decision a flanking column led by his most trusted subordinate, Stonewall Jackson. With Jackson dead, James Longstreet was clearly Lee's primary military asset. Longstreet did not want to fight on the offensive, however, and apparently spent July 1–3 sulking over Lee's variant view of things. Such defensive triumphs as the Battle of Fredericksburg appealed to Longstreet (and every other Confederate), but how often would one find a pliant Ambrose Burnside willing to slaughter his own army? Longstreet did not wish to take the initiative at all, so only grudgingly – and very tardily – moved away with Lee's maneuver element. The army commander remained near his other corps commanders, both of them brand new. After a sluggish march, marked by confusion and backtracking, Longstreet's column arrived opposite the Federal left in front of the two Round Tops.

The nature of the violent combat that swept across the fields and hills south of Gettysburg on July 2 was affected in a fundamental way by the impulsive actions of Federal General Daniel E. Sickles. The general came not from a military background but from the political realm, having been a powerful Congressman from New York. Sickles's legacy includes not just his Civil War service, but also a series of bumptious endeavors: he killed his wife's lover before the war, and escaped on a plea of temporary insanity; as postwar US ambassador to Spain, he had an affair with that country's queen; and he played the central role in preserving Gettysburg battlefield early in the twentieth century. In July 1863, Sickles always insisted, he had saved the battle itself for the Union, by pushing forward in front of the main line without Meade's permission. As Longstreet slowly approached action, Sickles moved forward into his path.

The assault by Longstreet's Confederates drove Sickles off his new position, and cost the Federal general his leg (after the war, a Congressman once again, Sickles took visiting constituents to the medical museum in Washington to show them his leg bones, donated as an exhibit). General William Barksdale of Mississippi, as fiery an antebellum politician as Sickles had been, led a dramatic charge into Sickles's line. Southerners swept east and northeast in a wide arc that resulted in bitter fighting across a landscape that became forever famous: The Peach Orchard; The Wheatfield; Devil's Den; Little Round Top. The last position held the key to that sector of the battlefield, looking down on the others and also commanding Cemetery Ridge to the north. After a desperate struggle, Confederates from Texas and Alabama receded from the crest of the hill, leaving a ghastly harvest of prostrate comrades behind them. As darkness fell, the Federals held the key ground and Lee's great opportunity had passed. Controversy still rages over the efficacy of Sickles's relocation, and about Longstreet's lassitude in moving to battle.

Impeccable hindsight shows convincingly that Lee's decision to attack the next day, July 3, against Meade's center, was his worst of the war. He doubtless undertook the forlorn hope because it seemed the only remaining option he had to get at his enemy. The Army of Northern Virginia had reached the end of a very long supply limb, about 120 miles (190km) from the nearest railroad-served depot back in the Shenandoah Valley. Stocks of commissary, quartermaster, and ordnance stores (particularly artillery ammunition) had dwindled and could not be renewed. Overwhelming tactical success on July 1 had yielded the opportunity for an even greater triumph on July 2, but that opportunity dissolved under frustrating circumstances. Lee's infantry had never failed to do what he asked of them. Might not a full fresh division of them, just arrived on the field, with support from other units and massed artillery, break the Federal center?

In the event, they could not. About 12,000 Confederates tried, in the most renowned attack in all of American military history. "Pickett's Charge" actually included about as many men from other units as from General George E. Pickett's division, which prompted postwar quarrels about the event's famous name. Confederate Colonel E. Porter Alexander massed artillery for a thunderous advance barrage, which used up much of the tenuous supply of shells. The barrage also fired too high against a target obscured by smoke and dust. When the infantry stepped out, they faced a maelstrom of shell-fire, then canister at closer range, and finally musketry in sheets as they charged past the humble farmhouse of the Codori family. A Virginian in Pickett's command wrote: "On swept the column over ground covered with dead and dying men, where the earth seemed to be on fire, the smoke dense and suffocating, the sun shut out, flames blazing on every side, friend could hardly be distinguished from foe."

Generals Lewis A. Armistead and Richard B. Garnett suffered mortal wounds at the front of the attack. Garnett's body was never recovered from the carnage, although his sword turned up in a pawn shop years later. Half of their men went down as well (Northern losses reached perhaps 1,500). A handful of brave Confederates broke into the Federal line for a time and hand-to-hand fighting raged around a battery near an angle in a stone fence. A Northern major marveled at how "the rebels ... stood there, against the fence, until they

Confederate General Lewis A. Armistead leads the desperate "Pickett's Charge" at the forefront, just before being mortally wounded. (Painting by Don Troiani, www. historicalartprints.com)

OPPOSITE PAGE:
Depiction of one segment of the fighting on July 3, from the immense 19th-century cyclorama painting by Philippoleaux, the largest piece of Gettysburg art and probably the most famous. (Ann Ronan Picture Library)

were nearly all shot down." They had reached what often has been called "the high-water mark of the Confederacy."

When the survivors turned back in sullen retreat, they suffered as dreadfully as on the way in. Among the Southern officers mangled was Colonel Waller Tazewell Patton, one of six brothers in the army and a great-uncle of the General Patton famous during the Second World War. The colonel had grasped a cousin's hand, said "it is our turn next," and leaped over the stone wall at the peak of the attack, then went down with his lower jaw shot away. As he lay dying in a Federal hospital, unable to talk, "Taz" scribbled a note to his mother: "My only regret is that there are no more brothers left to defend our country."

Fighting continued on July 3 in lesser volume on the far Federal right at Culp's Hill, and Jeb Stuart's cavalry engaged the mounted foe well behind the main Union line, but Pickett's Charge proved to be the final major engagement of the Battle of Gettysburg. Each army had lost about 25,000 men. During the night of July 4–5, Lee's army began to retreat toward the Potomac River through a violent rainstorm. The miles-long column of wagons bearing suffering and dying men became a train of utter misery. Meade pursued with some energy. Skirmishing flared along the route each day, but by July 14 Lee had managed to cross the rain-swollen river back into Virginia across a set of precarious pontoon bridges.

General Ambrose Powell Hill had been one of Lee's most capable division leaders, but at Bristoe Station and elsewhere he failed to perform to his commander's expectations. (Public domain)

General Meade came in for more calumny than praise. President Lincoln was disgusted that he had not captured the entire Confederate force, which looked far easier on a Washington map than on a muddy Maryland ridgeline. George Meade had won the war's largest battle, scant hours after taking command, and had done so against an enemy army that had been inevitably triumphant theretofore; but politicians and press, followed eventually by many historical writers, grumbled that he should have done more.

Meade commanded the Army of the Potomac for the rest of the war as by far its most successful leader. In a very real sense, he saved the Union – yet he has never received much recognition for his achievement. That is probably because General Ulysses S. Grant subsequently came east at a convenient moment, when numbers and materiel made it possible to end the war by simply shooting down many tens of thousands of men on both sides until arithmetic held sway.

The fall and winter of 1863–64

The perspective of years seems to suggest that Gettysburg turned the war onto a new axis, especially when taken with the Federal conquest of the Mississippi River through the fall of Vicksburg on July 4. History is, of course, lived forward but written backward. Americans struggling to further their opposite causes in 1863 saw little of what is now said to have been obvious. Confederates who fought at Gettysburg, and their families writing from home, rued the reverse they had suffered, but almost never displayed any notion of impending doom. When the Yankees came back across the Potomac, they believed, the invaders would be as susceptible to defeat as they always had been – and the veteran Confederate army set about to prove it.

Back on Virginian soil, Lee resumed his adroit maneuvering to counter each Unionist initiative, and proved to be almost uniformly successful in foiling his enemy. The armies edged southward and eastward, out of the Shenandoah Valley and into piedmont country, finally fetching up about 40 miles (64km) of latitude south of the Potomac. Through the late summer and fall of 1863, operations centered on a corridor between Warrenton and Culpeper and Orange. None of the sallies and probes evolved into a major engagement. Lee dispatched Longstreet in early September with a third of the army's infantry to the Western Theater, where the reinforcements would arrive just in time to play a crucial role in the Battle of Chickamauga. Two Federal corps followed Longstreet west, where they spent the rest of the war. Longstreet returned to Virginia in the following spring.

Lee's reduced strength threw him squarely on the defensive. Meade promptly pushed his foe south of the Rapidan River in mid-September, but on October 9 Lee grasped the initiative again, as he so much preferred to do. The Confederates advanced columns around both of Meade's flanks, forcing the Federal army to fall back north beyond Warrenton toward Manassas. A. P. Hill's troops took the lead. Hill had been almost invisible at Gettysburg during his first battle at the helm of the Third Corps. Now he had the advance at a portentous moment on October 14.

Unfortunately, Hill displayed more dash than judgment. Without reconnoitering the position, he threw two brigades of North Carolinians at a Union force ensconced behind a railroad embankment at Bristoe Station. The Northerners proved to be the entire Federal II Corps, veteran and unmovable. The Carolinians fell in windrows without any hope of success, losing about 1,400 men in a short interval. The Federal II Corps then withdrew unmolested. Lee conveyed his sad reaction to Hill in a typically restrained rebuke. As the two generals rode across the scene and Hill sought to explain how the disaster unfolded, Lee said quietly: "Well, well, General, bury these poor men and let us say no more about it."

Three weeks after Bristoe Station, the Federals inflicted another minor disaster on Lee's army. Confederates in Virginia were accustomed to achieving most of their goals, and had never been driven from a fixed, well-defended

The youthful Emory Upton had much to do with the striking Federal success at Rappahannock Station. He would be heard from again at Spotsylvania Court House and Cold Harbor, and after the war would play a central role in the reorganization of the United States Army. (Public domain)

position. When Lee fell back across the Rappahannock River in the aftermath of Bristoe Station, he incautiously left a *tête-de-pont* on the river's north bank at Rappahannock Station. A reliable brigade of Louisiana infantry occupied strong entrenchments north of the river, and artillery posted on the south bank offered supporting fire. When General Jubal A. Early, commanding the Confederates in the vicinity, noticed enemy strength concentrating nearby, he sent another brigade of infantry across to support the Louisianians.

Both brigades were doomed. Union General John Sedgwick closed in on the position with his VI Corps on November 7, 1864. A bright young West Point graduate (he had just turned 24), Colonel Emory Upton, led the advance with determination and swept over the works. Outflanked Confederates raced for safety across the pontoon bridges that connected the bridgehead with the southern bank. Only by means of a daring exploit were the Southerners able to cut loose the pontoon bridges and put the river between themselves and the victorious enemy. The Federals had inflicted about 2,000 casualties, most of them in the form of prisoners. The youthful Upton would be heard from again with another daring attack the following May, and then as a leader in reorganizing the United States Army after the war.

With the Rappahannock line breached, Meade could move into the excellent bivouac country south of that river and north of the Rapidan. For the next six months, the Rapidan River would constitute the military frontier in Virginia. (The river had been named in colonial times for British Queen Anne. Its rapid flow prompted settlers to call the stream the "Rapid Anne," subsequently shortened to Rapidan.) Skirmishing through the fall of 1863 and the following winter only threatened major operations once, at the end of November. On the 26th, Confederates who had been easing into what they thought would be winter quarters learned that Meade was moving in strength toward crossings lower on the Rapidan, not far west of the familiar ground around Chancellorsville.

Elements of the contending armies collided on November 27 at Payne's Farm and a hot, confused fight blossomed. Much of it raged in densely wooded country. Captain John C. Johnson of the 50th Virginia, "a large and stout man of about fifty years of age," who towered over most of his men at 6ft 7in of height, decided that his men "were not doing as well as they ought." To shame them into maintaining a steadier fire, Johnson stalked to the crest of the

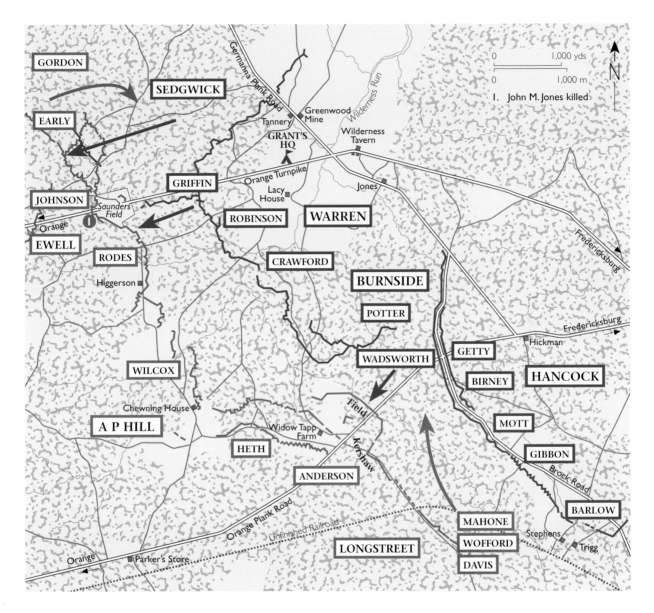

The Battle of the Wilderness, May 5–7, 1864.

position, lay down on the ground, "broadside to the enemy," and told his men that "if they were afraid … they could use him as a breastwork." Undaunted and pragmatic, several infantrymen did just that, resting their rifles on Johnson and firing "steadily from that position until the fight was over." Johnson survived the gesture, and also a chest wound he suffered in 1864 and two periods as a prisoner of war, to return home in 1865.

Once both sides had tested their opponents around Payne's Farm, the engagement there became the nexus upon which a long set of parallel lines spread across the countryside just south of the Rapidan. During the last three days of November and the first day of December, men in uniforms of both colors spent more time digging than shooting. A weather front brought in bitter cold and whistling wind on the heels of a long downpour, making everyone miserable at the same time that it reduced the potential for major military movements on the region's few and poor roads.

Meade's lines ran north–south, facing west toward Lee's position. Between the two ran Mine Run, which gave its name to the week-long action. Meade prepared a major turning movement around the Confederate right (southern) flank for the morning of November 30, but when the time came he recognized that his foe was ready to repulse the attack from strong works. The Pennsylvanian courageously cancelled the attack and two days later recrossed the Rapidan, having lost about 1,500 men south of the river. Lee and most of his soldiers were bitterly disappointed. "We should never have permitted those people to get away," Lee seethed.

Meade recognized that sending the vain assault forward would have been popular with President Lincoln and elsewhere in Washington, but he wrote officially, "I cannot be a party to a wanton slaughter of my troops for any mere personal end." To his wife, Meade admitted, "I would rather be ignominiously dismissed, and suffer anything, than knowingly and wilfully have thousands of brave men slaughtered for nothing." His estimate doubtless was correct: had he thrown in attacks that cost 10,000 (or even 15,000) more men, he surely would have enjoyed, and retain to this day, a glossier image. He might have retained independent control of the Army of the Potomac and emerged as the war's great hero in the North.

As the armies filed away from the Mine Run earthworks, they were ending a year of campaigning that had taken them on broad sweeps across Virginia, Maryland, and Pennsylvania. Only twice during 1863, however, had they fought full-scale, pitched engagements. Chancellorsville was the largest battle ever fought in Virginia, and Gettysburg the costliest of the entire war; but 1863 had produced far less intense combat than the armies had experienced in 1862. The soldiers who settled into winter camps in December 1863 faced, unawares, a new year that would bring far more fighting than the year just past, and under far different circumstances.

Into the Wilderness

In May 1864, the Federal army advanced across the Rapidan River and ended a period of six months during which that stream had, almost without interruption, constituted the military frontier between the United States and the Confederate States. General Robert E. Lee's Army of Northern Virginia had spent the winter spread across the rolling fields beyond the right bank of the river in Orange County, around Orange Court House and Gordonsville and Verdiersville. General George G. Meade's Federal Army of the Potomac wintered in the piedmont countryside north of the Rapidan, centered on Culpeper Court House.

Southern troops by this time had begun to suffer markedly for want of rations, both in volume and in quality, at least in part because the president of the key rail line in central Virginia was an antebellum immigrant from the North who secretly accepted pay from the Federal Secretary of War. Northern troops enjoyed infinitely better supplies. Their army also underwent a profound change during this winter. Meade remained its nominal commander, and would occupy that role to the war's end. The newly minted commander-in-chief of all Federal armies, however, established his headquarters next to Meade, leaving the army commander consigned to a secondary profile. Ulysses S. Grant had come east as the hero of benchmark Federal triumphs at Vicksburg and Chattanooga to be commissioned into the newly created rank of lieutenant-general. For the rest of the war, Meade's army commonly appeared in the press as "Grant's army" because the commander-in-chief was with it. Writing on the war still uses that locution, and in fact it will appear this way in most instances through the rest of this book.

As spring hardened the roads in 1864, "Grant's army" prepared to take the offensive with a new-found determination imparted by Grant himself. A reorganization consolidated some of the familiar old corps out of existence, leaving only the II, V, and VI Corps. General Ambrose E. Burnside's IX Corps also marched with the army. The once-disgraced Burnside had enough political currency to have landed back in corps command, and to be immune to Meade's orders. He would report directly to Grant, in awkward contravention of the most basic principles of unity of command.

The combined Federal force that crossed the Rapidan at the beginning of May numbered about 120,000 men. Lee could counter with only a few more than half as many troops, including Longstreet's infantry, newly returned from their adventures (and mis-adventures) in Tennessee and Georgia. Grant could – and did – draw on innumerable reinforcements through the coming campaign; the Confederate manpower cupboard by this time had become close to bare.

Grant intended to move south across the Rapidan east of Lee's army and slice straight through "the Wilderness" to get between his enemy and Richmond. That would force Lee to react rapidly under circumstances in which his enemy could choose the terms of engagement. Much late-twentieth-century writing has professed to recognize the striking wisdom that places did not matter, only the enemy's army. Lee and his government knew better. Richmond must be held for an array of fundamental reasons, industrial, logistical, military, political, and spiritual. When it in fact fell in April 1865, the war in Virginia ended almost concurrently. Grant's attempt to force Lee's small army to defend the approaches to Richmond in the spring of 1864 was precisely the right formula.

Getting through the Wilderness proved to be far more difficult than Grant had hoped. The dense second-growth thickets that gave the region its name covered about 70 square miles (180km²) on the south bank of the Rapidan–Rappahannock line, about 12 miles (19km) wide and six miles (9.5km) deep. When Lee received word that his adversary had crossed the

The Texans turn Lee back on the Widow Tapp Farm, Wilderness Battlefield. (Painting by Don Troiani, www.historicalartprints. com)

Rapidan into the Wilderness, he hurled his troops eastward and they struck the Federal right flank like a thunderbolt. The Brock Road offered Grant and Meade the only practicable route southward through the Wilderness. Two east–west roads served Lee as corridors of advance and attack. The old Orange Turnpike ran 2½ miles (4km) north of the parallel Orange Plank Road. Densely scrubby country separated them. The intersections of the two Orange roads with the Brock Road network became the focus of the strivings of both armies for three days, May 5–7, 1864.

The Battle of the Wilderness erupted on the Orange Turnpike on the morning of the 5th when Federal detachments in that quarter saw Confederates of General Richard S. Ewell's corps threatening from the west. Grant directed Meade to attack. Meade sent General Gouverneur K. Warren's V Corps. The Confederates had begun to build earthworks along the crest of a ridge at the western edge of a 40-acre (16ha) open space known locally as Saunders Field. When Warren's men marched in determined ranks into the field and started up the other side, they were inaugurating a pattern that defined much of the subsequent two days of fighting on the Turnpike. Confederate firepower pouring down the slope into Saunders Field, from behind defensive works, proved more than flesh and blood could stand – both at the first attack and through many others that followed. An early Unionist surge did attain the western crest, killing Southern General John M. Jones and breaking the line. However, Confederates pounding rapidly eastward on the Turnpike soon ejected the interlopers and restored the position.

Much of General John Sedgwick's Federal V Corps went to Warren's aid. Throughout May 5 men on both sides, particularly the blue-clad attackers, died in the struggle for Saunders Field. A section of guns stranded between the lines served as a magnet for repeated hand-to-hand strife. At day's end, the initial situation around the field remained unchanged despite a daunting expenditure of blood: Federals held the eastern edge, Confederates the western.

The thickets of the Wilderness, broken by only a few rude paths and desolate farmsteads, made maneuvering and fighting on a large scale impracticable between the Turnpike and the Plank Road. Both armies recognized the potential advantage of using the unoccupied middle ground as a means of threatening an exposed enemy rear; both made gestures toward exploiting the opportunity; neither ever managed to effect a serious lodgment.

Meanwhile, a separate battle raged on the Orange Plank Road, nearly in isolation from events a few miles to the north. General A. P. Hill's Confederate Third Corps moved eastward on the Plank Road. The sturdy Federal II Corps, commanded by the indomitable General Winfield Scott Hancock, interposed an obstacle between Hill and the crucial intersection. General George W. Getty's division, extracted from VI Corps up on the Turnpike, hurried south to help Hancock hold the Brock–Plank crossroads. Bitter fighting seethed through the confusing thickets. Men died by the hundreds and fell maimed by the thousands.

Federal strength threatened to overwhelm Hill, but at the end of May 5 he had held. A third of Lee's infantry, the First Corps under General James Longstreet, did not reach the battlefield at all on May 5. Hill's troops, weary and decimated and ill-organized, lay in the brush of the Wilderness that night with the desolate awareness that they could not withstand a serious attack in the morning.

The arrival of Longstreet's first troops early on May 6 salvaged a desperate situation for Lee and resulted in a moment of high personal drama for the Southern leader. Hancock had carefully arranged for a broad attack on both sides of the Plank Road. Soon after dawn, he launched his assault with characteristic vigor. It rolled steadily forward, scattering Hill's regiments and threatening to rupture Lee's entire front. Artillery had been of little use in the thickets, but a battalion of a dozen Confederate guns lined the woods at the western edge of the Tapp field, a 30-acre (12ha) clearing around the rude cabin and modest farm of a widow named Tapp – the only sizable open space anywhere in the battle zone along the Plank Road. The cannon flung canister across the Tapp Farm space in double-shotted doses, making the ground untenable for Union infantry. Northern troops filtered around the edge of the clearing to get in behind the guns and complete the victory. Then, without any

The final Confederate attack on May 6 swept all the way to the Brock Road, but could not hold the position. (Public domain)

time whatsoever to spare, the van of Longstreet's column reached the point of crisis.

Among the first units up was the famed Texas Brigade, perhaps Lee's best shock troops. The battles that had won the Texans their well-deserved renown had cost them enormous casualties: fewer than 800 of them remained to carry muskets into the Wilderness that morning. As the brigade moved resolutely through the hard-pressed artillery, Lee rode quietly beside them. The general recognized his army's peril, and had determined to take a personal role in repairing the rupture. When the Texans noticed him, and recognized his intention, "a yell rent the air that must have been heard for miles around." The Texans urged Lee to go back, shouting that they would not go forward until he did so. A soldier (there would later be dozens of claimants for the honor) grasped Lee's bridle and turned him back.

A participant in the event, writing soon thereafter, noted that Lee had not said much, but it was "his tone and look, which each one of us knew were born of the dangers of the hour" that "so infused and excited the men." A Texan next to the observer, "with tears coursing down his cheeks and yells issuing from his throat exclaimed, 'I would charge hell itself for that old man.'"

Lee went back. The Texans went forward and redeemed their pledge. Federal bullets hit nearly three-quarters of them within a few minutes, but they stabilized the situation and saved the day. The "Lee-to-the-Rear" episode immediately became an integral part of army lore. A monument at the spot today says simply, "Lee to the rear, cried the Texans, May 6, 1864."

Once Longstreet's reinforcements had stabilized the situation, the Confederate commanders looked for a means to regain the initiative. They found it in an unfinished railroad – graded and filled, but not yet tracked – that ran south of and parallel to the Plank Road. A mixed force of four brigades pulled from various divisions got astride the rail corridor, moved east until opposite the dangling Federal left flank, then turned north and completely routed Hancock's troops. In Hancock's words, the Confederates rolled up his line "like a wet blanket." Most of the attackers pushed as far north as the Plank Road. Some of them actually went into the woods north of the road.

In the ensuing chaos, a mistaken "friendly" volley tore into a cavalcade of Confederate officers reconnoitering on the road. It killed General Micah Jenkins and inflicted a dreadful wound on Longstreet. Lee's most capable surviving subordinate eventually recovered, but he would be out of service until long after the war had settled into a siege at Petersburg. The fatal volley, reminiscent of the mistaken fire that had mortally wounded Stonewall Jackson nearby exactly one year earlier, extracted all the energy from the Confederate success. An attack later in the day pressed all the way to the heart of the enemy line on the Brock Road, but in the end it produced nothing but more losses.

While Lee inspired the Texans and then regained the initiative on the Plank Road, General Ewell's Confederates continued to hold firm control of their crucial wood line up on the Turnpike. General John B. Gordon – a non-professional

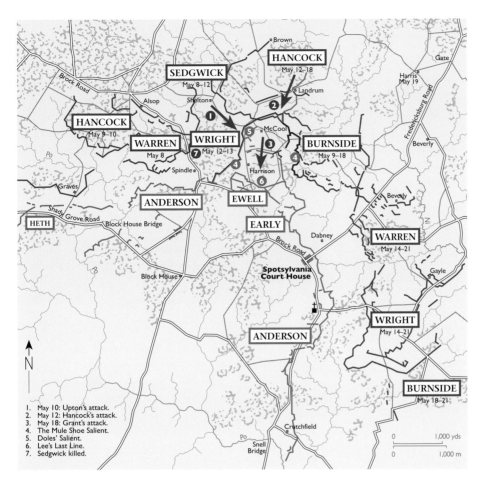

The Battle of Spotsylvania Court House, May 8–21, 1864.

1. May 10: Upton's attack.
2. May 12: Hancock's attack.
3. May 18: Grant's attack.
4. The Mule Shoe Salient.
5. Doles' Salient.
6. Lee's Last Line.
7. Sedgwick killed.

soldier who would bloom late in the conflict into a remarkable warrior – spent much of May 6 attempting to secure permission for an attack in the woods on the far left, where Grant had failed to protect his right flank. Timidity ruled Ewell's behavior by this time in the war (he had lost a leg and gained an extremely strong-willed wife, with deleterious impact upon his élan and *amour-propre*). By the time Gordon extracted authority to attack, daylight was dwindling. Even so, the surprise assault captured two Yankee generals and hundreds of men, and thoroughly shattered Grant's flank. In a ghastly aftermath to the Wilderness fighting, leaves and brush caught fire from muzzle flashes and hundreds of helpless wounded men of both sides burned to death.

The Battle of Spotsylvania Court House

After three days of intense combat in the Wilderness, Grant had lost about 18,000 men, Lee perhaps 8,000 (Confederate casualties for the last year of the war are difficult to ascertain with any precision). Wilderness was the only major battle in the Virginia Theater in which an army had both of its flanks shattered.

Hundreds of helpless wounded men of both sides burned to death when muzzle flashes set the thickets of the Wilderness on fire. (Public domain)

Grant had vivid, immediate proof that fighting Lee would be nothing at all like toying with generals Bragg and Johnston and Pemberton in the west. Nothing daunted, the Federal commander-in-chief calmly determined to press southward again, keeping the pressure on Lee.

Early on May 7, Grant issued orders to leave the Wilderness and head southeast toward Spotsylvania Court House, where the regional road net afforded a chance to slip between Lee and Richmond. When Grant turned south, despite having suffered as grievous losses as had prompted other commanders to return north, he put the war in Virginia onto a new track. Soldiers sensed the new resolve when they divined the direction of the move, and cheered boisterously. Tens of thousands of them would be shot in the next four weeks, but the army would continue to press steadily southward.

The march toward Spotsylvania Court House turned into a dramatic race fraught with mighty consequences. In a remarkable bout of prescience, Lee had ordered months before the improvement of a set of woods roads that paralleled the Brock Road, leading toward Spotsylvania. He selected General Richard H. Anderson, a phlegmatic officer, to replace temporarily the wounded Longstreet at the head of the First Corps. Anderson put his troops on the road to Spotsylvania, and found no good place to stop because of burning woods and narrow byways – so he kept marching all night long.

Federal progress on the far better Brock Road faltered in the face of scattered, but determined, resistance from Confederate cavalry. General Philip H. Sheridan, a Grant crony from the west, was new to command of the Federal cavalry, which should have shouldered the gray-clad skirmishers out of the way with ease. Sheridan was scheming this night, however, about getting out from under Meade's orders and instead reporting directly to his friend Grant. As a result, the Confederate resistance held on at one sketchy position after another all night.

Early on May 8 the race to Spotsylvania ended with Confederates controlling the key intersection on the Spindle Farm a matter of moments before Meade's advance arrived there. The consequence of Sheridan's indifference and Anderson's inability to stop was a very narrow margin of success for the Confederates. All day long, Federals trudged across an open field into Southern rifle fire, hoping to gain the intersection that they had lost in the race. They never succeeded, on May 8 or on several subsequent days. Thousands of them fell killed or wounded in the forlorn attempts.

The Battle of Spotsylvania Court House churned across a broad stretch of country for two weeks, from the meeting engagement on May 8 until May 21. Never before had field armies in Virginia remained in close contact for more than a few days. Now the war was changing, edging away from dash and maneuver toward mighty defensive works and, eventually, positional warfare resembling a siege.

Most of General Lee's defensive line at Spotsylvania took advantage of good ground along a ridge that covered 4 miles (6.4km) of farming country between the Po and Ni Rivers. From the point at which the May 8 race ended, units of both sides spread in both directions, entrenching as they went. Federal reinforcements pressed southwest toward the Po, hoping to get beyond Lee's flank; Confederates arrived to counter them. When both armies' flanks reached the Po, Federals began to push in the opposite direction, northeast from the Brock Road. Confederates countered that initiative too, but in the process created an unfortunate anomaly in their position.

General Edward "Allegheny" Johnson (the nickname came from an early war victory at a place called Allegheny) led his Confederate division northeast from the Brock Road long after sundown. In the inky darkness, Johnson's staff and the van of the division emerged from thick woods into the edge of a clearing. They could see Federal campfires in the distance at what seemed to be a lower elevation, so they stopped and began to erect defensive works. By morning, the Confederate line they had fortified and extended stretched far north of the generally east–west axis of the troops nearer the Brock Road. This "salient" swung up and back through a broad arc that prompted some of the farm lads who fought there to bestow upon it the name "Mule Shoe."

Confederates used felled trees covered with earth to fabricate an intricate set of field fortifications unlike anything that had been used earlier in the war. This view is in the vicinity of the nose of the Mule Shoe, near what became "the Bloody Angle." (Public domain)

The Mule Shoe salient, about a mile (1.6km) deep north-to-south and half that wide, became the paramount military feature through most of the Battle of Spotsylvania. The location of the line did take advantage of high ground, and it did afford protection for Confederate supply routes farther south; but it proved to be fatally vulnerable in a tactical sense. Southern infantry erected a vast, complex array of defenses of dirt and felled trees to strengthen the salient. They also constructed traverses – interior defensive walls perpendicular to the main line – to protect against fire coming in from hostile country opposite their flanks. No fortifications, however, could extinguish the elemental defect of a salient: an enemy who broke through at any point across the entire arc immediately had at his mercy the rear of every defending unit.

General Grant's strength in numbers and materiel gave him the luxury of dictating the action. For two weeks he intermittently probed at Lee's line, occasionally bludgeoning it with a massive attack. On May 9 the Army of the Potomac lost the reliable veteran commander of its VI Corps, General John Sedgwick. The corps commander's troops had been building breastworks next to the Brock Road when long-range Confederate rifle fire, from about 650 yards (600m) away, drove them from their jobs. Sedgwick sought to inspire them to do their duty by standing tall. "They couldn't hit an elephant at that range," he said. A dull whistle announced the passage of another well-aimed bullet which whistled past. The one after that hit Sedgwick beneath his left eye and killed him instantly. He was the highest-ranking Federal officer killed during the war.

Federals probed west of the Po, where Confederates blocked them successfully, but the heaviest fighting surged back and forth across the entrenched positions in the Mule Shoe salient. On May 10, General Emory Upton, the bright young New Yorker in command of a Federal brigade, sold army headquarters on the notion of attacking a vulnerable segment of Lee's line. Upton led a dozen regiments to the edge of a wood that looked across 150 yards (135m) of open field toward the northwest corner of the Mule Shoe. There a salient on the salient – a small bulge on the corner of the larger projection – offered an attractive target. The Federals waiting to attack dreaded the deadly fire they would face the moment they emerged from cover. "I felt my gorge rise," one of them wrote, "and my stomach and intestines shrink together in a knot... I fully realized the terrible peril I was to encounter. I looked about in the faces of the boys around me, and they told the tale of expected death. Pulling my cap down over my eyes, I stepped out."

Upton's direct assault surprised the Confederates – Georgians under General George Doles. It burst over the works, captured several hundred

Southerners, and seemed poised to rupture the whole Mule Shoe position; but Confederate reinforcements hurriedly sealed the shoulder of the breach, some of them led by Lee himself. Federal supports did not come forward with the same élan Upton and his men had shown. When the fighting waned at dark, the breakthrough had been repulsed.

General Grant apparently considered Upton's success as admonitory. In the Wilderness, all of Grant's efforts to maneuver against Lee had been less than successful, and he wound up with both of the Union flanks turned and shattered. Now Upton had gone straight ahead. Perhaps the solution was simply to overwhelm the outnumbered Confederates? On May 12, Grant launched an immense assault intended to do just that. The immediate result was the heaviest day of fighting at Spotsylvania and one of the most intense hand-to-hand combats of the war. In the longer term, Grant's preliminary success on the 12th probably convinced him to adopt the notion of full-scale, head-on frontal assaults that led to vast and futile effusions of blood over the next few weeks.

Through the night of May 11–12, Federal troops marshaled opposite the northeast face of the Mule Shoe. Relentless rain and a pitch-black night complicated their preparations (one general called the result an "exquisitely ludicrous scene"), but by 4.30am a force of about 25,000 men had consolidated into a dense mass, ready to attack. General Winfield Scott Hancock sent them forward in what would prove to be the most successful assault of its kind by Federals during the entire war in Virginia. Hancock's leadership and the men's bravery contributed to the attack's initial success, but it also benefited from two bits of happenstance: in a dreadful stroke of bad timing, the Confederate artillery had been withdrawn from the Mule Shoe to be ready in case Grant moved eastward; and the rain and humidity had rendered most of the Confederate infantry's weapons inoperative.

The noise of the gathering enemy had been audible all night to Confederates (McHenry Howard said it sounded "like distant falling water or machinery"), and they had scrambled to get the artillery back in position. When the attackers approached, they made an incomparable target for canister or other artillery rounds – rolling forward in a wide, deep formation, impossible to miss. Most of the Confederate guns scurrying back toward the nose of the Mule Shoe,

General John Sedgwick, commander of the Federal VI Corps, declared "they couldn't hit an elephant at that range" just moments before a sharpshooter's bullet killed him. (Public domain)

however, arrived just in time to be captured without firing a round. When the Southern infantry leveled muskets and pulled triggers, the commander of the famous old "Stonewall Brigade" expected the results he had seen many times before: volleys that knocked down the enemy in windrows and halted the assailants' momentum. But "instead of the leaping line of fire and the sharp crack of the muskets," General James A. Walker wrote in dismay, "came the pop! pop! pop! of exploding caps as the hammer fell upon them. Their powder was damp!" The military rubric, "Keep your powder dry," belonged to earlier wars fought with flintlock muskets. This affair on May 12, 1864 was the only major instance in which damp powder affected tactical events during the Civil War.

The Federal tide swept over the strong works at the nose of the Mule Shoe and roared on southward for several hundred yards. Then the chaos and disorientation, often as incumbent upon military success as upon military failure, dissolved the momentum. Desperate Confederates, some led by General Lee in person (as on May 6 and May 10), knit together new lines across the Mule Shoe and up its sides. By dint of intense, costly fighting they pushed Hancock's Federals back to the outer edge of the northern tip of the works. By then both sides had exhausted their initiative and the swirling fighting dissolved into a deadly, bloody, close encounter across the entrenchments. For 20 hours the contending forces occupied either side of a gentle bend in the works that

For hours the combatants struggled at hand-to-hand range, separated only by fortifications made of earth and wood. (Public domain)

stretched for about 160 yards (145m), making it forever famous as "the Bloody Angle" – a *nom de guerre* christened with the blood of hundreds of soldiers.

The Bloody Angle was made possible by the tall, thick earthworks, new to the war in this campaign. No one could have fought for more than a few minutes over the kind of primitive trenches in use only a few months before. The nose of the Mule Shoe featured embattlements made of tree trunks laid lengthwise, sometimes two parallel rows with dirt between. Dirt piled over the bulk of the fortification made it impenetrable by either bullets or shells. The ditch behind the works was deep enough to require a firing step for defenders to see to fire, through a space between the main wall and a head log perched above it.

About 2,000 men from South Carolina and Mississippi clung to the south face of the works. Far more Federals from the VI and II Corps threatened the Bloody Angle from the north, but numbers mattered little in that narrow front. Most Union troops went to ground behind the lip of a draw about 40 yards (37m) north of the works; others lay directly behind the north edge of the contested line. Brave men of both sides leaped atop the works to fire a round then drop back, if they survived. Others threw bayoneted rifles across like harpoons. A steady rain added misery to terror. The trenches filled with water "as bloody as if it flowed from an abattoir."

A Confederate called the scene "a perfect picture of gloom, destruction and death – a very Golgotha of horrors." A Federal general who visited the scene described the results of a fire so intense and long-continued "that the brush and logs were cut to pieces and whipped into basket-stuff … men's flesh was torn from the bones and the bones shattered." Toward midnight of May 12–13, an oak tree 22in (56cm) thick fell. It had been hit not by a cannonball, but by countless thousands of bullets, which gradually nibbled their way through its dense bole.

Just before dawn on May 13, the Confederate survivors finally received orders to abandon the Bloody Angle and fall back to a new line drawn across the base of the Mule Shoe – where Lee's position probably should have been formed from the outset. A Northerner who visited the newly won position at the nose of the salient left a graphic description of the place's horrors: "Horses and men chopped into hash by the bullets … appearing … like piles of jelly… The logs in the breastworks were shattered into splinters… We had not only shot down an army, but also a forest." In the aftermath of "this most desperate struggle of the war," one Mississippian who survived admitted that the tension and dread of the ordeal had shattered their nervous systems. Once they reached safe ground, the weary veterans simply "sat down on the wet ground and wept. Not silently, but vociferously and long."

Through the period May 13–17, the Federal army slipped steadily eastward, then southeastward, extending toward and around the Confederate right. This tactical measure foreshadowed Grant's strategic agenda for the next month, during which a crablike sliding movement to the southeast sought always to get closer to Richmond than Lee's army. Already he had unleashed Sheridan's cavalry to raid toward the Southern capital. The raiders did not get into

Richmond, but they did kill the Confederacy's incomparable cavalry leader, General J. E. B. Stuart, on May 11 in fighting around Yellow Tavern. Stuart had said, "I had rather die than be whipped." Lee would miss his skill in screening and reconnaissance functions.

Although fighting flared all across the lines with regularity, the next major Federal attempt did not come until May 18. On that morning, Grant launched another massive frontal assault against Lee's troops in their strongly entrenched new lines across the base of the Mule Shoe – a position that came to be called "Lee's Last Line." Upton's head-on attack on May 10 had worked; so had the Hancock onslaught on May 12; perhaps what was needed was simply to bludgeon Lee. This time, though, Confederate cannon stood ready. Without needing much help from supporting infantry, they slaughtered Grant's attackers without the least difficulty or danger.

The Army of the Potomac recoiled after heavy losses, never having come close to their enemies. As General Meade wrote wearily to his wife the next day, after the thorough repulse "even Grant thought it useless to [continue to] knock our heads against a brick wall." Most Southern infantry hardly mentioned the event in their letters and diaries, the repulse having been so easy that it required "but little participation of our infantry." A Confederate artillery colonel wrote regretfully that the Yankee infantry "*wouldn't charge* with any spirit." In the words of a boy from Richmond, "the Union troops broke and fled."

To the North Anna and the James

Fighting on May 19 at the Harris Farm, northeast of the old salient position and beyond the Ni River, brought to a close two weeks of steady combat. Grant moved southeast in his continuing efforts to intrude between Lee and Richmond and force battle on his own terms. The two armies clashed across and around the North Anna River, midway between Spotsylvania and Richmond, on May 23–27. They waged no pitched engagement during that time, but jockeyed steadily for position.

The river, running roughly perpendicular to the Federal line of advance, offered only three usable crossings. The left (northern) bank of the stream at the fords on the eastern and western edges of the battlefield commanded the right bank, making it possible for Grant to force troops across. At Ox Ford in the middle, ground made the Confederates masters of the locale. Nonchalantly, almost indifferently, Grant pushed his columns across on each flank, giving Lee a golden opportunity to defeat either side in detail. The river and its difficult fords markedly complicated Federal options, to Lee's advantage.

In 1862 or early 1863, such circumstances would have yielded a thorough thrashing for Grant. In May 1864, however, Lee did not have the means to gather in the toothsome prize. All three of his corps commanders were out of action, and a temporary illness had almost prostrated Lee himself. He could only seethe from his cot: "We must strike them a blow – we must never let them pass us again – we must strike them a blow."

Grant steered his army southeast once more, from the North Anna River toward Totopotomoy Creek, ever closer to Richmond. Lee's customary interposition kept nudging the Federals eastward even as they pressed south. Steady but desultory fighting at Totopotomoy led Grant toward scenes familiar from the earlier campaigns around Richmond.

By June 2 the armies were concentrating around Cold Harbor, where Lee's first great victory had been won on June 27, 1862 in the Battle of Gaines's Mill. The Confederate line that was hurriedly entrenched at the beginning of June 1864 ran right through the old battlefield; some of the 1864 fighting of greatest intensity would rage where the same armies had jousted two years before. A Northern newspaperman described the Southern entrenchments as "intricate, zig-zagged lines within lines, lines protecting flanks of lines ... a maze and labyrinth of works within works and works without works."

On June 3, weary of being blocked at every turn and always inclined toward brutally direct action, Grant simply sent forward tens of thousands of men right into that formidable warren of defenses, and into the muzzles of rifles wielded by toughened veterans. The young Northerners obliged to

Union engineer troops at work on the banks of the North Anna river, where Lee stymied Grant for four days in late May 1864. (Public domain)

General Evander M. Law's Alabama troops slaughtered attacking Federals at Cold Harbor. "It was not war," Law wrote, "it was murder." (Public domain)

participate in this disaster at Cold Harbor knew what the result would be. A member of General Grant's staff noticed them pinning to their uniforms pieces of paper bearing their names and home places, so that their bodies would not go unidentified. In very short order on that late-spring morning, 7,000 Union soldiers fell to Confederate musketry without any hope of success.

A Federal from New Hampshire wrote bluntly: It was undoubtedly the greatest and most inexcusable slaughter of the whole war… It seemed more like a volcanic blast than a battle… The men went down in rows, just as they marched in the ranks, and so many at a time that those in rear of them thought they were lying down." General Emory Upton, who had been so successful at Rappahannock Station and Spotsylvania with carefully planned attacks, wrote on June 4, that he was "disgusted" with the generalship displayed. "Our men have … been foolishly and wantonly sacrificed," he wrote bitterly; "thousands of lives might have been spared by the exercise of a little skill."

Some Southerners dealing out death from behind their entrenchments around Cold Harbor blanched at the carnage, but a boy from Alabama reflected on what was being inflicted upon his country and admitted that, "an indescribable feeling of pleasure courses through my veins upon surveying these heaps of the slain." A pronouncement by that Alabamian's brigade commander, General Evander M. Law, has been the most often-cited summary of Cold Harbor. "It was not war," Law mused, "it was murder."

The bloodshed northeast of Richmond settled into steady, but deadly, trench warfare for the week after June 3. Rotting corpses from the hopeless assault spread a suffocating stench across both lines; flies and other insects bedeviled the front-line troops; sniping between the lines inflicted steady casualties and made life difficult. Troops who had been scornful of digging earthworks earlier in the war now entrenched eagerly. Soon they had constructed elaborate lines and forts that stretched for miles across the countryside.

Much of the ten months of war that remained to be fought in Virginia would feature such horrors, but the site of most of those operations would be south of the James River. On June 12, Grant began carefully to extract substantial components of his army from the trenches and move them southward toward a crossing of the river. In managing that successful maneuver, Grant skillfully and thoroughly stole a march on General Lee, and achieved his most dramatic large-scale coup of 1864. Soldiers would continue to battle in the outskirts of Richmond for the rest of the war, but the focus of operations henceforth would move below the James to the environs of Petersburg.

Petersburg besieged

For ten months, the primary armies in the Virginia Theater of war struggled for control of Petersburg, Virginia. They fought pitched battles for possession of key roads and rail lines; they covered the surrounding countryside with massive forts and entrenchments; and Federals fired artillery into the city. The war came to Petersburg initially, however, not with a mighty roar, but in a slowly building rhythm.

General Benjamin F. Butler's 35,000-man Army of the James posed the earliest threat to the city when it landed at Bermuda Hundred on May 4, 1864. Because the omnipotent Federal navy could land Butler's troops with impunity, they found themselves unopposed and only 8 miles (13km) northeast of Petersburg. Confederate General P. G. T. Beauregard inherited the difficult task of knitting together the sparse and disparate units in the vicinity to keep Butler in check.

The Federal general's paramount goal was Richmond, but he turned first toward Petersburg. Although steadily outnumbered by odds of three-to-one, Beauregard managed to thwart Butler in four actions between May 9 and May 22 at Port Walthall Junction, Swift Creek, Chester Station, and Drewry's Bluff. The Confederates benefited immeasurably from Butler's ineptitude, timidity, and contentiousness with his own subordinates. By May 22, Butler had given up and begun to entrench the neck of the Bermuda Hundred peninsula. In the memorable phrase of a disgusted General Ulysses S. Grant, this left Butler's force "as completely shut off from further operations ... as if it had been in a bottle strongly corked."

On June 9, Butler tried again. He sent 6,500 men from inside the corked bottle to capture Petersburg, which lay almost entirely unprotected and apparently within easy reach. The Federal cavalry swung around to come in from the south while the infantry went at the town from the northeast. They

Grant's headquarters. (Public domain)

PREVIOUS PAGE:
The brave but hopeless charge of the 1st Maine Heavy Artillery at Petersburg, June 18, 1864. The Maine unit lost more men here in a single battle than any other regiment on either side of the war. (Painting by Don Troiani, www.historicalartprints.com)

Southerners called General Benjamin F. Butler "Beast Butler" for his attitudes toward civilians in occupied New Orleans in 1862. In 1864, Butler fumbled hopelessly in his operations around Petersburg. (Public Domain)

were repulsed in a desperate fight that became famous as "The Battle of Old Men and Young Boys." An array of citizens beyond the outer limits of military age (ranging in age from at least 14 to 61), ill-armed and untrained, threw themselves in the path of the invaders – and turned them back. One veteran battery arrived in time to play a crucial role in the narrow margin of victory. Nearly a hundred of the civilians became casualties as they saved their hometown. Anne Banister was standing on the porch of her home with her mother and sister when a wagon brought up "my father's lifeless body shot through the head, his gray hair dabbled in blood." On the evening of June 9, "universal mourning was over the town, for the young and old were lying dead in many homes."

By the time the rag-tag civilian assemblage had held Petersburg, Grant had decided to devote his main army to the task of capturing the city. The incredibly costly repulse of his troops at Cold Harbor on June 3 had eroded even Grant's oblivious determination. Taking Petersburg would sever most of the roads and railroads heading to Richmond, thus cutting the Confederate capital off from the rest of the Confederacy. On June 12, Grant began deftly to disengage major units of the Army of the Potomac from its trenches and move it by stages to the James River. On the 14th the crossing began, in part on transports and in part by way of an enormous pontoon bridge, more than 2,000ft (600m) in length, that was one of the engineering wonders of the war.

General Robert E. Lee's remarkable ability to divine his enemy's intentions stood him in good stead in many a campaign, but it deserted him in early June. Grant slipped away from Lee's presence without the Confederate chieftain learning of the move. When Beauregard reported the arrival south of the James of portions of the main enemy army, Lee discounted the news. Beauregard's tendency to concoct visionary schemes and embrace implausible notions contributed to Lee's uncertainty, but Grant thoroughly and unmistakably stole a march on his adversary. The result was a three-day span during which Petersburg stood almost defenseless against a Northern horde.

One of the war's great marvels is that Grant's men did not simply march into Petersburg during June 15–18. They surely would have done so had they not been enervated by the bloodletting of the previous month. On the 15th, more than 15,000 Northerners faced barely 2,000 Southerners. The defenders spread themselves in thin, widely separated clusters among works begun in 1862 to protect the city. Late on the 15th, a portion of that line fell to attacking Federals. "Petersburg," Beauregard wrote, "was clearly at the mercy of the Federal commander."

For two more days, Grant's troops swarmed around Petersburg without making a decisive move. Early on June 18, the first men from Lee's Army of Northern Virginia finally arrived, and Lee himself reached the town before noon. The Confederates bought time by abandoning their outer works on the 18th, leaving the first Federal attack to dissipate in a confusing complex of empty trenches.

When the blue-clad legions reformed and moved forward again, they attacked without concert – and without success. The First Maine Heavy Artillery, which Grant had extracted from a cozy post in the quiet forts around Washington and sent into the line with muskets, was butchered. More than 630 of the Maine men fell in an utterly hopeless assault. During the entire Civil War, no regiment suffered as many losses in one engagement. One of the minority who survived unscathed described the experience: "The earth was literally torn up with iron and lead. The field became a burning, seething, crashing, hissing hell, in which human courage, flesh, and bone were struggling with an impossibility... In ten minutes those who were not slaughtered had returned." The next morning a dense fog lifted to reveal a "field of slaughter, strewn thick with the blue-coated bodies ... decomposing in the fierce rays of a Southern sun."

While the bitter Maine veteran gazed across a field covered with his friends' bodies, major elements of Lee's Army of Northern Virginia were filing steadily into the defenses. Those sturdy troops would not be routed from their entrenchments by any kind of frontal assault. Petersburg had been saved, and for more than nine months would stand, with Richmond, as the last major Confederate citadel in Virginia.

The Crater

When the wretchedly managed Federal assaults of June 15–18 ended in an ineffectual welter of blood, Grant faced the necessity to begin a siege. He had lost more than 10,000 men in the awkward attempt to batter his way into Petersburg, as against appreciably fewer than half as many Confederate casualties. With characteristic determination, Grant quickly arranged to extend his lines southwestward across Lee's front. His purpose in this and several subsequent initiatives was to snap Southern railroads and other lines of communication and supply. At the same time, his almost limitless resources in men and materiel would benefit from ever-longer front lines. Eventually the limited Confederate strength would be stretched to the breaking point. Execution of those two initiatives constituted the story of the next nine months.

Grant's first move of his left beyond Lee's right came on June 21. The reliable II Corps, under the magnificent leadership of General Winfield Scott Hancock, moved across the Jerusalem Plank Road, permanently denying that artery to the Confederates, and on toward the Weldon Railroad. Lee could not surrender the vital rail link without a fight. He sent two divisions out to intercept Hancock's force. The tactical result was stunning. The glorious old Federal II Corps folded and ran in the face of a smaller force, losing 2,500 men, the vast majority of them as prisoners of war.

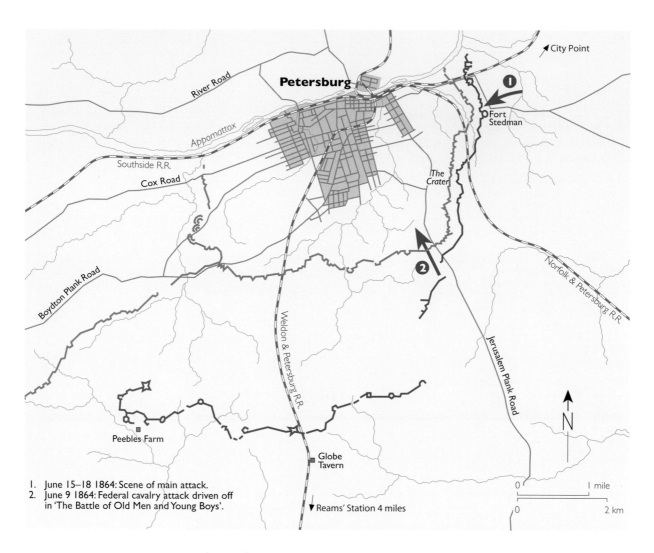

1. June 15–18 1864: Scene of main attack.
2. June 9 1864: Federal cavalry attack driven off in 'The Battle of Old Men and Young Boys'.

The battles around Petersburg, June–October 1864.

This embarrassing result, which could not have been imagined under any circumstances from that seasoned formation a few months earlier, highlighted the condition of Grant's army. It had been bled so thoroughly, and enervated so completely, that it had lost its hard-won and long-held prowess. Most of the army's field-grade officers, company officers, and non-commissioned officers lay moldering in graves between the Rapidan and James Rivers, or languishing wounded in facilities along the east coast.

Conventional historical wisdom has long credited Grant with a sort of quiet genius that recognized the necessity of slaughtering troops of both sides in endless hecatombs until arithmetic won the war. The unmistakable historical record shows that accepting about 200,000 combined casualties in getting to Richmond did end the war in a year of bloodshed. A minority opinion suggests that the immutable advantages of terrain and strategic

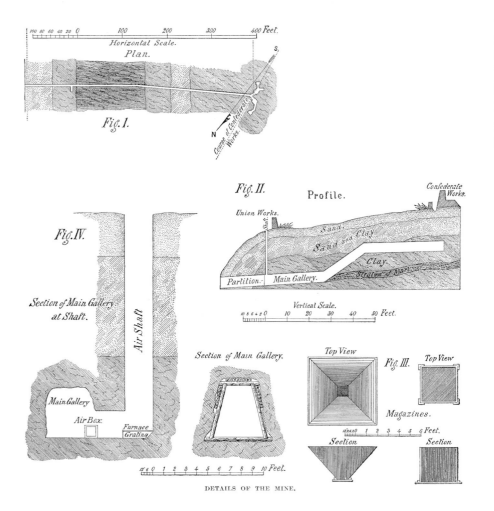

DETAILS OF THE MINE.

The sturdy coal minors who dug the tunnel between the lines faced considerable danger and discomfort even before it was packed with explosives. Their ingenious system for drawing fresh air into the tunnel made the project possible. (Public Domain)

imperatives available to the Federal cause around Petersburg would have set a far more desirable stage upon which to invoke elements of the military art. By the time the Army of the Potomac reached that advantageous ground in 1864, however, the army retained only a barely recognizable shadow of its former might. The months to come would feature operations in the image of the Weldon Railroad.

Through the summer of 1864, Grant intermittently pushed his left farther west, and Lee countered on his right. Most of the soldiers' energies, however, went into work with shovels rather than with rifles. A warren of forts and redoubts and trenches sprang up and ambled across the Virginia countryside. Men fought from behind works of wood and dirt, and lived in "bombproofs," as they called their rude homes hollowed out in the earth and reinforced with timber.

One of the war's most remarkable episodes, the product of an amazing engineering feat, grew out of the stalemate imposed by impregnable fortifications. Attacking a deeply entrenched enemy afforded little hope of success, against a guarantee of staggering casualties. A regiment recruited in coal-mining country, the 48th Pennsylvania Infantry, conceived the notion of digging a tunnel far beneath the earth's surface that would lead under the Confederate line, which then could be blown to smithereens. The Pennsylvanians undertook the novel project with a great deal of energy and ingenuity. They modified ration boxes to use for removing the dirt. They sent parties out to cut timber to shore up the excavation. They fabricated a complex but clever means to exhaust bad air from the lengthening tunnel and bring in fresh air through a wooden conduit. After three weeks of labor, the miners had completed a tunnel that ran 511ft (156m) and ended squarely beneath the main enemy line. For ten days they dug a lateral chamber and then packed it full of gunpowder – 4 tons of it. They planned to blow up the massive charge at dawn on July 30.

The Pennsylvanian soldier-miners had achieved an incredible success, but the Federal military hierarchy had not done nearly as well preparing to capitalize on the fruits of their labor. General Ambrose E. Burnside, who had failed so egregiously at Fredericksburg in 1862, was back with the army in command of the Federal IX Corps and responsible for the sector where the 48th had dug so diligently. He decided to assign his well-trained but untested all-black division to exploit the gap to be made by the explosion. General Meade refused to let Burnside use the black troops as the first wave because he knew that, if they took heavy losses, he would be pilloried by politicians and journalists. Burnside chose (by the mindless expedient of drawing straws) to substitute the least effective of his white divisions, commanded by the inept – and perhaps drunken – General James H. Ledlie.

Exploding the mine involved moments of high drama. An officer of the 48th lit the long, long fuse at 3.00am and thousands of men in blue waited in breathless silence for the explosion. Thousands of Confederates in deadly danger dozed in innocence. Nothing happened. By 4.15am it had become apparent that nothing was going to happen without intervention. Two brave Pennsylvanians, Lieutenant Jacob Douty (a doughty fellow indeed) and Sergeant Harry Reese, crawled into the long, dark mine to investigate. They found that the fuse had failed at one of its several splices, relit it, and scurried to safety. Finally, at 4.45am the "earth trembled for miles around," as a Virginia soldier put it, under the echoes of a mighty explosion. The blast killed or wounded nearly 300 South Carolinians.

When Smith Lipscomb, who survived, tumbled out of the air and landed on his feet, his thighs "felt like they were almost shivered." Lipscomb thought that he must have been badly crippled, but a Federal volley "convinced me I was not as badly hurt as I thought I was," he recalled later. The injured man staggered back under cover and began rubbing his painful legs. Before long he had found a rifle and began shooting at the enemy. The carnage continued until Lipscomb "saw the blood run down [a] little drain ditch several feet."

Ledlie's troops dashed forward toward the breach and gazed in awe at a chasm about 170ft long, 80ft wide, and 30ft deep (50m x 25m x 10m). While they stared at the place known ever since as "the Crater," Confederates behind the gap and on either side began to rally. Federal reinforcements pushed into the Crater and beyond, but fire from either flank limited their penetration. General Lee pulled Southern reinforcements from points all around his front to use in reestablishing his line. For several hours, an opening blown in the Confederate position beckoned Federals to lunge through and capture the city just beyond. Eventually Burnside received permission to commit the black division to the fight, but long after the crucial moment for which those troops had been trained. The black soldiers simply added to the chaos in the muddy, bloody Crater.

As Confederate units closed in, Federals in the Crater became defenders instead of attackers. Artillery shells, some of them from newly deployed high-angle mortars, exploded above the Crater and flung shards into its corners. The Confederate charge that retook the position erupted over the lip of the Crater and surged through its midst in hand-to-hand combat that turned the pit into "one seething cauldron of struggling, dying men." General J. C. C. Sanders of Alabama, who commanded a brigade at the scene, wrote that Southern guns "literally mowed down the enemy piling up Yankees and Negroes on each other." Confederate artillerist Frank Huger used similar language: "our men literally butchered them." A Massachusetts officer described the crowded situation inside the Crater as so tight that "many of those killed were held in a standing position until jostled to the ground."

The performance of the black troops generated considerable controversy. Some Northerners applauded their efforts; others damned them. A private

The fight for control of the Crater developed into a savage hand-to-hand struggle. (Public domain)

from Massachusetts, writing the next day, called the black soldiers "cowardly rascals" and declared that they "didn't get far before they broke and skedaddled … one might as well try to stop the wind." The Yankee lad expressed a wish that the newspapermen so fond of extolling black troops should go into battle with them. General Sanders, watching from across the lines, admitted that the black troops "fight much better than I expected but … many of them were shot down by the [Yankees]." Southerners who had never fought against freed slaves before relentlessly fired into the Crater and killed men under circumstances that would usually have resulted in captures. "This day was the jubilee of fiends in human shape," a Southerner wrote, "and without souls." A conflict in which slavery had become a steadily more significant issue had now reached a point where former slaves fought directly on the front line for their freedom and that of their brothers.

When the last Federal survivor dashed back to the lines beyond the Crater, an unusually dramatic battle ended and a dazzling opportunity had disappeared. The Union army lost 4,000 men on July 30; the Confederates about 1,500. General Grant removed Burnside and Ledlie from their commands, and summarized the Crater in regretful benediction: "It was the saddest affair I have witnessed in the war." There would be no other chance to go straight at Petersburg until the war's final week. For Grant, it was back to striking westward toward the railroads.

The struggle for the railroads

Ten days after the fight for the Crater, another gigantic explosion rocked the region. In the war's most dramatic incident of espionage and sabotage, Confederate agent John Maxwell blew up a time bomb on a barge full of explosives at Grant's headquarters complex at City Point, a few miles below Petersburg. The result, a colonel wrote to his wife, was "terrible – awful – terrific." The blast and secondary explosions killed 50 Federals, destroyed several structures, and did millions of dollars' worth of damage. The North's seemingly bottomless industrial capacity easily replaced the losses, but Southerners had occasion to cheer a daring and dramatic act.

Supplies and their transportation took center stage through the summer and fall of 1864. Railroads and wagon roads leading into Petersburg from the west and southwest sustained Lee's army around the city and also supplied sustenance for both troops and civilians around the national capital, 30 miles (48km) northward. Lee had to fight to keep those lines open. Grant welcomed the chance to close them, and to meet Lee's dwindling strength in the open, away from the powerful fortifications that neutralized the armies' differences in strength.

In mid-August, Grant moved again toward the Weldon Railroad. This time he stuck there. On the 18th, Warren's Federal V Corps effected a lodgment near Globe Tavern on the railroad. Two Confederate brigades hurried to the site and routed an isolated Union detachment, but did not have nearly enough strength to drive Warren away. The next day a further Confederate effort, this time in more strength, again achieved localized success. A Virginian fighting near Globe Tavern called it "the warmest place" that he ever had been in, "subjected to fire from the front, right flank, & rear all at the same time."

In fact, it was Warren's right flank that came under the greatest pressure. He lost most of two seasoned regiments as prisoners, and the situation seemed desperate for a brief interval. Reinforcements enabled Warren to hold fast on August 19, and on August 21 he handily repulsed a series of Southern attacks. In one of them, a bullet tore through both of General John C. C. Sanders's thighs and he bled to death. He had reached his 24th birthday four months before. A few days later his sister back in Alabama wrote to a surviving brother of her wrenching loss. Fannie Sanders described dreaming of John every night, then awakening to the living nightmare of the truth. "Why! Oh why, was not my worthless life taken instead of that useful one!" Fannie cried. "I have been blinded with tears." Families on both sides of the Potomac had abundant cause for grief. The fight for Globe Tavern and the railroad cost some 4,300 Union casualties, and 2,300 Confederate.

With a new anchor on the Weldon Railroad, Grant's lines stretched farther westward, requiring Lee to match the expansion, despite the direly thinning Southern resources. Grant immediately sent his once-powerful II Corps right down the Weldon line to destroy it as far south as possible. He could not permanently occupy that zone south of Globe Tavern, but he welcomed the chance to destroy more Southern transportation. The II Corps had been eviscerated in May, though, and repeated its poor showing of June in the Battle of Ream's Station on August 24–25.

Confederate General A. P. Hill led out a mixed reaction force of eight infantry brigades drawn from various portions of the line, forming what in later wars would be called a "battle group," brought together for a specific mission. The infantry joined with General Wade Hampton's Southern cavalry to surround and batter the Federals, who put up only a feeble resistance. General Hancock, the superb commander of the Union corps, rode among his men, waving his hat and his sword, shouting "For God's sake do not run!" His bravery accomplished little. Hill inflicted about 2,700 casualties, many of them captured, and lost only 700 men himself. The new Union bulwark at Globe Tavern, however, remained intact.

On September 29, 1864, a determined Federal assault captured Fort Harrison on Lee's main defensive line outside Richmond. (Public domain)

During September 14–17, Hampton's mounted troops executed one of the most successful raids of the war – "the Beefsteak Raid." About 4,000 Confederate horsemen dashed far behind the Union army and rustled a huge herd of beef cattle from under their enemies' noses. Hungry Southern troopers found most of the cattle guard "cozily sleeping in their tents." Hampton lost only a few dozen men and returned with 300 human prisoners and 2,500 cattle. The hunger rampant in the South by this time made the beef a tantalizing prize of war.

Elsewhere, September was a bad month for Confederate arms in Georgia, where Atlanta fell to General William T. Sherman, and in Virginia's Shenandoah Valley. Late in the month Federal initiatives also brought on some of the heaviest fighting of the year along the Richmond–Petersburg lines. Between September 29 and October 7, 1864, intense action erupted below Richmond and north of the James, and also around Petersburg west of the new Union establishment at Globe Tavern. Grant had attacked unsuccessfully north of the James twice before near Deep Bottom, in coordination with his offensives around Petersburg. This new effort fell with impressive might on the Confederate defensive line around Chaffin's Bluff and New Market Heights. Federal attackers ran headlong into a linchpin of the defensive complex at Fort Harrison, and captured it at the climax of a bloody assault. A New Hampshire soldier described the deadly work: "Our men fall riddled with bullets; great gaps are rent in our ranks as the shells cut their way through us, or burst in our midst; a solid shot or a shell … will bore straight through ten or twenty men; here are some men literally cut in two, others yonder are blown to pieces."

The cost of the success, which included the death of General Hiram Burnham, commander of an attacking brigade, drained away momentum in the Union ranks. Once again a temporary advantage wilted for lack of immediate exploitation. Lee directed a counterattack in person the next day, hoping to retake Fort Harrison, but it failed. The Southern leader faced the necessity of carving out a new position closer to Richmond. Fighting in the area continued intermittently for a week, killing General John Gregg of the famous Texas Confederate brigade on Darbytown Road on October 7, but no decision resulted. Confederate territory on the Richmond–Petersburg lines continued to shrink.

While Lee struggled to maintain his position outside Richmond, Grant simultaneously renewed his pressure south and west of Petersburg. General Warren again commanded a mixed force vectored toward that sensitive Confederate flank. His target this time was the Boydton Plank Road, west of Globe Tavern. Beyond that road ran a truly significant target – the South Side Railroad, Lee's last rail link into Petersburg. Warren found early success, but Confederate countermeasures directed by General A. P. Hill yielded results by now familiar: tactical victories for the Confederates against dispirited Yankees; but strategic success for Grant in the form of farther extension of his lines to the west. On September 30 and October 1, the troops fought fiercely on the Peebles Farm and the Jones Farm. Hill's men held Warren away from the Boydton Plank Road, and far short of the South Side Railroad, inflicting about 3,000 losses as against 1,300 Confederate casualties. When the smoke cleared, however, Unionist forts and earthworks had begun to sprout in this new sector.

In late October, the final major Federal effort to westward in 1864 moved toward the same target that had eluded Warren at Peebles Farm. While the customary diversionary demonstrations unfolded near Richmond, a mighty force composed of troops from three infantry corps, supported by a strong cavalry detachment, would push once again to the Boydton Plank Road and then beyond toward the much-coveted South Side Railroad.

On October 27, General Hancock and his II Corps succeeded in brushing aside Confederate cavalry and reaching the Boydton road, breaking across it near Burgess Mill on Hatcher's Run. In that vicinity the victorious Yankees came up against infantry and artillery in a good position. Warren's Federal V Corps floundered through tangled brush in a vain attempt to help. Meanwhile, the customary Confederate reinforcements pounded rapidly down the roads from Petersburg. Late on the 27th, those new troops attacked Hancock's men with vigor. Although they did not break the Union line, the Southerners hammered it so hard that Hancock retreated overnight and left his wounded behind. Burgess Mill had cost him 1,800 casualties, the Confederates 1,300.

As winter spread its grip across Virginia, and major operations became impracticable, Lee's line stretched far wider than the Southern leader would have preferred. When next the weather would allow Grant to move farther west, Lee would have little chance of resisting effectually. The armies retired into watchful winter quiet in their heavily entrenched lines. Desertion increased on both sides. War-weary Confederates slipped away steadily. Even the ever-more-powerful Union armies suffered more than 7,300 desertions nationwide per month on average during 1864.

The Shenandoah Valley campaign of 1864

In the spring of 1862, General Thomas J. "Stonewall" Jackson had catapulted to lasting fame by waging a campaign in Virginia's fertile and lovely Shenandoah Valley that captured the imagination of the South and transformed the nature of the war. By turns careful and then dazzling in his maneuvers, Jackson utilized the valley's features to his own advantage. The two forks of the Shenandoah River served as moats, being crossed at only three places in 100 miles (160km) by bridges. The Massanutten Mountain massif ran down the heart of the valley for 50 miles (80km) as an immense bulwark and shield. The northeastern end of the valley reached a latitude north of Washington, and looked like a shotgun pointed at the Northern capital. A Unionist who fought in the region described its military character: "The Shenandoah Valley is a queer place, and it will not submit to the ordinary rules of military tactics. Operations are carried on here that Caesar or Napoleon never dreamed of. Either army can surround the other, and I believe that both can do it at the same time."

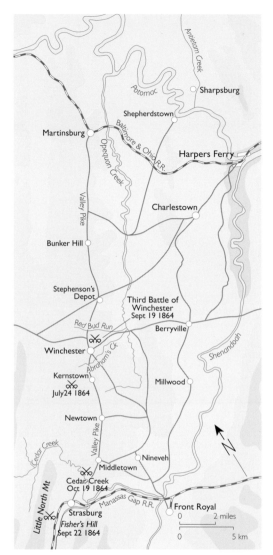

The Shenandoah Valley campaign, September–October 1864.

OPPOSITE PAGE:
The victorious charge of the youthful cadets of the Virginia Military Institute at New Market, as painted by Benjamin West Clinedinst, a postwar graduate of the Institute. (Virginia Military Institute Museum)

As Confederate options near Richmond and Petersburg narrowed in 1864, General Lee determined to take advantage of the valley again. He sent his trusted and able lieutenant, General Jubal A. Early, to raise Jackson-like hell in that vulnerable sector.

Significant operations had been under way in the valley for several weeks by the time Early arrived. General Grant's comprehensive plan to keep pressure up all across the Confederacy's frontiers included the dispatch of two tentacles toward the valley. General William W. Averell led an expedition in southwestern Virginia against the Virginia and Tennessee Railroad. He was successful in a stubbornly contested action at Cloyd's Mountain on May 9, 1864, but Averell's mission did not have a major direct impact on the war's main theater.

At the same time, General Franz Sigel pushed a force of some 10,000 men south up the valley (the rivers run nominally northward, so south is "up" the valley) toward the vital Confederate depot and rail junction at Staunton. The German-born Sigel offered Grant and President Lincoln more political energy than military prowess, appealing as he did to the large population of German-born immigrants living in the North. A non-German in Sigel's army described the men's "most supreme contempt for General Sigel and his crowd of foreign adventurers." Even Grant admitted that he could not "calculate on very great results" in western Virginia.

Against Sigel the Confederates mustered an army about half the size of their adversary's, led by General John C. Breckinridge. The disparate fragments that made up Breckinridge's army included a detachment of boys who would become famous in the impending fighting, the teenaged cadets of the Virginia Military Institute (VMI). On May 15, 1864 the two small armies clashed at the crossroads village of New Market, with control of the valley at stake. A steady rain complicated the brutal business of firing muskets and cannon, holding the acrid gunsmoke close to the ground and making the battlefield an eerie stage. Men from Massachusetts, Pennsylvania, Ohio, and Connecticut peered down from a commanding crest on the Virginians pressing toward them. Colonel George S. Patton I commanded a key Southern brigade; his grandson and namesake would win fame 80 years later in a very different war.

In the midst of the Confederate line marched the 250 young cadets. Several had just turned 15 years of age. "They are only children," Breckinridge said worriedly to an aide, "and I cannot expose them to such fire." The exigencies of

The irascible but able General Jubal A. Early fought against heavy odds in the Shenandoah Valley. General Lee called him "my bad old man." (Public domain)

the moment left him no choice, and the youngsters dashed forward through sheets of lead so "withering," their commander wrote, that "it seemed impossible that any living creature could escape." The boys charged in a torrential thunderstorm across a fire-swept field so muddy that it sucked some of their shoes from their feet, then dashed into the midst of the Federal cannon. Regular troops on either side of them had played an important role, but the VMI cadets had behaved like veterans. Their youthful assault fostered a legend. Fifty-seven of them (21 percent) fell as casualties, ten of those mortal. Among the dead boys was a grandson of Thomas Jefferson.

Breckinridge and his men chased Sigel north for miles, but the victory proved to be temporary. Breckinridge hurried across the Blue Ridge Mountains to help General Lee around Richmond. Sigel's military debits had finally outweighed his political assets and President Lincoln shelved him. General David Hunter reorganized Sigel's command and led it south again. On June 5 he destroyed a small, hurriedly assembled force led by Confederate General William E. "Grumble" Jones (the nickname being well earned on the basis of Jones's personality) in the Battle of Piedmont. Ill-disciplined Confederate cavalry failed to perform at the crisis. When Jones fell dead his rag-tag army dissolved, and for the first time during the war, a Northern force gained control of the invaluable railroad junction and warehouses of Staunton. Hunter then moved south to Lexington, burning homes as he went – some of them belonging to his own kin, who seemed to receive especially harsh treatment. Soldiers torched the home in Lexington of Virginia's former governor, John Letcher, denying the family's women and children the chance to remove even clothing from the house before it became engulfed by the flames.

When Hunter crossed the mountains and closed in on Lynchburg, another vital railhead and supply depot, General Lee determined that he must be checked. To that end, he ordered Early to lead the Second Corps of the Army of Northern Virginia westward. The corps made an obvious choice: it had been in the famed 1862 Valley campaign under Stonewall Jackson, and many of the men lived in or near the valley. Early was an equally good choice because of his energy and determination. The fiery Virginian stood up in his stirrups while scouting the lines around Lynchburg, shook a fist at the Yankees, and bellowed his scorn for both his enemy and the irregular Southern troops he was replacing: "No buttermilk rangers after you now, you God-damned Blue Butts!" Early used the derisive term "buttermilk rangers" to refer to stragglers, especially cavalry, ranging to the rear for refreshments instead of doing their duty. His difficulties with poor cavalry would bedevil operations for the next five months.

Early's seasoned troops chased the Federals away from Lynchburg on June 17–19, 1864. Hunter's men straggled through the trackless mountains in West Virginia on a weary march that took them out of operations for weeks. Early promptly turned north and moved steadily down the entire length of the valley and into the very outskirts of Washington, DC. En route he fought an engagement on July 9 near Frederick, Maryland, on the banks of the Monocacy River. A blocking force under Federal General Lew Wallace (who would write the classic novel *Ben Hur* after the war) fought all day to delay Early's advance toward Washington. Wallace's troops eventually recoiled, but they had achieved their purpose.

President Lincoln worriedly wired to General Grant at Petersburg, urging him to come in person. Grant instead sent most of two corps of infantry to reinforce Washington – precisely the sort of result Lee had desired when he unleashed Early. Lincoln went to the forts on the line outside Washington and came under desultory long-range fire. The Confederates did not get into the capital city proper, and could not have held it had they done so. As Jubal Early commented in summary: "We haven't taken Washington, but we've scared Abe Lincoln like hell!"

Union forces pursued Early to the Potomac River as he retired, then to the slopes of the Blue Ridge, and then beyond to the Shenandoah River. Early's rearguard repulsed them along the way, then savagely turned on the Federals at Kernstown on July 24, just south of Winchester. There the Confederates inflicted one of the most unmitigated thrashings of the war on their enemies, who suffered more than 1,200 casualties as against fewer than 250 Confederates lost. A few days later, General Grant sent a new commander to the Shenandoah Valley, with strong reinforcements. His instructions to General Philip H. Sheridan were to whip Early, and then to turn the beautiful valley into "a barren waste."

Despite an enormous preponderance in numbers, Sheridan had a far easier time accomplishing the "barren waste" element of his orders than he did in whipping Early. In the decisive battles of September and October, Sheridan was able to deploy more cavalry than Early had troops of all arms combined. Those cavalry, furthermore, enjoyed wide mobility on good horses, and carried weapons that dramatically out-performed the equipment available to the Southern horsemen. Early did not trust his cavalry. He had more than ample cause for queasiness, but his fractious relationship with the mounted arm only exacerbated a deadly situation. In postwar quarreling with General Thomas L. Rosser, his chief cavalry subordinate during the campaign, Early referred to Rosser as "a consummate ass," compared him to Judas Iscariot, and suggested that if Rosser were to emulate Judas and hang himself, it would be "the most creditable act" he could perform.

For more than six weeks, Sheridan followed Early's detachments hither and yon through the northern valley as the Confederates tore up the Baltimore and Ohio Railroad – a vital Federal artery – and feinted at supply depots as far north as the Potomac River. Early's energetic deployments convinced Sheridan that he faced far more enemy strength than actually existed. Finally, on September 19, Sheridan hurled two corps through a narrow canyon east of Winchester and brought Early to pitched battle.

In bitter fighting that swirled across fields and woodlots between Red Bud Run and Abraham's Creek, exploding shells took a steep toll among ranking officers. Federal General David A. Russell, an accomplished brigade commander who had graduated from West Point and served in the antebellum army, fell instantly dead when a shell fragment went through his heart. A piece of shell hit Confederate General Archibald C. Godwin in the head and killed him instantly. The highest-ranking casualty on either side was Confederate General Robert E. Rodes, perhaps the best division commander in the Virginia Theater, who also died from a shell fragment in the head.

Despite being direly outnumbered, the Southern infantry east of Winchester held their ground and inflicted staggering casualties on Sheridan's attackers. The moment of decision came from behind the sturdy defenders, northwest of the scene of the heavy fighting. A wall of Union cavalry swept into the northern outskirts of Winchester and simply overwhelmed the Confederate horsemen in front of them. Early had no choice but to collapse his outflanked main line and fight for time to get away before the enemy's mounted troops could deploy entirely behind his army. He succeeded in that effort, aided by the onset of darkness, falling back 20 miles (32km) to a strong position at Fisher's Hill.

George S. Patton, who had done so well at New Market, fell mortally wounded by another exploding shell during the retreat. Artillery fragments reaped an especially deadly harvest of braided officers on this day. The Third Battle of Winchester extracted more than 5,000 casualties from Sheridan's attackers. Early lost 1,700 men killed and wounded. He reported 1,800 men missing, but declared that many of them were "stragglers and skulkers," not prisoners.

Twice more in the next month Early would fight Sheridan. Each time the formula would resemble that of Winchester: Early's indomitable infantry would attack successfully or bloodily repulse their enemies, then Confederate cavalry on Early's left flank would collapse and unravel the entire line.

Sheridan pressed briskly forward toward Fisher's Hill on September 20 and on the 21st he skirmished as necessary to secure the ridges opposite Early's new position. Keeping steady pressure on his outnumbered and reeling opponent made good sense. General George Crook, who would later achieve notable success in the Indian Wars in the southwestern United States, conceived a bold plan to unhinge Early's line. Crook proposed taking his entire corps up onto the slopes of Little North Mountain, which anchored the Confederate left, then moving south until he was in a position to turn the enemy line. Sheridan cavalierly, and characteristically, claimed for himself all of the credit for this battle plan, although his own preliminary proposal had been to launch an utterly impractical frontal assault on the opposite end of the line.

On September 22, while the rest of Sheridan's army demonstrated straight ahead toward Fisher's Hill, Crook put his plan into action. It worked fabulously

well, in part because Early had again positioned his unreliable cavalry at the most vulnerable segment of his position. The Confederates reeled southward again in total disarray, losing prisoners and cannon as they went. Early's defeated fragments did not stop until they had scampered more than 50 miles (80km). An onlooker heard a weary Confederate chanting a home-spun ditty that began, "Old Jube Early's gone up the spout." Early blamed his army for the rout. When a passing soldier yelled irreverently at the army commander, Early spat back, "Fisher's Hill, god damn you," believing that the very name of that embarrassment was opprobrium enough.

Sheridan had cause to believe that he had forever removed Early's little army from serious consideration, and set about destroying the valley systematically. His men killed thousands of animals, burned countless barns and mills, and destroyed crops everywhere. The vandalism loosened or destroyed the reins of discipline in some instances, and Unionists went beyond warfare on agriculture to burn houses and savage civilian women in what Virginians called "The Burning." Ironically, the region most heavily affected included one of the largest concentrations of unflinching pacifists on the continent, most of them Mennonites or Dunkards; their buildings burned as briskly as anyone else's.

Southern cavalrymen, many of them watching their own homes aflame, could not stem the onslaught, but they took the chance to execute groups of enemy arsonists when they cornered them. War never treads gently, especially

Early's Confederates fought Sheridan's Federals to a standstill east of Winchester on September 19, 1864, but Northern cavalry eventually overran Early's left and decided the day. (Public domain)

Starting on October 6, Sheridan's Federals systematically burned out the Shenandoah Valley. (Public domain)

civil war, but the American strife in the 1860s had been amazingly civilized – until the fall of 1864. Rosser's enraged Confederate cavalry eventually stretched too far from infantry support and suffered a resounding beating on October 9 at Tom's Brook by Union cavalry under generals George A. Custer, Wesley Merritt, and Alfred T. A. Torbert.

Incredibly, Early pushed back northward once more soon after Tom's Brook, a phoenix risen from the ashes, and by mid-October had again reached the vicinity of Fisher's Hill. Sheridan had concluded that his foe had been permanently vanquished, but the small Southern force launched against him one of the most amazing surprise assaults of the war. Lee had sent Early reinforcements from Richmond, among them some of the army's most dependable units. Confederate generals reconnoitered Sheridan's camps from a towering aerie atop Massanutten Mountain and discovered that the Federals were strewn randomly across a wide stretch of rolling country north of Strasburg and Cedar Creek, with scant attention to tactical considerations. They hatched a daring plan.

General John B. Gordon led a long, stealthy, circuitous march along a trail so primitive that he called it "a pig's path." Gordon's column crossed the North Fork of the Shenandoah, crept across the nose of a mountain, and came back to the river opposite the unsuspecting left flank of Sheridan's force. At dawn on October 19, they splashed into the stream and dashed up the opposite slope into camps full of sleeping Yankees, screaming the chilling "Rebel Yell" as they ran. The onslaught routed the entire Federal VIII Corps. The Federal XIX Corps fought bravely for a time, but the momentum of the Southern surprise attack overwhelmed them too, and swept north to the vicinity of the village of Middletown.

Only the Federal VI Corps remained unassailed and unbroken. Together with the unhurt Northern cavalry, the VI Corps numbered as many men as Early's entire army, but staying the Rebels' momentum proved to be a difficult task. General Horatio G. Wright, commander of the corps, was acting as army commander that morning in Sheridan's absence. Wright deserves far more credit than he has been given for his calm, courageous stand which diluted Confederate momentum and restored the day for his army.

Early has received considerable blame for not pressing Wright more firmly to keep astride the momentum that was his only major advantage under the circumstances. The Confederate commander's quandary was compounded by the behavior of his troops: many of the weary, lean, hungry Southerners could not resist the array of food and booty in the captured camps. Their absence thinned Early's ranks and limited his options. Early's own summary to a member of his staff is telling: "The Yankees got whipped," he said, "and we got scared." When the aide prepared to leave for Richmond with a report, Early directed him "not to tell General Lee that we ought to have advanced" farther during the morning, "for … we ought to have done so."

Sheridan dashed back from Winchester to the sound of the guns around Middletown, sent his immense force of cavalry sweeping around the Confederate left (for the third time in three battles), and advanced all across the line. With the momentum of the Southerners' surprise attack evaporated, there could be no doubt whatsoever about the outcome. Early's survivors fled south once more. All the bright hopes of the morning had vanished in the face of unchecked disaster. The Confederates had captured 20 cannon in their triumphant attack; now they lost all of them, and as many more of their own. Early's troops had inflicted 5,700 casualties on the Federal army, and lost 2,900 themselves. They also, by day's end, had for all intents and purposes lost the valley for the remainder of the war.

General Lee recalled most of Early's infantry to help with the desperate defense of Richmond and Petersburg. Cavalry detachments roamed the valley through the winter of 1864–65, raiding for the scant supplies available and harassing one another without major results. Both sides afflicted such of the civilian population as had not fled, and eked out a cold, bitter, costly existence. The small remnant with Early collapsed after only a faint struggle at the Battle of Waynesboro, in the southern valley, on March 2, 1865. The general himself was among the handful who escaped. By then, Lee's lines beyond the mountains were close to the breaking point.

From Richmond and Petersburg to Appomattox

Winter weather and its effect on a bad road system stymied Grant's steady probing westward toward the railroads through the war's last winter. The only major operation through that period unfolded on February 5–7, 1865 in the Battle of Hatcher's Run. Once again the Federals hoped to seize and hold the Boydton Plank Road; and once again they coveted the invaluable South Side Railroad, which ran just beyond the road.

A strong Federal force moved into the area. It included II Corps, now under General Andrew A. Humphreys (long-time, much-admired corps commander Hancock had left the army), and Warren's V Corps returning to familiar ground.

On February 5, Humphreys battered Confederates who had hurried out from Petersburg. The next day, further Southern units swarmed over Warren and inflicted serious damage, but without lasting results. On the 7th, Lee concluded that he could not evict the Federals from their new perch, so both sides once more went back to entrenching. This latest extension of the line left Lee with 35 miles (56km) to defend. About 1,500 Federals had fallen, and 1,000 Confederates.

The battles around Petersburg, 1865.

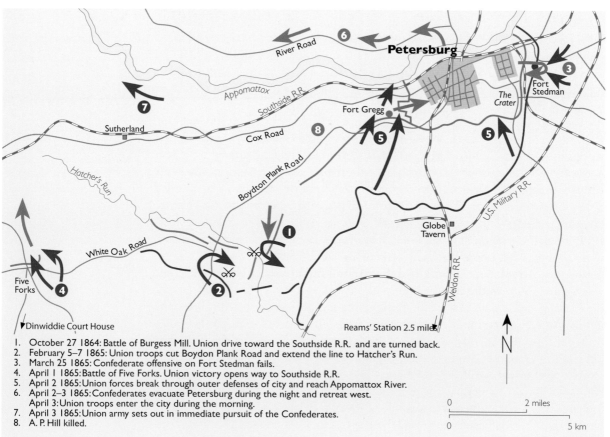

1. October 27 1864: Battle of Burgess Mill. Union drive toward the Southside R.R. and are turned back.
2. February 5–7 1865: Union troops cut Boydon Plank Road and extend the line to Hatcher's Run.
3. March 25 1865: Confederate offensive on Fort Stedman fails.
4. April 1 1865: Battle of Five Forks. Union victory opens way to Southside R.R.
5. April 2 1865: Union forces break through outer defenses of city and reach Appomattox River.
6. April 2–3 1865: Confederates evacuate Petersburg during the night and retreat west.
   April 3: Union troops enter the city during the morning.
7. April 3 1865: Union army sets out in immediate pursuit of the Confederates.
8. A. P. Hill killed.

Among the Southern casualties was General John Pegram. One contemporary remembered him fondly, if oddly, as "a delightful & artistic whistler." The handsome young officer had been married in Richmond at St Paul's Church on January 19 to Hetty Cary, a widely admired belle – "the most beautiful woman I ever saw in any land," enthused a Confederate officer. Five days after his wedding John celebrated his 32nd birthday. Two weeks later and he was back at St Paul's in a casket.

By mid-March, Lee's options had all but vanished. He accepted a desperate scheme hatched by the innovative General Gordon, back with the main army after leading the secret march at Cedar Creek in the Shenandoah Valley. Gordon would marshal as many men as could be spared from the attenuated lines and lead them in a late-night assault against the Federals at Fort Stedman, not far from the Crater and on precisely the ground where the 1st Maine Heavy Artillery had been slaughtered the preceding June.

Careful planning and steady bravery brought Gordon initial success. Picked troops silently removed the defensive obstructions in front of the Confederate works opposite Stedman, then crawled up a ravine toward their enemy. Small detachments of volunteers silenced Federal pickets and deftly opened a corridor through the enemy obstacles near the fort. Storming parties followed and burst upon their surprised foe, capturing the fort and spreading down the line on either side. More Southern infantry followed, Gordon in their midst, to exploit the breakthrough.

A major Federal supply depot only a mile (1.6km) behind Fort Stedman must have seemed to some of the starving Confederates to be the quintessential prize. Daylight brought stunning reality, however, as Federals farther down the lines on both sides brought artillery to bear. By 8.00am Yankees were swarming back toward Stedman. "The whole field was blue with them," a dismayed Southerner wrote. In the succinct summary of a disappointed North Carolinian, the fleeting success resembled a "meteor's flash that illumines for a moment and [then] leaves the night darker than before."

The Confederate horizon would darken even further during the next fortnight, then flicker out permanently. The advent of early spring gave Grant the chance to push west and southwest again. Lee obviously could not hold out much longer in Petersburg and Richmond, but the Federal commander feared that his wily adversary might find a way to slip away through the lines and head for North Carolina to join forces with another retreating Confederate army there.

Confederate General John Pegram married a young woman acclaimed among the most beautiful in the South, then was killed a few days later. (Public Domain)

Before Lee could attempt such a stratagem, his thinly manned lines snapped. Fighting by Union cavalry around Dinwiddie Court House on March 31 went well for Confederate General George E. Pickett, but to Lee's dismay Pickett fell back north to the invaluable Five Forks intersection on the White Oak Road. On April 1, Pickett, ever the dilettante, played host at a fish fry. Generals Fitzhugh Lee and Tom Rosser joined him at what became infamous as "The Shad Bake." While the generals enjoyed the respite from winter's short rations, Warren's diligent V Corps crashed into the exposed Confederate left and completely shattered it. Instead of applauding Warren's coup, Sheridan, commanding on the field, relieved him from command and assumed the mantle of the hero of Five Forks.

With Five Forks in Unionist hands, there remained nothing to keep them from the long-sought South Side Railroad. The next morning Grant ordered attacks all along the line and ended the siege of Petersburg. Horatio Wright's VI Corps rolled through A. P. Hill's troops almost at will. In a random encounter in the woods, two Federal enlisted men met Hill, who ranked behind only Longstreet among Lee's subordinates, accompanied only by a courier. After a nervous exchange of challenges, one Yankee fired a bullet that went through Hill's thumb and into his heart.

Farther northeast, closer to Petersburg, a tiny Confederate detachment held desperately to Fort Gregg to buy time for Lee to knit together a new line, and for the Confederate government to evacuate Richmond. Fort Gregg's defenders counted only two Mississippi regiments, one section of Louisiana artillery, and a handful of artillerists pressed into service as infantry – perhaps 300 men in all. The entire fresh Federal XXIV Corps attacked across an open field against the small work. Although it seemed to one witness that the Federal flags created "a solid line of bunting around the fort," the Southerners repulsed the first assault. Another fell back in confusion, leaving a bloody wake behind. Attacking Northerners wrote of "withering fire" that "mowed down our men most unmercifully." Finally the defenders collapsed under an overwhelming assault from all sides. They had shot more than 700 Federals. Only a handful of unwounded Southerners survived to be captured.

The sacrificial stand in Fort Gregg bought Lee time to protect Petersburg by means of a hastily connected interior line, but that night he had to abandon the city that for so long had been a focus of military operations in Virginia. For six days, April 3–8, 1865, Lee's Army of Northern Virginia wove a weary trail westward, hoping against hope to find a means of escape. Federal detachments, both infantry and cavalry, darted in and out of the desperate Southern columns, snaring prisoners and disrupting the retreat. Lee hoped to find rations for his men near Amelia Court House and Farmville; there were none. On April 6, the last pitched battle of the war in Virginia broke out on the banks of Sayler's Creek. The fighting did not rage hot or long. Federals closing in from three sides captured about 8,000 men, including eight general officers. Lee fought off pursuit at Cumberland Church on April 7 and kept heading west.

On the night of April 8, near Appomattox Court House, Lee found the enemy directly in his path as well as closing in from all sides. The next day he surrendered to Grant. The ceremony took place in the home of Wilmer McLean. By remarkable coincidence, four years earlier McLean had moved to Appomattox from his farm along Bull Run, to get away from the war that the Battle of Manassas had brought to his property. Not coincidentally, and entirely characteristically, Grant did not even invite Meade to the ceremony.

With four years of bloodshed at last ended in Virginia, other Confederate forces across the South faced imminent surrender. It now remained for Northerners to implement their hard-won victory, and for Southerners to find the means of sustenance in a destroyed country.

PORTRAIT OF A SOLDIER: McHENRY HOWARD'S WAR

In September 1814, Francis Scott Key of Maryland wrote a poem as he watched British ships bombard Fort McHenry in the harbor of Baltimore. When an actor sang Key's "The Star-Spangled Banner" to the tune of an old drinking song, it at once became a popular patriotic air, and many years later the official national anthem of the United States.

Francis Scott Key's grandson, McHenry Howard, did not hesitate about going to war against the Star-Spangled Banner when Northern troops invaded his hometown of Baltimore in 1861. Federal authorities simply threw into jail those of Maryland's elected legislators who would not do as they were told. Howard and thousands of other young men from the state hurried southward, eager to fight for restoration of self-government. Their purpose, Howard wrote, was "not merely to aid the cause of the Confederacy as it was constituted, but believing that they were serving their own State – in subjection – in the only way that was left to them." Francis Scott Key had about 60 descendants living in 1860, and "every man, woman and child was Southern," Howard recalled, although "I cannot recall that any owned slaves in 1861."

When war interrupted Howard's civilian pursuits, he had been studying law after graduating from Princeton University. The 22-year-old lawyer in training belonged to a volunteer organization, the "Maryland Guard," that served purposes at least as much social as military. The guardsmen affected gorgeous uniforms of the "Zouave" variety, modeled after the outfits of French colonial troops who had caught the popular fancy in North America. Howard later described his garb with amusement provided by hindsight:

The full dress was a dark blue jacket, short and close fitting and much embroidered with yellow; a blue flannel shirt with a close row of small round gilt buttons (for ornament merely) down the front, between yellow trimming;

OVERLEAF:
Grant and Lee meet near the Appomattox Courthouse following Lee's surrender, Union and Confederate soldiers are shown in the background. (Anne S. K. Brown Military Collection, Brown University Library)

blue pantaloons, very baggy and gathered below the knee and falling over the tops of long drab gaiters; a small blue cap, of the kepi kind, also trimmed with yellow; and, finally, a wide red sash ... kept wide by hooks and eyes on the ends.

Private Howard would soon discover, in the world of a real soldier in the field, that "this gaudy dress, which made a very brilliant effect on street parade ... was totally unsuitable for any active service."

For nearly a year Howard served (more suitably attired, of course) in the ranks as an enlisted man with the 1st Maryland Infantry, Confederate States Army, made up of 1,000 young men who had escaped across the Potomac River to join the Southern cause. In the spring of 1862 he won a commission as lieutenant and aide-de-camp to fellow Marylander General Charles S. Winder. Lieutenant Howard remained at that lowest of the commissioned ranks for the final three years of the war. In his staff role, he had an opportunity to observe much of the conflict's most dramatic events, and many of its most significant leaders. After a Federal shell killed General Winder at Cedar Mountain in August 1862, Howard did staff duty with generals Isaac R. Trimble, George H. Steuart, and George Washington Custis Lee, son of army commander General Robert E. Lee.

When Lee's Army of Northern Virginia headed north after the Battle of Chancellorsville, Lieutenant Howard followed as a supernumerary. His chief, General Trimble, had not reported back to the army after convalescing from a bad wound. That left Howard without a role, but he could not ignore his comrades' aggressive move northward and headed across country toward the Potomac to catch up with the army. When he splashed up the left bank of the river, the exiled Marylander noted sadly that it was the first time he had been on the soil of his native state in one month more than two years.

In Greencastle, Pennsylvania, Howard and a half-dozen other stray Confederates wound up in a hot street fight against mounted Yankees. Pistol bullets shattered windowpanes on all sides, dust obscured galloping horses, and the little band of Rebels had to flee. Later Howard and his mates chased a lone horseman for miles, only to discover that he was a Confederate major and an old friend.

During the army's subsequent retreat back toward Virginia, Howard rode through a Maryland town and thought wistfully, "Oh, that it was Baltimore!" On July 14, as the Army of Northern Virginia abandoned Maryland, Howard wrote in his diary: "Feel very much depressed at the gloomy prospect for our State. I look around me constantly to see as much of it as I can before leaving it." As the army crossed the Potomac into Virginia, bandsmen gladly struck up "Sweet Home," but that seemed "a mockery" to the Marylanders. Howard "could not refrain from some bitter tears as I ... looked back to our beloved State."

For ten months after Gettysburg, the exiled lieutenant performed staff duty under General George H. Steuart, a West Point graduate with "Old Army" ideas about organization and discipline. The summer after Gettysburg passed without

McHenry Howard, 1838–1923.
(Public domain)

a major engagement. During the lull, Howard and his comrades fought against the elements and against logistical defects – just as has every army in every era. In September 1863, he wrote disgustedly in his diary: "Raining like pitchforks – very disagreeable… Regular equinoctial storm – have had nothing to eat for almost twenty-four hours." Violent downpours had drowned every fire for miles. Through one uncomfortable day, Lieutenant Howard, General Steuart, and three others huddled unhappily in a storm-shaken tent all day long, hungry and miserable.

Howard missed the campaigning around Bristoe Station in October 1863 because he had gone to the Confederate capital for religious reasons – to be confirmed in the Episcopal faith in Richmond's elegant St Paul's Church. He had returned to duty by the time of the Battle of Mine Run, where his staff chores brought him under heavy fire: "the bullets coming through the switchy woods sounded somewhat like the hissing of a hail or sleet storm." He also noticed in that engagement one of the benchmarks of the war's evolution. Confederate soldiers had reached the conclusion that substantial protective fortifications made really good sense in the face of rifled musketry. They used "their bayonets, tin cups, and their hands, to loosen and scoop up the dirt, which was thrown on and around the trunks of old field pine trees" that they cut down and stretched lengthwise.

During the winter of 1863–64, genuine hardship became a constant companion of Southern soldiers. Lieutenant Howard described his diet, at a point in the food chain well above the privates and corporals, as consisting mostly of "corn dodgers" – corn meal cooked with water – for both breakfast and dinner. In good times, dinner also included "a soup made of water thickened with corn meal and mashed potatoes and cooked with a small piece of meat, which … was taken out when the soup was done and kept to be cooked over again."

Events in the spring campaign in 1864 threw McHenry Howard into the cauldron of combat, then yanked him out of action as a prisoner of war. At the Wilderness, the night of May 5 echoed mordantly with the "moans and cries" of wounded men from both armies who lay between the lines and beyond succor. "In the still night air every groan could be heard," Howard wrote, "and the calls for water and entreaties to brothers and comrades by name to come and help them." The next morning, fires started in the underbrush by muzzle flashes spread through the Wilderness and burned to death some of the helpless wounded.

Spotsylvania followed Wilderness immediately. On May 10, 1864, a brutal cross-fire caught and pinned down Howard and his friends. They had no option but to hug the ground and wait for darkness. "A more disagreeable half hour," he wrote in retrospect, "with a bullet striking a man lying on the ground every now and then, could not well have been spent." Two days later a Federal assault swept over the nose of the Confederate works near the point soon to be christened "the Bloody Angle." Yankee bayonets surrounded Howard and he went into a captivity that would last for six months. Howard's concise sketch map of the Angle at Spotsylvania remains an important artifact for studying the battle.

As his captors herded Lieutenant Howard to the rear at Spotsylvania, he began a prison experience shared by hundreds of thousands of Civil War soldiers. Howard wound up at Fort Delaware, in the middle of the Delaware River downstream from Philadelphia. There he enjoyed reasonably civilized treatment, by the uncivilized standards of the day. The fort's commander liked Howard and others of the Confederates, but some of his subordinates took the opportunity to abuse their power, as humans are wont to do. In November

1864, Howard went back south under a program for the exchange of prisoners. Once released in Georgia, he used a flask of brandy to bribe his way into a good railroad car on a Confederate train and by the end of 1864 had reached Richmond again.

Through the war's waning weeks, young Howard assisted General G. W. C. Lee in the effort to turn an accumulation of home-front troops, raw levies, and naval ratings into a hodge-podge brigade for emergency use. The emergency arose on April 2, 1865. The lieutenant was sitting in a pew at St Paul's, where he had been confirmed a few years earlier, for the 11.00am Sunday service, when a courier informed Jefferson Davis that the army's lines had been broken. Richmond must be abandoned. For four days the *ersatz* brigade under G. W. C. Lee took part in the retreat west and south from Richmond. In a mix-up that especially depressed and horrified Howard, the green troops loosed a volley against friends that killed several men, victims of mistaken friendly fire just a few hours before the army surrendered.

Howard fell into enemy hands again on April 6 at Sayler's Creek. This time his prison camp was Johnson's Island in Lake Erie. There he took the oath of allegiance to the United States on May 29 and made his long way home. Awaiting him in Baltimore was a demand, dated September 1862, that he report to Yankee conscript officers to be drafted into Federal service. Men had come to his mother's house and asked the names and occupations of all the family's males. Howard's mother responded that her husband and eldest son were being held unconstitutionally as political prisoners in northern Bastilles. Four sons were serving in the Confederate army. "McHenry," she told her interrogators, was "with Stonewall Jackson and I expect he will be here soon." The officials wrote out the conscription demand and left. McHenry Howard kept the souvenir the rest of his life.

Lieutenant Howard enjoyed a long and fruitful career after the war. He completed his legal training and practiced law in Baltimore for decades, finding time also to write extensively about his Confederate experiences. McHenry's lively, urbane recollections appeared in periodicals both North and South. He eventually turned his story into a charming and important – and sizable, at 423 pages – book that is a classic piece of Confederate literature: *Recollections of a Maryland Confederate Soldier and Staff Officer under Johnston, Jackson and Lee* (Baltimore: Williams & Wilkins Company, 1914). Howard died in his native Maryland on September 11, 1923, two months before his 85th birthday.

THE WORLD AROUND WAR

While soldiers carrying arms under both flags faced death or maiming at the battle front, their families at home coped with a wide variety of fundamental changes and challenges. Some home-front Americans met with fabulous economic opportunities; others with dire economic suffering. Millions of civilians struggled with numbing grief at the loss of loved ones, and millions more faced personal danger from scavengers – both "friendly" troops and invaders.

"The world around war" section in chapter 1 of this volume describes those trends on a war-wide basis, including the impact of the war on the growth of government; women's roles in society and commerce; inflation and wages; speculation; corruption in the production of war materials; taxation; refugees; slavery and freed ex-slaves; and politics. In every context, the impact of the war upon civilians became broader and deeper during 1863–65 in the Virginia Theater than it had been during the war's first half.

Since all but a few days of the armies' campaigning in the theater unfolded on Confederate terrain, the impact on Southerners was far greater. Millions of Northern firesides mourned deeply and bitterly when the casualty lists from Virginia arrived, but on the economic and social front most Northern institutions actually gained strength, while the Confederacy was in the process of utter destruction. Southerners carefully watched the news about the price of gold in New York, and relished evidence of inflation. They were deluding themselves. The North thrived, as victorious nations' war economies generally do. Only on the battlefield could Confederates hope to create circumstances in which they might generate enough war-weariness to win their independence.

Southern civilians faced war's brutality on a far more intimate level than their quondam fellow-citizens in the North. Until fairly recently it had been conventional wisdom that mid-19th-century mores kept occupying soldiery in check. A recent careful survey and indexing of United States Army courts-martial during the war has banished that old-fashioned notion. More than 83,000 Union soldiers came before courts. Nearly 5,000 of them were charged with crimes against civilians, including 558 for murder and 225 for rape. The number of formal trials, of course, only begins to reflect the volume of untried crimes, especially in areas where civilians were utterly powerless to protect themselves.

For millennia, European wars have trampled the citizens of the continent, shattering property and minds and leaving millions of non-combatant dead. In the two and a quarter centuries that comprise the relatively short life span of the United States however, no large body of American civilians has ever felt war's horrors up close – except Confederates during the final stages of the Civil War. As a direct result, soldiers from desolated areas of the South came under immense pressures to go home and protect their families. A letter from home came into evidence at a desertion trial of one of Lee's men. "I have always been proud of you," wrote Mary to Edward, "and since your connection with the Confederate army, I have been prouder of you than ever before … but before God, Edward, unless you come home we must die." Edward went home. Provost guards brought him back to the army. After the trial Edward was returned to duty, perhaps on the strength of the emotions provoked by the letter. Soon thereafter he was killed in action.

The personal suffering and loss would gradually heal in many instances, but the destruction of more than 620,000 lives could not be erased. Margaret

Junkin Preston, one of the leading female authors in the country, wrote a condolence letter to a friend whose brother had just fallen victim to what Preston called "this horrid and senseless war." Maggie's heart-felt emotions capture what so many millions of others went through.

> I cannot refrain from mingling my grief with yours… It is dreadful to have our loved ones die… [We are] utterly shaken by the uncontrollable outthrusting of our mere human grief at seeing the pleasant face never never more … the tender eyes shut, not to be opened again – the sweet interchange of thought, feelings, emotions – all all over!… The Blessed God comfort you under this sense of loss which will press upon you so agonizingly.

A few weeks after she wrote this tender letter, Maggie faced the same ordeal when her own 17-year-old stepson fell mortally wounded in action.

PORTRAIT OF A CIVILIAN: ELLA WASHINGTON AND THE FEDERAL ARMY

George Armstrong Custer became forever famous when he led more than 250 cavalrymen to annihilation on the Little Big Horn River in 1876. A dozen years earlier he had been infamous among Virginians for destruction of civilian property and executing prisoners. Before either of those notable episodes of Custer's life and death, he had been the gallant savior of a hard-beset Virginian woman who lived near Richmond.

Ella Bassett grew up on her father's sizable plantation "Clover Lea," a dozen miles northeast of Virginia's capital city. She had been born in September 1834 at another family estate, "Eltham," in New Kent County. In May 1862, the Civil War came to Eltham, and the next month it washed up on the grounds of Clover Lea as well. Two years later the war, by then a hard-eyed, unforgiving monster, descended on Clover Lea in an episode fraught with terror for Ella. Her descriptions of the ordeal she experienced in May and June 1864 serve as an example in microcosm of the suffering of hundreds of thousands of civilians at the mercy of invading troops.

By 1864, Ella had been a married woman for three years. Her husband, Colonel Lewis Washington, was a direct descendant of the first President, George Washington (through George's wife and family; he had no natural children). So was Ella. She and Lewis each had ancestry back to the first President's family on both sides of their own parentage, and accordingly Lewis and Ella were themselves distant cousins by multiple connections. Lewis was more than two decades older than Ella and had been married before. Ella evidently had little or nothing to do with his two daughters, who lived with relatives in Maryland, but she was fond of stepson James Barroll Washington.

The war's preliminaries had fallen on Lewis Washington with alarming savagery the year before he married Ella. On an October morning in 1859, several men used a fence rail to batter down the door of Washington's home, "Beall Air," near Harpers Ferry, Virginia. The intruders – a detachment from the marauding party directed by John Brown – knew that Lewis owned relics of George Washington and demanded them as booty. They carried Lewis off as a hostage. He witnessed, as a prisoner, the storming by United States Marines of Brown's hideout at Harpers Ferry. Directing the storming party was Colonel Robert E. Lee, United States Army. Among the first men to the door of the stronghold was Lieutenant J. E. B. Stuart, United States Army, acting as an aide to Lee.

The year after Lewis's brief ordeal at the hands of Brown's merry band, his new bride, cousin Ella, moved into Beall Air. In late 1861, the couple moved from Beall Air to Ella's family place at Clover Lea. She attributed the need to relocate to "the critical condition of my health." Since Lewis's home stood in a mountainous region, and Clover Lea plantation lay in the relatively swampy ground near Richmond, contemporary notions would have suggested (not inaccurately) that health considerations would actually militate in favor of Beall Air. Perhaps Ella's concern was to be near her own family to secure their assistance. Not long after the Washingtons relocated to Clover Lea, their baby daughter Betty died. In June 1863, Ella bore a son, William D. Washington.

The 1862 campaign around Richmond nearly resulted in the capture of the Confederate capital and an early end to the war. Fortunately for the Southern army, its timid commander fell wounded at the end of May and General R. E. Lee assumed command. In the week of fighting denominated the "Seven Days battles," Lee slowly and at great cost drove away the besieging Northerners and bottled them up against the James River. Lee won the week's biggest battle with the largest charge he ever launched during the war, at Gaines's Mill, just 5 miles (8km) from Clover Lea.

In the aftermath, suffering wounded men clogged the entire countryside. A major hospital mushroomed next to the Bassett-Washington property. The Richmond *Whig* three times published appreciative notices of the kindness bestowed on sick and wounded soldiers by women of the neighborhood, "especially … the ladies of 'Clover Lea.'" A few weeks later, the same newspaper reported the death of baby Betty. It is hard to avoid the speculation (but impossible to prove) that microbes from the hundreds of sick, wounded, and infected soldiers convalescing in the vicinity might have brought on the infant's demise.

Although the Federals failed to capture Richmond during that spring of 1862, they did capture Ella's stepson, Lieutenant James Washington. The youngster, who had been serving on the staff of Confederate army commander Joseph E. Johnston, found himself in the hands of a friend from West Point days, George A. Custer. The quondam classmate treated Washington to a cigar and something to drink, and rounded up some other friends serving in the Union army. That evening, Ella wrote later, the prisoner and his captors enjoyed "rather a jollification in one of the headquarters tents," reminiscing about their cadet days at the famous Benny Haven's Tavern near the military academy grounds.

When the provost guard took young Washington away to head for a prisoner-of-war camp, Custer stuffed some US currency in his friend's vest pocket to help smooth his captivity. "You must have some money, Jim," Custer said, "those pictures in your pockets [Confederate currency] don't pass up there." The cartel for exchange of prisoners had not yet broken down at that stage, so James went back to Confederate service upon exchange after a short period in captivity. Two years later, George Custer would be in a position to help James Washington's stepmother in a more substantial fashion.

War's mailed fist went rampaging northward for nearly two years after the fighting around Richmond in May and June 1862 – but in May 1864 hostile troops swept across the grounds of Clover Lea and threatened to destroy everything that the Bassetts and Washingtons owned. On May 28, Ella could hear rifles rattling in the near distance. It was a time "of dreadful suspense and anxiety." She wondered in her diary that evening whether her brothers had been in the fighting, and whether they had survived. A few Confederates galloped past, pausing only briefly. "God bless you, boys," Ella's father said as they hurried away. As their horses' hoofbeats faded, Ella thought they left behind "a strange silence, brooding over nature like a pall."

The next morning, after a terrified night and little sleep, Ella had to face the invasion of her property by swarms of uncontrolled enemy foragers. This "most

OPPOSITE PAGE:
Ella Bassett Washington, 1834–98. (Courtesy of the Mount Vernon Ladies' Association)

horrible set of creatures I ever saw" took everything in sight and made the women fear for their safety. Ella longed for a guillotine to "take their heads off in just as rapid a style" as they were killing the farm animals.

In desperation, Ella Washington sent notes off to her stepson's friend, General Custer, hoping that he might come to assist her. One of the messages did reach the Federal cavalry general and on the 30th he arrived in person at Clover Lea, where he at once promised to protect the stepmother of his friend James Washington, and her property. Custer behaved gallantly with the pretty Virginian, who despite being his school chum's stepmother was not much beyond his own age. Ella wrote of the pleasure of finding someone, in the midst of "this host of enemies, with whom we can feel some human sympathy."

Even though they enjoyed intermittent protection afforded by the connection with Custer, Clover Lea and its civilians still suffered under the hostile occupation. Despite her gratitude for Custer's aid, Ella told her diary: "In wickedness and impudence no nation ever equalled the Yankees." Years later, in contrast, she still wrote warmly of the enemy general's "generous and kindly deeds done under trying circumstances."

Mrs Washington's experience as a helpless pawn on the chessboard of war was of a kind shared by countless thousands of other women. Her own vivid words describe some of what she saw and felt:

> the dreadful Yankees... I feel so much fatigued I can scarcely dress... What a day of horrors and agony, may I never spend such another... The demon of destruction [was] at [our] very door, surrounding, swallowing [us] up in its fearful scenes of strife... How can such an army of devils not human beings ever succeed?... I fancied (though it seems a very ridiculous idea) that there was something almost human in [the dying farm animals'] screaming voices... I was glad when the last had been killed... I am feeling physically and mentally oppressed, never found my nerves so shaken, and my courage so tried.

As General Custer took his leave of Clover Lea and went back to war, Ella described to him the frustration of being helpless to affect her own fate. "You men don't know how much more intolerable the martyrdom of endurance is than the martyrdom of action." "Some of us," he replied, "can comprehend, and sympathize, too. War is a hard, cruel, terrible thing. Men must fight, and women weep." Ella gave Custer as a token of her appreciation a button from George Washington's coat. The general set the button as a brooch and presented it to his wife, who eventually donated the relic to the US Military Academy. It survives today in the collection of Custer Battlefield National Monument, Montana.

Custer subsequently played a role in making war "a hard, cruel, terrible thing" in the Shenandoah Valley. In September, his troopers murdered six Confederate prisoners in a churchyard and the streets of Front Royal. One was a 17-year-old youngster whose widowed mother screamed in horror as she

pleaded in vain for his life. A girl in the village wrote of how that "dark day of 1864 … clouded my childhood" and haunted her dreams forever. The famed Confederate partisan leader John S. Mosby ordered execution of a like number of Custer's captive men, but the Southerners blanched after carrying out half of the brutal job and let the rest go. Twelve years later, Custer himself wound up at the mercy of merciless men and died with scores of his troopers at the Battle of the Little Big Horn.

James Barroll Washington became a railroad president after the war and died in 1900. His father, Ella's husband, died in 1871, leaving the widow without many resources. Ella used her Washington connections to assist ex-Confederates in procuring Federal pardons after the war. When that lucrative but short-term business died down, she subsided into genteel poverty and died in New York in 1898.

Federals stand in review as their defeated foemen march past at Appomattox, en route to surrendering their arms. (Painting by Don Troiani, www.historicalartprints.com)

HOW THE PERIOD ENDED: FROM APPOMATTOX TO LIVERPOOL

Lee's surrender at Appomattox Court House on April 9, 1865 essentially ended the war in the Virginia Theater. Many thousands of men had slipped out of the weary, retreating, Confederate column as the cause became patently hopeless, thus escaping the final surrender. Some of those soldiers attempted to head south into North Carolina to join the Southern army still fighting there under General Joseph E. Johnston. That forlorn hope evaporated when Johnston surrendered to General William T. Sherman near Durham Station on April 26, after complicated negotiations involving Washington politicians.

In the weeks that followed, Confederates who had not signed paroles at either Appomattox or Durham Station gradually made their way to occupied towns and took the oath of allegiance to the United States. Some troops from the Deep South took weeks or even months to reach homes, many of them desolated, in Alabama or Louisiana or Texas. Soldiers who surrendered with Lee, or took the oath separately later, missed the ordeal suffered by their comrades who had been taken prisoner just a few hours before the Appomattox ceremony. Confederates captured during the retreat from Richmond and Petersburg, including thousands of men who surrendered at Sayler's Creek, went off to prison camps as though the war still raged on. Most did not secure their freedom until mid-June 1865.

Meanwhile, the triumphant Federal armies converged on the national capital for a mass celebration of the war's end. On May 23 and 24, hundreds of thousands of blue-uniformed veterans marched in serried ranks. As the victorious divisions and brigades and regiments began to muster out of service, far-flung Confederate detachments continued to fight forlornly, and finally to give up the struggle. On June 2, General Edmund Kirby Smith formally accepted terms at Galveston, Texas, and surrendered the Confederate forces in the Trans-Mississippi. Weeks later the Confederate cruiser CSS *Shenandoah* was still capturing whalers in the Bering Sea. Lieutenant James I. Waddell, CSN, finally surrendered the *Shenandoah* to British officials at Liverpool on November 6, 1865.

The reconstruction of the desolated Southern states remained to be done, and the healing of divisions, and the reunion of the United States in fact as well as in law. None of those tasks would be easy; nor could they be accomplished to the satisfaction of everyone.

OPPOSITE PAGE:
Lieutenant James Barroll Washington and Captain George Armstrong Custer in 1862, while Washington was a prisoner of war in the keeping of his old friend from the US Military Academy. (Little Bighorn Battlefield National Monument, National Park Service)

CHAPTER 4
THE WAR IN THE WEST JULY 1863-1865

THE FIGHTING: THE FINAL STAGES

Crisis in Missouri

Since the Missouri campaign of 1861, the entire Missouri region had been torn by savage guerilla warfare, fueled by continuing raids from Kansas. William Quantrill and William Anderson led the Rebel bushwhackers. Among their followers were acclaimed robbers Frank and Jesse James and Cole and Jim Younger. From Kansas, pro-Union guerrillas included the diminutive "Big Jim" Lane and Charles Jennison.

In an effort to check the acts of partisans, Union occupation troops under Major-General David Hunter and John Schofield nearly ruined their careers with repeated failures. They tried building forts in guerrilla-infested areas, but local partisans blended into the community and struck when they discovered soldiers at a disadvantage. Next, they experimented with population removal. Because guerrillas drew from friends and families for support, in 1863 Brigadier-General Thomas Ewing had arrested the wives and family members of notorious guerrillas as leverage against them. On August 25, 1863, Ewing announced he would transport those under arrest as well as the families and other supporters of the Confederacy to Arkansas. Before he could do that, though, the rickety building where he housed some of the women collapsed, killing five and

The Battle of Chickamauga. (Anne S. K. Brown Military Collection, Brown University Library)

crippling another. Two victims were sisters of William Anderson, already known for his violence. He now vowed to kill every Yankee he could find, and it was not long before he earned the nickname "Bloody Bill."

In retaliation, Quantrill led his party of 450 on a raid against Lawrence, Kansas, a hotbed of abolitionism. En route, they forced Kansas farmers to act as guides and then executed them. On August 21, they slipped into town and disposed of the small number of soldiers there. The town soon surrendered, but those words meant nothing to Quantrill and his followers. All told, they murdered 150 males, wounded 30 more, and torched 185 buildings.

Federals responded to the raid by ordering all western Missourians who did not live in certain cities to migrate. Those who pledged loyalty to the Union could settle around forts, and all others would have to abandon the area. Union authorities hoped to deprive guerrillas of local support and establish free-fire

Sterling Price, a Mexican War veteran and an original opponent of secession in Missouri, soured on the Union after Frank Blair and others took aggressive action to block the governor's pro-Confederate policies. He commanded Missouri's secessionist militia in 1861, led a Confederate division as a major-general at Pea Ridge in 1862, and directed the last raid into Missouri in 1864. After suffering a defeat at Westport near Kansas City, he began his retreat, enduring Union harassment along a roundabout route back to Arkansas.

zones in the area, thereby eliminating much of the worry of distinguishing friend from foe. The policy had little if any effect on the bushwhackers.

What ultimately led to the demise of guerrilla activities actually stemmed from their own success. Various partisan activities had impressed Major-General Sterling Price, particularly the work of Quantrill, and when they insisted that Missourians would rise up in support of the Confederacy if he raided into the state, Price jumped at the opportunity. With 12,000 cavalry, half of whom lacked arms, Price crossed into Missouri on September 19, 1864.

In support of the movement, various pro-Rebel bushwhackers had attacked isolated posts, towns, and pockets of soldiers, massacring troops and civilians, armed and disarmed alike. Simmering divisions began to bubble to the surface among guerrilla leaders. Anderson wanted to attack the fortified garrison at Fayette; Quantrill opposed it as too dangerous. When Anderson and his men suffered a repulse and the loss of 13 men, it only infuriated them more. A few days later, they entered Centralia in search of plunder and news of Price's whereabouts. There they pulled 25 unarmed Union soldiers off the train and executed them. When some Missouri militiamen stumbled on the guerrillas, they attacked and suffered a horrible defeat. Out of an original 147 militiamen, 129 were cut down. The guerrillas then committed a host of atrocities, including cutting off the genitals of a living soldier and placing them in his mouth.

Price, meanwhile, had advanced well into Missouri. On September 27, 1864, the same day as the Centralia Massacre, his command attacked Federals under Ewing at Ford Davidson, or Pilot Knob, suffering heavy losses in the repulse. As Union reinforcements arrived in Missouri, Price pressed westward along the south bank of the Missouri River. Anderson and his people met up with them, and Price sent them on a destructive spree north of the river. Before October ended, Anderson fell to two militiamen's balls. They placed his body on display, then severed his head, and eventually buried him in an unmarked grave.

As Price's columns pressed toward Kansas City, Union forces closed in on them. With Curtis to his front and Major-General Alfred Pleasanton closing from his rear, Price attempted to beat them at Westport. He attacked Curtis first, and pushed the Union command back initially, but the Federals stiffened and launched their own counterattack. To the rear, Pleasonton drove back the Rebel cavalry, and Price began his retreat on October 23. Federals continued to press him, capturing 1,000 men in Kansas. Eventually, his command limped into Arkansas with only half of his original 12,000.

Price's raid was the last major Confederate undertaking west of the Mississippi River. Guerrilla fighting continued in Missouri, however, and extended well after the war, as unreconstructed bands like the Jameses and Youngers continued to rob and plunder. Quantrill, having suffered the humiliation of a rebellion in his ranks, elected to shift his base of operations to Kentucky. In May, he was shot in the back and paralyzed by Union troops. He died almost a month later.

The Tullahoma and Chattanooga campaigns

During the Vicksburg campaign, Halleck and even Grant pleaded with Rosecrans to advance. Since early in the war, the idea of liberating Unionists in East Tennessee had intrigued Lincoln. Once Grant had crossed the Mississippi River and engaged Pemberton's forces, the administration had even more reason to demand that Rosecrans attack: Union leaders feared that Bragg's army would rush reinforcements west to defeat Grant. If "Old Rosy," as his men called him, would advance on the Confederate Army of Tennessee, Bragg would be compelled to hold on to all he had. In fact, Johnston did draw troops from Bragg, as well as units from the Atlantic coastal defense. Yet Rosecrans would not be rushed. Finally, after word that Union troops under Major-General Ambrose P. Burnside would push toward East Tennessee, the Union Army of the Cumberland moved out from Murfreesboro on June 23, 1863, 169 days after the Battle of Stone's River.

Rosecrans may have been slow, but he was not without skills. He used a portion of his army to swing around and threaten the Confederate rear. In an effort to protect the Confederate base at Tullahoma, Bragg pulled his forces back, thereby uncovering valuable gaps in the Cumberland Plateau. With powerful Union columns pressing through them and then in on his flanks, and a raid that threatened his rear, Bragg decided to abandon Tullahoma and fall back to Chattanooga.

Major Union campaigns, 1863–65.

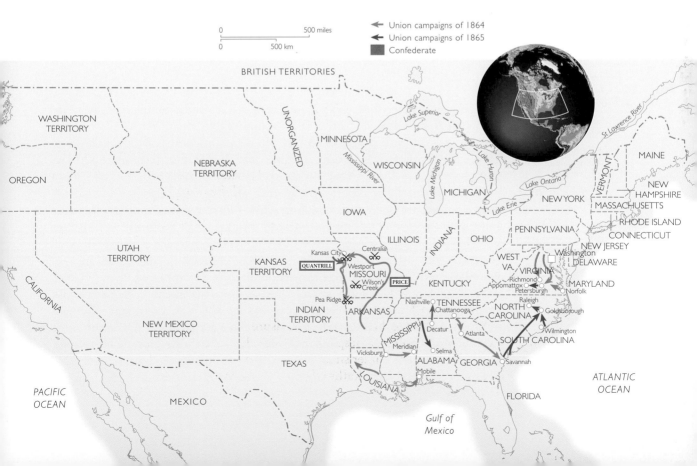

George H. Thomas, a Virginian by birth, served as corps commander under Rosecrans. His defense at Chickamauga saved the Army of the Cumberland and earned him the nickname of the "Rock of Chickamauga." Appointed its commander before the Chattanooga battles, he served in the Atlanta campaign. Late in 1864, Thomas routed Hood's army at Nashville. (Library of Congress)

Leonidas Polk. Polk violated Kentucky's neutrality in one of the great blunders of the war. As a corps commander, he promoted unrest with Bragg. Polk was killed during the Atlanta campaign. (Library of Congress)

At comparatively little cost, Rosecrans had driven his enemy back 80 miles (129km). But he deemed further pursuit impossible. Heavy rains had impaired movements on both sides, converting roads into muck. "Tulla," so noted one Confederate officer, was Greek for "mud," and "homa" meant "more mud." The halt, however, did not sit well with authorities in Washington. They could neither see rainfall nor experience the mud; all they could envision was a delay that would allow Bragg to fortify. And when Old Rosy took time to repair the railroad from Nashville, they interpreted it as his usual temporizing behavior and balked. Finally, under threat of removal, Rosecrans's army rumbled forward again in mid-August 1863, in conjunction with Burnside's advance on Knoxville, which was taken on September 2.

Bragg, meanwhile, had lost the faith of his army and had begun to lose confidence in himself. His corps commanders, Polk and Lieutenant-General William J. Hardee, had voiced displeasure over his leadership. For the most part, Bragg's soldiers despised him for his strict discipline and lack of battlefield success. Under stress, especially during campaigns, he himself grew ever more despondent. Rather than view the mountains around Chattanooga as a defensive advantage, Bragg transformed them in his own mind into a Federal asset.

Because those mountains and the Tennessee River provided strong protection for Chattanooga and its defenders, Rosecrans executed a march of deception, as he had done in the Tullahoma campaign. He sent a portion of his army north of the city, to convey the impression that he was uniting with Burnside. The bulk of his army, though, crossed the Tennessee River to the southwest. By the time Bragg realized what had happened, Union forces were barreling down on his rear. On September 8, he abandoned Chattanooga to the Federals, who entered the city the next day.

To this point, in spite of delays, Rosecrans had conducted a skillful campaign. But then he got sloppy. He assumed the Rebels would fall back once again, and he divided his army for another maneuver campaign, spreading it out far too wide for the hilly terrain. Fortunately for Old Rosy, Bragg could not exploit the opportunity. Twice the Rebel commander tried to pounce on portions of Rosecrans's isolated forces, and in both instances subordinates failed to execute. In haste, Rosecrans consolidated his command near a stream known as Chickamauga.

Since the spring, Confederate officials had debated the possibility of reinforcing Bragg or Pemberton from Lee's army. At the time, Lee had his own plans, a raid into Pennsylvania, and he demurred. With Bragg in need that fall, and the Union Army of the Potomac exhibiting little initiative, President Davis sent west two divisions from Lee's Army of Northern Virginia, under the command of Lee's "Old War Horse," Lieutenant-General James Longstreet. Traveling in a roundabout way, it took them nine days to reach Bragg's army. Major-General John Bell Hood's division also arrived the day before the fight, September 18, giving Bragg numerical superiority. The next evening, Major-General Lafayette McLaws's division reached the battlefield.

On September 19, Union and Confederate troops began to skirmish over control of a clearing. Reinforcements joined the fray piecemeal. Each time that one side extended beyond the enemy flank, a fresh batch of troops stretched beyond them. Neither Bragg nor Rosecrans could coordinate anything effective, in part because of the heavy timber around the battlefield. All they had to show for the day of fighting were lengthy casualty lists.

That night, Longstreet arrived with McLaws's division. A frustrated Bragg gave him command of the Rebel left wing and directed Polk to initiate the fight on the right the next morning. As usual, Polk made little progress, due partly to his tardiness and partly to the stout resistance of Major-General George H. Thomas's corps. In exasperation, Bragg called on Longstreet to launch an assault.

Never before on a battlefield had Longstreet fallen into such good fortune. Rosecrans had begun to pull units over to his beleaguered left, as additional support for Thomas. When a Union staff officer mistakenly reported a gap in the line on the right – the troops were actually well concealed in some woods – Old Rosy shifted some units over, this time creating a gap. Into this breach

Longstreet's men fortuitously charged. Two Union divisions collapsed, racing back to Chattanooga. In their flight, they took the Union army commander with them. Once the Rebels penetrated the line, Longstreet ordered them to wheel right, to envelop the bulk of Rosecrans's command. Union units melted away, until the old stalwart, Thomas, held firm. With some timely reinforcements, the native Virginian Thomas refused to budge from Snodgrass Hill, and repeated Rebel attacks could not drive him off. At dark, he withdrew his men, earning the sobriquet "Rock of Chickamauga" for his efforts.

In triumph, Bragg emerged in lower standing than before the battle. No one was impressed with his leadership during the course of the fight, and the bloodbath – over 18,000 casualties on the Rebels' side and more than 16,000

Murfreesboro to Chickamauga, June–September 1863.

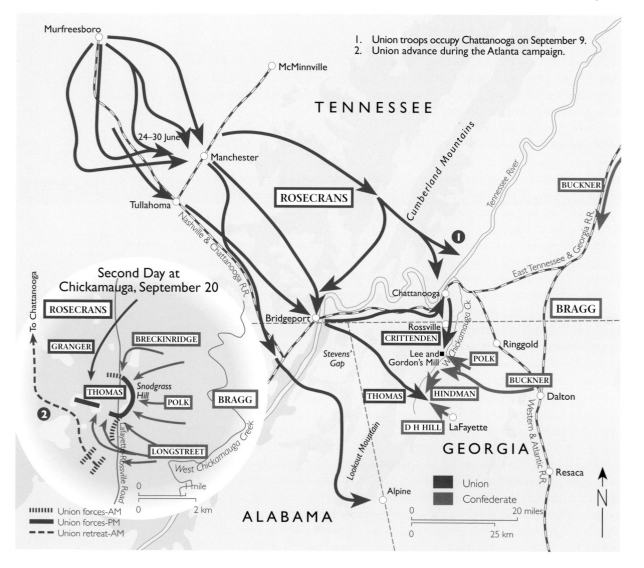

1. Union troops occupy Chattanooga on September 9.
2. Union advance during the Atlanta campaign.

for the Yankees – seemed to have paralyzed him. He contributed nothing after the breakthrough, and despite pleas by Forrest and others to follow up the victory, he stalled. The Federal troops made good their escape and fortified. Eventually, Bragg took up positions to lay siege on September 23, attempting to cut off all supplies, but he lacked the resources to do so completely.

After Bragg wasted a splendid opportunity to crush the bulk of the Army of the Cumberland, old and new wounds began to fester among the Confederate high command. Bragg suspended Polk and two others for refusing to obey orders. Several generals petitioned Davis to remove Bragg, and Longstreet wrote to the Secretary of War, pleading with him to send Lee. Forrest rejected such niceties. He threatened Bragg to his face. "I have stood your meanness as long as I intend to," thundered the brilliant cavalryman. "You have played the part of a damned scoundrel, and are a coward, and if you were any part of a man I would slap your jaws and force you to resent it." Forrest then made clear that if Bragg ever interfered or crossed paths with him, "it will be at the peril of your life." Bragg, as well as everyone else in the army, knew Forrest would do it, too.

The best cavalry commander in the Western Theater and probably on either side in the war, Nathan Bedford Forrest was a scourge to Union soldiers. Forrest's disgust for Bragg was so great after Chickamauga that he threatened to kill him. Forrest also gained notoriety when his cavalrymen slaughtered black soldiers at Fort Pillow. (Library of Congress)

Finally, Davis traveled out to Chattanooga to resolve matters himself. The Rebel President relieved D. H. Hill, a good yet cantankerous officer, and transferred Polk to Mississippi. With Davis's assent, Longstreet took 15,000 men to recapture Knoxville. Yet the President failed to address the major problem, Bragg.

On the other side, Rosecrans's days were numbered. Officials in Washington tolerated his seemingly interminable delays as long as he won, but after the Chickamauga débâcle they lost all faith in him. Lincoln thought Rosecrans acted "confused and stunned like a duck hit on the head." The Assistant Secretary of War, Charles A. Dana, visited Chattanooga and reported that the army lacked confidence in him. What the administration needed was someone to take charge. That man was Grant.

Battles around Chattanooga

Secretary of War Edwin M. Stanton caught a speedy train westward to rendezvous with Grant in Louisville. Instead, he caught up with him at Indianapolis, and the two rode together that last leg. The administration had decided to create the Military Division of the Mississippi from the Appalachians to the river, and it assigned Grant as the commander. Stanton then gave Grant a choice: he could keep Rosecrans as commander of the Army of the Cumberland, or replace him with Thomas. Grant chose Thomas.

The Union plan did not call for Federal forces to break through the Confederate line in the center, but men from the Army of the Cumberland did just that. In the excitement of battle and their desire to restore their reputation after the disaster at Chickamauga, these Federals exploited the steep incline along Missionary Ridge, pursuing the defenders so closely that Rebels near the top could not fire for fear of hitting their own men. In a massive rush, depicted here in the sketch, Yankees carried the heights in one of the greatest assaults of the entire war. (Library of Congress)

Before Grant arrived at Chattanooga on October 23, the administration had already taken steps to improve the situation there. It had transferred the XI and XII Corps under Major-General Joseph Hooker from the idle Army of the Potomac by rail, and Sherman, with another 17,000, had been on the march from Mississippi. Rosecrans and his staff had prepared plans for opening supply lines. Grant's presence instilled confidence, and he soon had the "cracker line" open.

With reinforcements under Sherman and Hooker there, Grant implemented his plan. Additional manpower had doubled Union strength, while Bragg depleted the size of his command by detaching Longstreet and 15,000 men. Grant could use this considerable numerical superiority to his advantage. He ordered Hooker to attack up Lookout Mountain on the Rebel left, while Sherman's forces would roll up the right. Thomas's army, which, Grant assumed, suffered from a lack of confidence after Chickamauga, would play a less active role. It would threaten the enemy center, a long, steep hill called Missionary Ridge.

The battle opened up well for the Federals. On November 23, 1863, Thomas's people attacked and secured Orchard Knob, from which they threatened an assault on Missionary Ridge. The next day, Hooker assailed a lightly defended portion of Lookout Mountain with almost three divisions. The successful operation amid pockets of fog created quite a spectacle and

gained the nickname "The Battle Above the Clouds." Sherman, meanwhile, had crossed the Tennessee River and planned to roll up the Rebel right at Missionary Ridge, while Hooker rushed down on the left.

Yet two factors operated against Sherman. The narrow ground and rough terrain limited his options and restricted the amount of troops he could deploy for battle. The second factor was a superb Confederate division commander named Patrick Cleburne. An Irishman by birth, Cleburne had run afoul of officials in Richmond by proposing the use of black slaves as soldiers. Although he was the best division commander in the army, authorities somehow managed to overlook him for advancement, no doubt as a result of his controversial suggestion. As usual, Cleburne's men fought like tigers, and Sherman could make little headway against such a determined and well-led foe.

With Union plans stymied, Grant directed Thomas to order his men forward on November 25. The Union commander hoped that if men from the Army of the Cumberland seized the first row of rifle pits, it would draw Confederate reinforcements from the flanks and assist Sherman and Hooker. To the shock of both Grant and Thomas, who were standing together, soldiers in the Army of the Cumberland not only crashed through the first line of defense, they kept on going. An annoyed Grant asked who gave that order, saying there would be "hell to pay." Thomas admitted knowing nothing. As the defenders fell back, the Yankee troops pursued so closely that Rebels

This is the crest of Missionary Ridge, where Thomas's men charged without orders on November 25. The steepness of the hill, and the Confederates in flight, provided protection for the attackers, who dislodged and routed Bragg's army. (Library of Congress)

OVERLEAF:
The Army of the Cumberland before Chattanooga. (Anne S. K. Brown Military Collection, Brown University Library)

higher up the slope could not fire for fear of shooting their own men. Confederates, moreover, had chosen their primary line on the actual, not the military, crest, which created dead spaces where gunfire could not touch anyone. Federals discovered that as they clambered up the incline, they gained these pockets of protection from enemy fire, and Rebels could not depress their artillery guns enough to hit them. On November 25, the Army of the Cumberland exacted revenge for the Chickamauga disaster. They utterly shattered the center of Bragg's line.

Cleburne's division acted as rear guard and blocked Union pursuit. Still, Bragg had to fall back 30 miles (48km) to Dalton, Georgia, to regroup. The men in the Army of Tennessee had no confidence in Bragg's leadership; the turmoil of high command and the detachment of Longstreet's men had caused severe damage to the morale of the men. A week after the débâcle at Chattanooga, Bragg resigned as army commander.

Nor did Longstreet's Knoxville expedition reap benefits to the Confederate cause. He advanced on Burnside, delayed, and when he did finally attack on November 29, he failed. After the rout of Bragg's army, Grant rushed Sherman with two corps to help relieve Burnside. As the Federals approached, Longstreet slipped away.

Shake-up in the high commands

Now that Chattanooga was firmly in Union hands, Grant hoped to revive plans for a major campaign against Mobile, a valuable port still under Rebel control. Instead, the administration offered a litany of missions, none of which would significantly advance the Union toward its ultimate goal of defeating the Rebels. What Grant wanted to do was launch a campaign from New Orleans to Mobile, and from there press northeast toward Atlanta, while Thomas moved from Chattanooga to Atlanta. The administration countered with a proposal that he strike into Texas.

Before they worked out their differences, though, Lincoln and Congress had concluded that the nation's most successful combat commander should direct the war effort. Congress passed legislation to create the rank of lieutenant-general, and Lincoln signed it into law. There was no disagreement over who should receive the promotion. They established the law with Grant in mind.

In early March, Grant traveled to Washington to receive the promotion in person. Originally, he had intended to stay in the nation's capital briefly, just long enough to draft plans for the spring campaigns and resolve some command issues. Before he went, Sherman had advised him to return west. The politics in Washington were poison; all Grant had to do was look at Halleck to see how the pressures had affected him.

Once there, Grant soon realized that he must establish his headquarters in the east. Everyone from the politicians to the press to the public at large expected him to oversee the campaign against Lee. In their eyes, Lee's army had come to symbolize the viability of the rebellion, and until Grant

The battles for Chattanooga, October–November 1863.

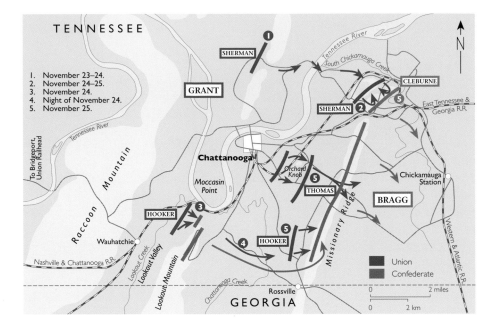

TENNESSEE

1. November 23–24.
2. November 24–25.
3. November 24.
4. Night of November 24.
5. November 25.

vanquished the Army of Northern Virginia, the revolt would continue. At the same time, Grant knew that he could not endure the endless distractions of life in the nation's capital.

As his solution, Grant formulated a novel command structure. To avoid the continual barrage of visitors and to oversee the operations of the Union forces against Lee's troops, he elected to travel alongside the Army of the Potomac. There, he could observe and, if necessary, supervise the army and its generals directly, while leaving Major-General George G. Meade in command. At the same time, he could remain relatively close to the political epicenter, Washington, DC. To handle everyday military affairs, Grant would retain former commanding general Halleck under a new title, chief of staff. A superb staff officer, Halleck would be Grant's connection to various field commanders, summarizing their messages and relaying them to Grant for decisions and instructions. Occasionally, Halleck would issue orders or advise field commanders on his own. In the shake-up, Sherman replaced Grant as head of the Military Division of the Mississippi on March 18. Trusted subordinate McPherson took charge of the Army of the Tennessee, Sherman's old command.

The Confederates, too, underwent a command change. With Bragg's resignation, Jefferson Davis needed a new army commander, someone in whom the soldiers had faith. Hardee agreed to act as commander until the President secured someone, but he would not do it permanently. Hardee proposed Joe Johnston. Davis's old friend, Polk, also suggested Johnston, as did Robert E. Lee. Although Davis still harbored resentments for Johnston's failure in Mississippi, he had little choice. It was either him or Beauregard, and Davis opted for the lesser evil, Johnston.

Banks's Red River operation

Because of French presence in Mexico, a desire to seize valuable cotton, and a distant hope to secure complete control of Louisiana and to begin the reconstruction process, in spring 1864, Lincoln called for an expedition under Major-General Nathaniel Banks up the Red River. Banks would march overland to Alexandria, Louisiana, where he would link with 10,000 veterans from the Army of the Tennessee under Major-General A. J. Smith, whom McPherson would loan temporarily. Their goal was Shreveport. Admiral Porter with an assortment of ironclads and gunboats accompanied Smith. In addition, Major-General Frederick Steele would march from Little Rock, Arkansas, with another 15,000. To oppose this force, the Confederates had some 15,000 men under Major-General Richard Taylor, Davis's former brother-in-law and one of Stonewall Jackson's old brigade commanders.

On March 25, Banks began the Red River campaign. Even though Sherman instructed Banks that he must conduct the campaign promptly and return McPherson's troops for the spring offensive, Banks began late and arrived at Alexandria eight days after Smith's men had taken the town. Taylor's Confederates fell back beyond Natchitoches and halted around Mansfield, forming their defense at Sabine Crossroads. On April 8, Federals stumbled into an unanticipated fight and suffered a rout, losing 2,500 as prisoners. Yankees fled pell mell to Pleasant Hill, where Banks prepared a defense built around Smith's corps.

The Red River campaign, March–May 1864.

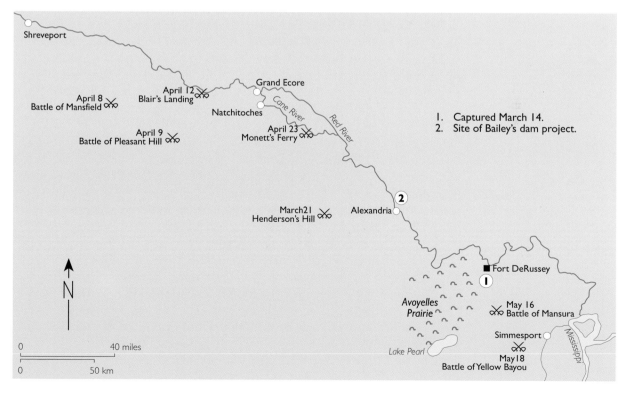

The next day, Taylor attacked, and although Federals blocked the advance, Banks withdrew the next day. The Rebels pursued, harassing Banks's command and Porter's fleet at every opportunity. By the time the Yankees had reached Alexandria, low water trapped the vessels. An ingenious engineer, Major Joseph Bailey from Wisconsin, erected a dam to build up the water level. When they broke the dam, the rushing water carried Porter's fleet to safety. Still, Confederates continued to strike at retreating Union columns until May 18, at the battle of Yellow Bayou. Not only had Banks suffered a severe repulse, and nearly lost Porter's expeditionary force, but delays deprived McPherson of critical manpower in the early days of the great spring campaign. Banks's retreat allowed the Confederates to concentrate on Steele's command and defeat it as well.

Poor leadership was only part of the Federal problem, though. The Red River campaign was the product of misdirected strategy on the part of Lincoln and Halleck. They ordered the expedition over the objections of Grant and Sherman, and even Banks preferred an advance on Mobile. The administration committed (and risked) valuable resources to an enterprise that, in the final analysis, would not have brought the rebellion appreciably closer to its conclusion, even if it had been extremely successful.

Plans for the spring campaign

The appointment of Joe Johnston sent a bolt of electricity through the Army of Tennessee. After a year and a half of the obstreperous and unsuccessful Bragg, the men felt as if they had finally secured a real leader. Johnston possessed an extraordinary charisma that drew soldiers to him. Troops felt as if he cared about them, and, at least initially, the men in the Army of Tennessee rejoiced over his appointment. Unlike the commander-in-chief, the soldiers did not blame him for the loss of Vicksburg, and he had the great fortune of having been removed well before the Bragg fiasco of mid- to late 1863.

Johnston's mere presence revived the Confederates' sinking morale, but despite his prewar experience as the Quartermaster-General of the United States army, he could not conjure supplies from nothing. He addressed basic necessities like food and clothing as well as he could, but the army suffered from serious shortages of mules, horses, and wagons, none of which he could overcome.

Johnston took on the job of commanding general with a legacy of mistrust between him and Davis that virtually doomed the assignment from the start. He believed that Davis installed him in positions that would inevitably fail, thereby ruining the general's reputation. Davis thought Johnston did not live up to his potential as a military man. He was too immersed in petty command prerogatives, and he dabbled far too heavily in the opposition to Jefferson Davis.

The Confederate President instructed Johnston to communicate freely and call on him for advice. He wanted Johnston to produce a campaign plan, particularly one with an offensive punch to it. Davis had read and digested only the misleading, positive reports of the army and convinced himself that it should assume the offensive that spring. Johnston kept his own counsel and refused to provide the kind of information his commander-in-chief expected. The Army of Tennessee, moreover, did lack the essential resources to undertake major offensives. The best it could hope for, Johnston believed, was to fight on the defense, repulse a major attack by Sherman, and then counterattack.

Johnston determined to fight on the defensive around Dalton,

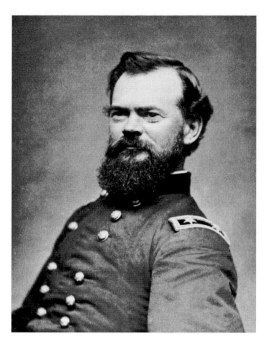

A Grant and Sherman protégé in the war, James B. McPherson graduated first in his class at West Point. He began the war as an engineer and rose to command the Army of the Tennessee. He was killed at the Battle of Atlanta. (Library of Congress)

seeking an error by the enemy to exploit. Yet in the event he had to fall back to Dalton, he failed to prepare alternate defensive positions to his rear and to design traps for Sherman's army. Throughout the campaign, when his army retreated, he and his staff had to scramble to find new defensive locations. Inevitably, he yielded the initiative and sacrificed the operational level of war for strictly tactical defensive positions.

On the Union side, upon Grant's return from Washington, he summoned Sherman from Memphis to discuss plans for the campaign season. Sherman would succeed him out west. To save time, they took the train to Cincinnati together, plotting strategy and discussing personnel changes. Two weeks later, Grant issued his plan in writing. He intended to assume the initiative on as many fronts as possible, "to work all parts of the army together, somewhat toward a common center," something the Union had attempted yet failed to accomplish for two years. "You I propose to move against Johnston's army, to break it up, and to get into the interior of the enemy's country as far as you can, inflicting all the damage you can against their war resources." Grant refused to dictate the specifics of the campaign plan; he merely requested that Sherman submit a general plan of his operations.

Rather than a single army, Sherman commanded what modern soldiers would call an army group. At his disposal for the campaign against Johnston, he had Thomas's Army of the Cumberland, McPherson's Army of the Tennessee minus A. J. Smith's people, and a small corps under Major-General John M. Schofield, head of the Department and the Army of the Ohio. Hooker remained with Sherman's forces, commanding the XI and XII Corps, which he merged

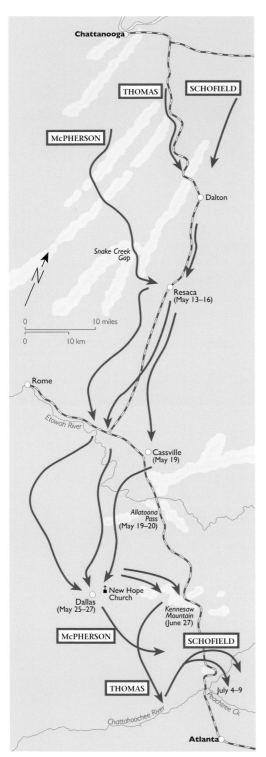

to form the XX Corps. Sherman's total force, infantry, cavalry, and artillery, totaled around 100,000.

Extremely sensitive to logistical issues, Sherman worried about Confederate cavalry raids striking his lengthy supply line on the campaign. He gathered large numbers of locomotives and rail cars to service his army. During the months before the campaign began, Sherman accumulated supplies and stockpiled all sorts of other necessities, such as rails, ties, and material for bridging. He directed the construction of blockhouses to protect vital positions along the rail route, and he devoted considerable numbers of troops to protecting that line of support.

After three years of active service, and years of army experience and contemplation, Sherman had concluded that the search for the climactic battle, especially against a competent opposing commander like Johnston, was a bootless one. Large armies, sustained by industrialization, advanced agriculture, and more modern supply methods, could withstand great losses, as the Rebel Army of Tennessee and the Yankee Army of the Potomac had, and still be effective forces. Where Sherman could damage the Rebel war effort was by taking Atlanta. A manufacturing city second only to Richmond, it was also a critical rail nexus.

Originally, Sherman had planned for Thomas and Schofield to hold Johnston in place while McPherson's Army of the Tennessee sliced down from northern Alabama to seize Rome, Georgia. The move might compel Johnston to fall all the way back to the Atlanta defenses. When it became clear that Banks could neither return A. J. Smith's men to McPherson nor undertake a strike on Mobile, which would help protect the Army of the Tennessee in its isolated march, and that two more of McPherson's divisions were delayed up north, Sherman had to revamp everything. Thomas, who had honed intelligence gathering to a fine art, ascertained that gaps in the mountainous country to the south and west of Johnston's army were lightly defended. Sherman determined that a bold flanking movement might be able to push into Johnston's rear, sever his rail link to Atlanta, and then strike the Rebel flank as the army retreated.

In early May, in conjunction with Grant's campaign against Lee, Sherman opened the offensive. Thomas held Johnston in place with an excellent feint, while McPherson slipped around the Rebel left flank. On May 8, Union troops

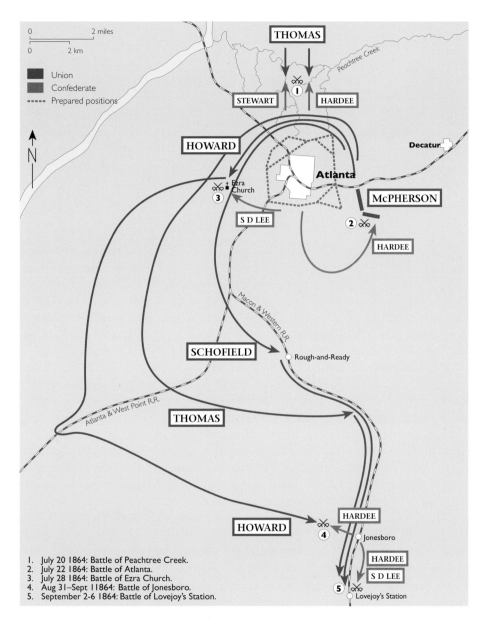

Battles around Atlanta, July–September 1864.

1. July 20 1864: Battle of Peachtree Creek.
2. July 22 1864: Battle of Atlanta.
3. July 28 1864: Battle of Ezra Church.
4. Aug 31–Sept 11864: Battle of Jonesboro.
5. September 2-6 1864: Battle of Lovejoy's Station.

advanced into Snake Creek Gap, not far from Resaca and the railroad. But the next day, Federal troops discovered a body of Confederates in a fortified position. Uneasy over his isolated situation, McPherson decided that he lacked the strength to assail the enemy. He withdrew to the gap, but this alone forced Johnston to retreat. Had McPherson's army possessed its full complement of troops, or had Sherman accepted Thomas's offer of lending some of his army, the campaign might have proved disastrous for Johnston. As it was, the flanking movement dislodged the Rebels from a great defensive position.

OPPOSITE PAGE:
Union advances during the Atlanta campaign.

The Western & Atlantic Railroad, which ran from Chattanooga to Atlanta, became part of Sherman's and Johnston's lifeline during the Atlanta campaign. From a military standpoint, Allatoona Pass proved extremely important. The photograph, looking northward, demonstrates the narrowness of the area and indicates how important control of it was for both sides.

As Johnston's command retreated, it picked up some valuable reinforcements. Polk brought what amounted to another corps, to join with those under Hardee and Lieutenant-General John Bell Hood, who had earned a great reputation in Lee's army as a brigade and division commander and had possessed the great fortune of spearheading the drive through Rosecrans's gap at Chickamauga.

Johnston took a defensive position around Resaca and then to the southwest along the northern bank of the Oostanaula River. After some fighting, especially on the Confederate right, Sherman's men forced a crossing over the Oostanaula, and by May 16, Johnston had to fall back again.

The pattern of Sherman fixing and turning his enemy continued. When Johnston planned a counterstroke, as he did at Cassville, Hood hesitated. The corps commander accepted a report that Union troops were approaching his rear and canceled the attack. Johnston then fell back to the Etowah River and a formidable defensive position at Allatoona. But he could not lure Sherman into an assault. The Union command slipped again to the west, and the Rebels retreated to the area around Dallas and New Hope Church, tossing up strong field works for protection. The Federals followed suit. The two sides then skirmished with each other, attacks breaking out at two points in the line.

By shifting to the west, Sherman had drawn Johnston away from the Western and Atlantic Railroad, the Confederate supply line to Atlanta. The Union commander tried to swing his army around the Rebel right flank, gain control of the railroad, and compel the Confederates to attack him. Instead, Johnston beat him there and occupied some high ground near Marietta. In mid-June, Sherman's command butted up against the Rebels, probing for any weaknesses or opportunities. Finally, on June 27, Sherman committed the kind of blunder that Johnston had sought weeks earlier. Believing that the Confederates had extended their line so far that it was weak in the center, Sherman hurled men up slopes in two locations. Troops in both Thomas's and McPherson's army were repulsed. At these encounters, collectively called the

With the help of slave labor, the Confederates erected some stiff defensive works around Atlanta. The photograph, taken from the viewpoint of the Rebel cannoneers by George Barnard in 1864, shows the protection afforded them, the open terrain for effective firing, and some obstructions to impede attackers. (Library of Congress)

Battle of Kennesaw Mountain, the Union suffered 3,000 casualties, while inflicting only 600.

With Johnston and much of the Confederate army distracted by the attack around Kennesaw Mountain, Schofield's troops slid past the Rebels on the Union right and, again, Johnston had to fall back toward Atlanta, occupying a prepared line. By July 5, McPherson had bypassed that position, and the Union flanks touched the Chattahoochee River. To get his army over the river, Sherman feigned a crossing on his right, had Thomas fix Johnston's army, and

directed Schofield to cross the river upstream. As Federals worked their way over the river, Johnston had to abandon yet another powerful defensive position. He retreated to the south side of Peachtree Creek, only 3 miles (5km) from the heart of Atlanta.

As Johnston fell back closer to Atlanta, people began to lose faith in their highly touted commander. Soldiers grumbled; some cast aside their weapons and went home; still others turned themselves in to the Yankees. How far Johnston would retreat, no one knew, but soldiers and civilians alike grew more and more concerned.

Back in Richmond, Davis worried about the loss of Atlanta. He had received reports, including private messages from Hood, complaining that Johnston refused to fight. From the army commander himself, Davis learned little. Johnston grumbled that he lacked the manpower to assume the offensive, or that he needed additional cavalry to strike Sherman's supply line, the Western and Atlantic Railroad. In fact, the disparity between the two armies was not that severe. During Johnston's retreat, he shortened his supply line to Atlanta and picked up some additional defenders. Sherman, meanwhile, had to peel off almost 20,000 soldiers to guard his supply line.

To get at the real situation, and to explain the issues from Richmond's perspective, Davis sent his military advisor, Bragg, to Atlanta to meet with Johnston. After speaking to subordinate commanders and Johnston over a few days, Bragg reported to the President, "I cannot learn that he has any more plan for the future than he has had in the past." Bragg did suspect, though, that Johnston "is now more inclined to fight."

The Confederacy could not afford to lose Atlanta, and Davis had to act. He needed assurance from Johnston that he would hold the city. "I wish to hear from you as to present situation," telegraphed Davis, "and your plans of operation so specifically as will enable me to anticipate events." In reply, Johnston insisted, "As the enemy has double our number, we must be on the defensive. My plan of operations must, therefore, depend on that of the

A year after the war, George Barnard snapped this photograph of Kennesaw Mountain and the remains of some field works. Sherman thought that the Confederates had stretched their lines too thin and ordered an attack up the slope. The Rebels repulsed this attack and inflicted heavy losses. (Library of Congress)

At the Battle of Atlanta, Hood attempted to roll up the Union flank. Federals observed the wide flanking movement, but Rebel delays misled Federal troops into believing that no attack would occur. Hardee's men drove the Union forces back, but Federals eventually counterattacked and held the line. Major-General James McPherson was killed while riding to the sound of gunfire, and Major-General John A. Logan oversaw the victory. (Ann Ronan Picture Library)

enemy. It is mainly to watch for an opportunity to fight to advantage." He then expressed a hope to employ the Georgia militia in the Atlanta defenses, to free up his army for movements.

That was the last straw. Davis needed to hear that he would defend the city and that he had a plan of action. Johnston offered neither. The next evening, July 17, Davis removed Johnston and placed Hood in command.

By all accounts, Hood was an aggressive fighter. Personally courageous, he fought in the front and suffered the consequences. A ball had shattered his arm at Gettysburg, and he had suffered the amputation of his leg from a wound at Chickamauga, which impaired his ability to move about and afflicted him with chronic and severe pain. He also lacked experience at high command. Yet despite his disabilities, there was no denying his aggressive spirit.

With Johnston's plan, Hood attacked Thomas's army on July 20, as it tried to cross Peachtree Creek. Veterans in the Army of the Cumberland beat them back. On July 22, at the Battle of Atlanta, he attempted to send Hardee's corps on a lengthy march around Sherman's left to roll up the flank. Even though Federals had seen them on the march, Hardee's late attack caught them off guard. In the battle, the Yankees lost McPherson, who accidentally rode into advancing Confederates and was shot and killed. Major-General John A. Logan, probably the best of the political generals on the Union side, replaced the fallen leader and repulsed the assault. When Sherman then swung to the southeast, stretching for the Macon and Western Railroad, Hood struck once more at Ezra Church. The new commander of the Army of the Tennessee, a pious, one-armed West Pointer named Oliver Otis Howard, repelled the attack on July 28. In three battles over nine days, Hood had done what Davis had asked him to do: fight. But in the process, he had suffered two and a half times as many casualties as Sherman's army, and he was in a worse position to hold on to Atlanta.

Sherman knew that if he could just cut the Western and Macon Railroad, Hood would be compelled to abandon the city. His cavalry failed to do the job, and he planned to pull back part of his army for defense, freeing up others for offensive operations to the southwest. Slowly, he wheeled his forces toward the railroad. In order to protect that last, vital line, Hardee launched a vicious attack against Howard's men at Jonesboro, but he could not dislodge them. With Thomas's and Schofield's columns gaining parts of the line, too, Hood had no choice but to abandon Atlanta. He exploded rail cars loaded with ammunition and evacuated his armed forces from the city. On September 2, 1864, a gleeful Sherman wired, "Atlanta is ours, and fairly won."

The presidential election of 1864

No doubt, Sherman knew just how important the fall of Atlanta was to the cause of reunion. More than a precious industrial and transportation center, Atlanta signaled the success of the commanding general, Grant, and the commander-in-chief, Lincoln. It could not have come at a more vital time.

Both the Union and the Confederacy understood the consequence of battlefield decisions that year. November 1864 would see a presidential election, and by choosing Grant as his commanding general, Lincoln had linked his political future to Grant's military success. The Rebels, too, recognized its significance. If they hoped to win independence, they must extract a political decision from antiwar forces in the North at the polls. And the key to that would be military success in 1864.

The year had opened with Banks's Red River fiasco, followed by stalemates in the two major campaigns. Grant incurred staggering losses in his campaigns in the east – some 60,000 casualties in seven weeks – and eventually locked into a siege with Lee around Petersburg. Sherman's columns had not suffered the same number of losses as Federals back east had done, but to observers it appeared as if the Rebels under Johnston were holding their own for quite a few weeks.

More than just the antiwar supporters, more than just the loyalists of the Democratic Party, Lincoln had generated a fair amount of opposition within his own party. Conservative Republicans saw him as caving in to the Radicals, while the Radicals believed that Lincoln catered too much to the opponents of abolitionism and to those who interpreted the Constitution narrowly. Secretary of the Treasury Salmon P. Chase tested the political waters with certain elements of the Republican Party, and Major-General John C. Fremont, the party's nominee for president in 1856, openly courted support to replace Lincoln on the ticket. Both insurgencies failed, but they represented uneasiness with Lincoln's candidacy.

During the summer months, the situation had grown tense for Lincoln. After the President withheld his signature and prevented the Wade–Davis Bill,

OVERLEAF:
The Battle of Atlanta, showing the death of General James B. McPherson, July 22, 1864. (Anne S. K. Brown Military Collection, Brown University Library)

a congressional plan for reconstruction, from becoming law, Wade and Davis drafted a critical manifesto that stoked the fires of opposition against Lincoln. In July, Jubal Early's raid northward had nearly seized Washington. The value of Union currency plummeted. And for a while, a sullen Lincoln believed his defeat at the polls was a real possibility. He drafted a letter which he required every cabinet member to sign unseen, declaring,

This morning, as for some days past, it seems exceedingly probable that this Administration will not be re-elected. Then it will be my duty to so co-operate with the President elect, as to save the Union between the election and the inauguration; as he will have secured his election on such ground that he can not possibly save it afterwards.

But just as quickly, the tide shifted. The Wade–Davis manifesto went too far, and it pulled Republicans together, at least for the election. The Democratic Party endorsed a peace platform, and then nominated Major-General George B. McClellan, who promptly announced his continued support for the war. The fall of Atlanta sent assurances to the Northern public that the Union was going to win the war, and that Lincoln was the nation's proper steward. Then, three weeks later, a large Federal force under Major-General Philip Sheridan delivered a powerful blow against Early's raiders and followed it up with yet another.

On November 8, 1864, Lincoln won reelection with overwhelming support from the army. Although not all soldiers were old enough to vote, and some states prohibited their troops in the field from participating, they rallied behind their commander-in-chief and aided his election cause any way they could. Of those who could vote, close to 80 percent cast their ballot for Lincoln, compared to 53 percent of the civilian population. In Sherman's army, about 90 percent cast their ballots for Old Abe. And whether they could vote or not, they clearly expressed their preferences to the folks at home. A Wisconsin man explained

Inauguration of President Lincoln following his reelection in 1894. (Mary Evans Picture Library)

to his brother that every man who voted against Lincoln was "a soldier's enemy." An Illinois fellow coached his dad to "Shun all disloyal company and do not vote the copperhead [Democratic] ticket, no matter who might say it is right." But the bluntest talk came from an Ohioan, who instructed his sister, "Tell Ben if he votes for Mc[Clellan] I will never speak to him again."

Bursting with confidence after their victory at Atlanta, soldiers were assured that they would win by Lincoln's victory at the polls. "We go with our Hartes contented," an infantryman explained to a friend, "nowing that we have a President that will not declare peace on no other tirmes then an Uncondishnell Surrender."

Planning for the great march

After the fall of Atlanta, Sherman decided not to pursue Hood's army. The two forces had been in continuous contact for over 100 days, and Sherman believed his men needed a rest. He doubted that the Rebel Army of Tennessee possessed enough strength to be much of a threat to the Union cause, and he much preferred to recuperate, refit, and then undertake a very different type of campaign from the grind toward Atlanta.

Hood's army, badly worn down but not whipped, eventually limped to Palmetto, about 25 miles (40km) from Atlanta. Morale declined over the loss of the campaign, but some rest, hot food, and time for reflection away from the boom of guns helped to restore their attitude, as did a religious revival that roared through camp. With a rejuvenated spirit, members of the Army of Tennessee began to look at the past campaign in a different light. The fall of Atlanta, concluded most of the troops, was merely a setback. Through a vast numerical superiority, the Federals had forced them out of the city, but had by no means crushed the Army of Tennessee.

During this hiatus, the Confederate President decided to pay the army a visit. Jefferson Davis had heard reports of dissatisfaction with Hood's performance throughout the Army of Tennessee and had also sensed a dramatic decline in public morale throughout the region. He hoped that a personal inspection of the army and a few public speeches on the way back to Richmond were just the solution. Upon his arrival, Davis immediately began to speak with Hood and several of his key subordinates, and it soon became clear

Before Sherman's army abandoned Atlanta, it destroyed the railroads. Groups of soldiers picked up rails and dislodged the ties. They then started large fires with the ties and laid the rails over them. Once the rails got red hot, men twisted the rails. Since the Confederacy had no other foundries outside Richmond that could produce rails, Sherman's men did not have to undertake the backbreaking work of filling in the rail gradings. They employed this technique through the Savannah and Carolinas campaigns, destroying 443 miles (713km) of railroad. (Library of Congress)

that a major shake-up was in order. Davis promptly transferred corps commander Lieutenant-General William J. Hardee, at his own request, to the Department of South Carolina, Georgia, and Florida. Hood, however, stayed. Davis had always been fond of Hood's aggressive style, and he strongly approved Hood's new plan to strike at Sherman's long supply line and retake Atlanta. To silence critics Davis placed a more experienced officer, General P. G. T. Beauregard, in a supervisory position over Hood. Hood would still command the Army of Tennessee; Beauregard's job was merely to give Hood advice.

In addition to sorting out the command problems, Davis also hoped to give the members of the Army of Tennessee a lift. He spoke to them of the upcoming campaign and announced that they would soon advance into Tennessee and Kentucky. The President insisted that Atlanta, like Moscow for Napoleon, would be Sherman's downfall. For the most part, the Confederate troops responded favorably to Davis's predictions, yet a few of the more superstitious men feared that "his coming is an omen of ill luck." The last time Davis had spoken to the Army of Tennessee was just before the catastrophe at Chattanooga.

While Major-General Joseph Wheeler and his cavalry looked after the Federals in Atlanta, on September 28 Hood embarked upon a series of rapid marches along Sherman's supply line, the railroad from Atlanta to Chattanooga, destroying track and bridges and gobbling up garrisons en route. At first, Sherman jumped at the bait. He left one corps to occupy Atlanta and pursued the Confederates vigorously with the rest of his command, and on a few occasions they nearly cornered Hood's elusive army. Yet by the time the Rebels reached eastern Alabama, the Federal commander had decided to call off the hunt. It was useless for the Federals to surrender the initiative, particularly when they could not move as rapidly as the Confederates.

Since late 1862, when Grant and Sherman wrestled with guerrillas and civilian problems in Tennessee and Mississippi, they had thrashed out a strategy of raiding. Rebel cavalry had been effective against the Union army and its supply lines. Think how much disruption a Federal army could cause, the two generals speculated, if it could destroy the Confederate infrastructure, seize their slaves, damage or consume their property, and disrupt lives. The Union could demonstrate unequivocally to the Southern people just how futile continued resistance would be. In February 1864, Sherman had tested the concept in a march on Meridian, Mississippi, living off the land and wrecking anything of military value. The best thing to do, Sherman concluded, was to launch an even grander campaign. He proposed that he send a portion of his army back to Tennessee under Thomas, in case Hood pushed farther north, while he struck west for Savannah with 65,000 men.

Neither Lincoln nor Halleck liked the plan, and Grant was at best lukewarm. The commanding general much preferred that Sherman eliminate Hood's army first. But Sherman kept tossing out more and more reasons why he should go and, ultimately, he struck a responsive chord. "Instead of being on the defensive, I would be on the offensive," he reminded his friend, "instead of guessing at what he means to do, he would have to guess at my plans. The difference in war is full 25 per cent." From that moment, Grant blocked any challenges to Sherman's raid, even though he raised questions himself. Grant believed in Sherman.

For his campaign, Sherman retained four corps – the XV and XVII from the Army of the Tennessee and the XIV and XX from the Army of the Cumberland – totaling about 60,000 infantry and artillery, along with a cavalry division of 5,000. These he grouped into two armies, the Army of the Tennessee under Howard and the Army of Georgia under Major-General Henry W. Slocum. To Chattanooga or Nashville under Thomas, Sherman sent back two corps, the IV and the X, plus some cavalry, from Schofield's troops on October 30.

Even though Confederate scouts detected the passage of troops and supplies back and forth, Hood decided not to try to block Sherman's advance deeper into Georgia. The Confederate commander had come to the conclusion that he could inflict more damage on the Federal war effort by invading Tennessee and possibly Kentucky without Sherman's army hounding his rear than by chancing a battle with the larger Federal force. Although Hood still had doubts about his army defeating superior numbers in a pitched battle, he was fully confident in its ability to conduct an effective raid against the smaller Federal numbers to the north. Thus, in an anomaly of warfare, both the Federals and the Confederates terminated the campaign intentionally by marching in opposite directions from one another without having given battle.

The March to the Sea

On November 15, 1864, in preparation for the campaign, Sherman's troops began to destroy anything of military value 60 miles (96km) back from Atlanta. Some private homes along the railroad were also torched. In Atlanta, Sherman's soldiers overstepped their bounds, lighting fires throughout the town and damaging an estimated 4,000–5,000 structures. Fortunately, the population in Atlanta was light. After seizing the city, Sherman had shipped out some of the inhabitants. He saw no need to strain his food supplies for Rebel supporters.

Sherman took about 1,200,000 rations with his army and a couple of weeks' worth of fodder for his animals. He had studied census records before the campaign and determined that he could supply his army from the people of Georgia, as long as his army kept moving. The key to the campaign was his reliance on the experienced nature of his soldiers. Eighty percent of his enlisted men had joined the army in 1861 or 1862. Nearly 50 percent qualified as veteran volunteers, having reenlisted for a second term of service. They knew how to handle themselves on the march, on the battlefield, and in camp. To feed his army, Sherman would have to disperse foragers into the countryside, often with loose supervision, and here that experience proved critical.

Against his army of 65,000, for much of the campaign the Confederates could only muster Major-General Joseph Wheeler and his 3,500 cavalrymen and some militia. On the march, Sherman intended to interpose his army between two valuable military targets. The Confederates could either protect one or

OVERLEAF:
Sherman's march to the sea.
(Anne S. K. Brown Military Collection, Brown University Library)

277

The storming of Fort McAllister. Sherman needed to seize Fort McAllister in order to open supply lines with the Union navy. Hazen used sharpshooters to pin down the defenders, and he assembled his men in a relatively thin line to reduce casualties. In 13 minutes, Hazen's troops captured the fort, with a loss of 24 killed and 110 wounded, mostly from land mines. His men inflicted 250 casualties. The sketch appeared in *Harper's Weekly*, January 14, 1865. (Anne S. K. Brown Military Collection, Brown University Library)

divide their forces, weakening resistance more. Thus, Sherman positioned his army between Macon and Augusta, two valuable industrial sites. Sherman realized that he did not have to capture those cities, which could prove costly and tie down his army. All he had to do was destroy Confederate facilities for moving their products, specifically the railroads, to accomplish his goal.

Sherman's army swung down as if to threaten Macon, home of an arsenal, armory, and laboratory, and then shifted up toward Augusta, which housed the great Arsenal and Gunpowder Works and the Naval Ordnance Works. Meanwhile, his army ripped up railroad track, burning ties and twisting rails. They did not have to waste time filling in the rail grade, because if his men did their work properly and twisted the rails (sometimes, they only bent them), the Confederacy had no facilities outside Richmond to melt down and roll rails. As Sherman advanced toward Augusta, he again maneuvered his army between Augusta and Savannah, confusing the Confederates as to his real destination and enabling his men to do their work. On the Savannah campaign, Sherman's troops destroyed over 300 miles (480km) of rail.

The campaign caused quite a sensation among people North and South. Few knew Sherman's true destination, Savannah, and the way he cut a swath right through the state of Georgia fascinated Northerners and terrified Southerners. By marching through the countryside, Sherman's soldiers frightened the people of Georgia. Hordes of bluecoats poured over farms, plantations, and towns, stripping the area of foodstuffs, livestock, and able-bodied male slaves, and destroying any items of military value they could not carry. Confederate soldiers in distant armies grew extremely uneasy over the welfare of loved ones and their life's work. Just as Sherman made Confederate commanders in Georgia choose between Macon and Augusta, so he forced Georgia soldiers to decide whether their ultimate responsibility lay with their beleaguered families or with the army. Before the campaign, he had vowed, "I can make the march, and make Georgia howl." And he did. On November 23, Milledgville, the capital of Georgia, fell to Sherman.

By the second week of December, Sherman's columns were approaching the area around Savannah. Grant had notified the Union navy of Sherman's

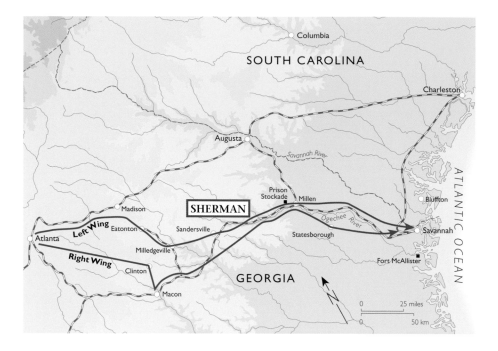

The Savannah campaign, November–December 1864.

intention, but no one knew for sure when he would surface. To open communications, Sherman's troops stormed Fort McAllister south of the city on December 13, and then stretched out to trap the garrison in Savannah. Some 13,000 Confederates under Hardee defended the city and were able to keep open one route of escape. On the night of December 20/21, Hardee withdrew before Sherman could complete plans to box the Rebels inside the city. The next day, Sherman announced to the President, "I beg to present you, as a Christmas gift, the City of Savannah." In reply, Lincoln admitted his uneasiness over the operation and that he had acquiesced only because "you were the better judge" and "nothing risked, nothing gained." The President then insisted, "the honor is all yours."

Hood's Tennessee campaign

Although Hood had lost Atlanta, Confederate President Davis retained his faith in him. Davis had appointed Hood because he was a fighter, and that was exactly what Hood did. Yet the Rebel President detected a lack of seasoning in high command, and to assist Hood, Davis assigned Beauregard as commander of the Military Division of the West. Beauregard had restored his reputation somewhat with Davis by performing well as commander of the Department of South Carolina, Georgia, and Florida, and then around Petersburg. Davis did not intend for Beauregard to supersede Hood. Rather, he wanted Hood in command, but felt that Beauregard could help shape Hood's plans and provide the kind of advice that the young, aggressive warrior needed.

Hood convinced himself that he had achieved a great success by striking Sherman's supply line, and now he planned to invade Tennessee and perhaps Kentucky. If Sherman pursued, he could give battle on his own terms. If Sherman refused to follow his army, then Middle Tennessee and perhaps more would be easy pickings. Beauregard weighed in by sending Forrest's cavalry to cooperate with Hood's army and by shifting the Rebel supply base to Tuscumbia, Alabama, on the Memphis and Charleston Railroad. Beauregard then offered some advice on how to conduct the campaign: to succeed, Hood must move rapidly.

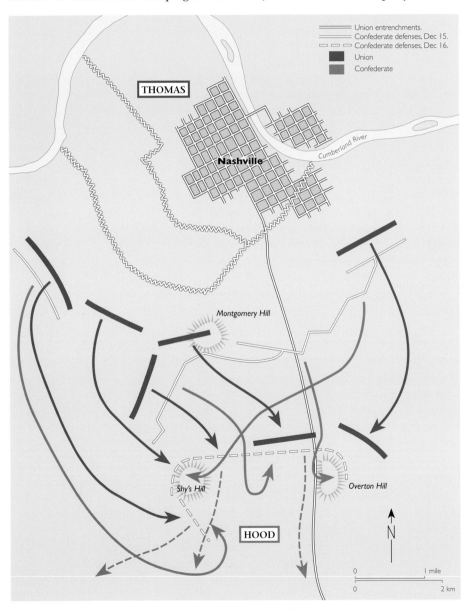

The Battle of Nashville,
December 15–16, 1864.

Instead, Hood dawdled. He wasted time trying to capture a Federal garrison at Decatur, Alabama, and struggled to find an acceptable crossing at the Tennessee River. Finally, he marched to Tuscumbia and waited for fresh supplies before entering Tennessee. This indecisiveness, so uncharacteristic of the impulsive Hood, may have been purposeful. Had the Rebel army advanced into Middle Tennessee along the railroad to Nashville, Sherman might have pursued, blocking Hood's escape route southward. By shifting his army to north central Alabama, Hood discouraged Sherman from chasing him.

On the Union side, Hood's movements may have baffled Sherman temporarily, but Grant assessed the Confederate commander's intentions exactly. Once the Army of Tennessee marched to Tuscumbia, Grant realized that any pursuit by Sherman made no sense. His trusted lieutenant must strike out for the coast with the bulk of his army, yet return enough men to Nashville for Thomas to defend Middle Tennessee.

A large part of Thomas's command came from Sherman's army during the Atlanta campaign. Major-General James Harrison Wilson took back 12,000 unmounted cavalrymen, armed with seven-shot Spencer repeating carbines, and began combing the region for fresh horses and equipment. Schofield's X Corps and the IV Corps under Major-General David Stanley gathered around Pulaski, Tennessee, to check a northward advance. Grant directed A. J. Smith's two divisions of 10,000 veterans, fresh from the defeat of Price, to move by rail from Missouri to Nashville, and Major-General James B. Steedman brought back 5,200 men from occupation duty along Sherman's old railroad supply line. In Nashville itself, Thomas had some post guards, quartermaster troops, and 14 artillery batteries to supplement the command.

Finally, on November 19, 1864, Forrest's cavalry led Hood's advance, followed by the three corps. Scouts estimated Schofield's forces at around 15,000. With about 30,000 infantry and artillery and 5,500 horsemen, Hood hoped to push north rapidly, slip around the Federal force, and seize Columbia, compelling Schofield to fight his way to Nashville. Despite nasty weather and deep mud, the Confederates made good progress. After some initial hesitation, Schofield detected Hood's plan and narrowly beat Forrest's cavalrymen back to Columbia. The Yankees occupied some prepared trenches on the south side of Duck River. Several days later, as the great Rebel horseman began to force river crossings, Schofield fell back once again.

Schofield did not believe that Hood could move his army along a roundabout and difficult course and still beat him to Spring Hill. He was wrong. Confederate cavalry and then some infantry arrived before many of Schofield's troops, yet they could not check the Union retreat. Stanley had rushed a division back in the afternoon of November 29, and a second one around sunset. With the aid of some artillery, these Yankee troops repelled piecemeal Rebel attacks. That night, miscommunication among the Rebel high command and a string of unfortunate decisions enabled Schofield to march unhindered right past the Confederate forces and through Spring Hill. By the morning of the 30th, weary Federals had stumbled into Franklin, on the south side of the Harpeth River, 18 miles (29km) from Nashville. Immediately, officers put them to work fortifying some old, overgrown trenches, while engineers built two pontoon bridges across the river.

When Hood realized that the Yankees had escaped, he seethed with anger. Everyone was to blame except, of course, himself. Hood had long believed that entrenchments stripped soldiers of their aggressiveness, and he determined to teach the officers and men of the Army of the Tennessee a lesson. The Rebels pursued rapidly, and when they came upon Schofield's troops at Franklin in the mid-afternoon, Hood ordered them to storm the works.

The relatively open, gently inclined terrain offered the Yankees an excellent line of fire. Still, Hood's men struck, and did so with fury. In the center of the Federal fortifications, where the Union maintained an advanced post, Rebels penetrated by following on the heels of those in flight. A vicious counterattack restored the line. Elsewhere, despite extraordinary bravery on the part of thousands of Confederates, Schofield's men repulsed the assaults.

On the last day of November, in less than three hours, Hood's army suffered almost 5,500 casualties. It was not a matter of courage; these Rebels exhibited plenty of that. The fact was that, in most instances, attackers were no match for veteran defenders fighting from behind breastworks, well armed with rifled muskets and supported by artillery. When the Union retreated to Nashville that evening, they took with them 702 prisoners, most of them captured as Federal troops sealed the penetration. The Yankees suffered 2,326 casualties.

At Franklin, Confederate commanders fought from the front and suffered staggering losses as a result. Twelve generals went down, six of them killed, and 54 regimental commanders fell in the fighting that day. Among those who lost their lives was Patrick Cleburne, the great Confederate division commander.

The next morning, Hood's soldiers marched past the grisly sight of the previous day's débâcle, crossed over the Harpeth, and began a slow advance up near the Union defenses of Nashville. At the time, Hood assumed that Thomas had not received substantial reinforcements, but he also believed that the Battle of Franklin had cut any offensive inclinations out of his army. Lacking the strength to lay siege to the city, he stretched his army out to cover the major roads heading southward and hoped that his presence might induce Thomas to attack him. A few days later, Hood detached some infantry and cavalry under Forrest to harass a Union garrison at Murfreesboro. It was Hood's hope that fear of losing those troops might induce Thomas to abandon his works and attack the Rebels.

Back in Nashville, Thomas had worried that he might not have enough soldiers to cope with Hood's army. But on December 1, as Schofield's columns entered the city, A. J. Smith's and Steedman's troops arrived as well. Now all Thomas needed was enough good mounts and saddles so that Wilson's cavalry could compete with Forrest's vaunted horsemen and some good fighting weather. Yet just before Wilson accumulated enough horses and equipment,

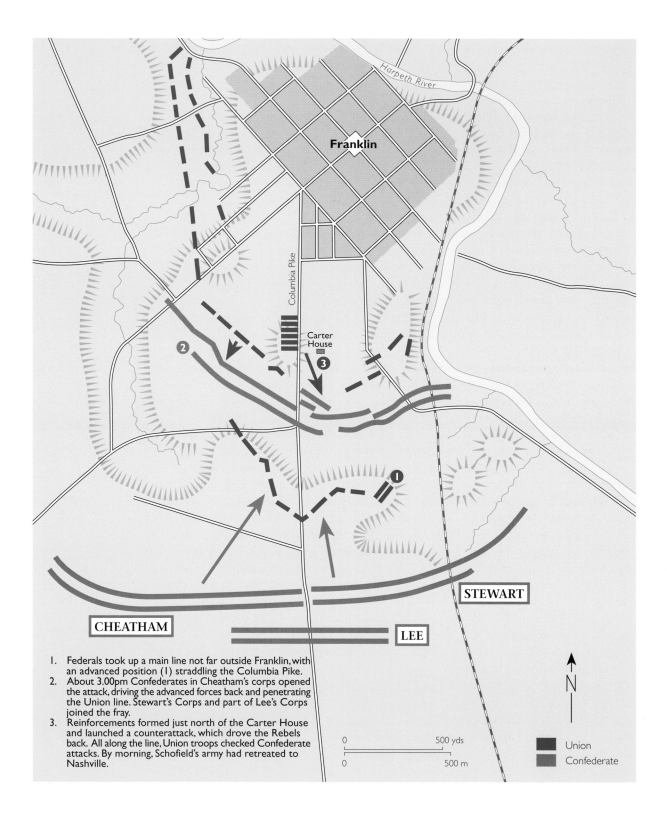

Franklin

Harpeth River

Columbia Pike

Carter
House

2

3

1

STEWART

CHEATHAM

LEE

1. Federals took up a main line not far outside Franklin, with an advanced position (1) straddling the Columbia Pike.
2. About 3.00pm Confederates in Cheatham's corps opened the attack, driving the advanced forces back and penetrating the Union line. Stewart's Corps and part of Lee's Corps joined the fray.
3. Reinforcements formed just north of the Carter House and launched a counterattack, which drove the Rebels back. All along the line, Union troops checked Confederate attacks. By morning, Schofield's army had retreated to Nashville.

N

| 0 | | 500 yds |
| 0 | | 500 m |

Union
Confederate

snow and sleet descended on Middle Tennessee, and for five days it scarcely let up. A thick sheet of ice blanketed the ground, making it nearly impossible for land movement by man or beast.

Meanwhile, Grant and officials in Washington had become increasingly uneasy over Thomas's delay. By the Union commanding general's calculation, Hood possessed fewer than 30,000 infantry and artillery, and while he thought it was possible that Forrest had more cavalry, Wilson's men carried repeating carbines which gave them an incredible firepower advantage. At one point, Grant nearly removed Thomas. He feared Hood would swing around Nashville and raid northward, wreaking havoc wherever he went. Only when Halleck balked did Grant yield. After Grant implored him to attack, Thomas declined. The ice storm prevented movement. Once it melted, Thomas vowed to attack immediately.

For a few days, Grant accepted the explanation, but impatience got the best of him. He ordered Major-General John A. Logan to travel to Nashville and take over from Thomas, and after some consideration, Grant decided to go himself. As Grant waited to board a train in Washington, word arrived that Thomas had attacked and won. Grant traveled no farther.

On December 15, Thomas launched a massive and extremely successful attack. His plan called for the Union to feint on the Rebel right and overwhelm their left. Under a cloud of fog, Steedmen's black soldiers delivered a powerful blow on the Confederate right that distracted them. On the opposite flank, A. J. Smith's troops and Wilson's cavalry crushed or completely bypassed the Rebel left. Then, late in the afternoon, Thomas hurled Schofield's men into the fight, and a massive Union assault compelled Hood's army to abandon the field.

The Rebels fell back to a new, more defensible position, but when Thomas attacked the next afternoon, the results proved even more disastrous for Hood. Once again, Thomas struck the Rebel right first, and with Rebel attention riveted there, Union infantry and cavalry swamped the left. As Federal infantry and dismounted horsemen penetrated into Hood's rear, the Rebel line crumbled, and the rout was on. Thousands of Johnny Rebs surrendered. One Confederate described the flight as a "stampede" and "a sad, shocking sight to behold." Unlike the last Confederate disaster, Wilson ordered his men back to get their mounts, and the Yankees, both cavalry and infantry, pursued with vigor.

During the two-day battle, Thomas's men took nearly 4,500 prisoners, including four generals. Wilson's pursuit snared another 3,200, of whom nearly 2,000 were men wounded at Franklin. Through Christmas Day 1864, Federal cavalry pressed the retreating Confederates. Not until Rebels crossed the Tennessee River, and Forrest assumed command of the rear guard, did Wilson ease up. Union infantry kept pace for a while, but by December 22, Thomas had directed them to proceed at a more leisurely speed and root out Rebel stragglers. For the campaign, Thomas's army took 8,635 prisoners and 320 Confederate deserters. As the attacking force, the Federals lost 3,061 and killed or wounded about 1,800 Rebels.

OPPOSITE PAGE:
The Battle of Franklin, November 30, 1864.

Thomas's campaign broke the back of the Army of Tennessee. While some of its members would fight again, and fight well, it no longer existed as an army in the true sense. The resounding Union victories at Franklin and Nashville, moreover, added great luster to Sherman's March to the Sea. Only such a resounding triumph would vindicate Sherman's decision to send back two corps and cavalrymen and head to the coast on his raiding strategy.

Campaign through the Carolinas

When Sherman arrived safely in Savannah, in December 1864, Grant had great plans to transport his army by water to the Petersburg area. With the addition of 65,000 veterans, the Federals could easily stretch around Lee's flanks and bring an end to the war in the east. But Sherman had other ideas. He hated the prospect of shipping his troops by water. Would it not be better, he proposed, to march his army through the Carolinas to Virginia, destroying railroads and anything of military value en route, as he had done in Georgia? Once Grant learned that it would take weeks and weeks to assemble enough transport ships, he authorized the Carolinas campaign.

This is a sketch by artist William Ward, who accompanied Sherman's army, of part of Logan's XV Corps as it waded across the Little Salkahatchie River in South Carolina in February 1865. Sherman's soldiers endured considerable hardships, like wading a swamp and a river in wintertime, during the Carolinas campaign. The sketch was published in *Harper's Weekly*, April 8, 1865. (Joseph T. Glatthaar)

Like their commander, Sherman's soldiers much preferred to march to Virginia by way of South Carolina. They viewed that state as the hotbed of the secession movement and blamed its people for all the lives lost, bodies maimed, and hardships endured. They were almost giddy at the prospect of exacting vengeance for instigating the war.

By comparison with the advance on Savannah, the Carolinas campaign was far more difficult. Federal troops had to march through swampy country in wintertime, often amid heavy rains. Because of the terrain, South Carolina lacked the bountiful food harvests of central Georgia. And as the Federals entered North Carolina, the Confederacy had assembled a sizable force to contest the advance, which in the previous campaign occurred only as Sherman's troops approached Savannah.

Once again, Sherman used two prized targets to confuse Rebel resistance about his initial destination. Two corps appeared as if they were marching on Charleston, while the other two threatened Augusta. Instead, Sherman employed the XV and XVII Corps to uncover the route for the XIV and XX more inland. Then, his army, often taking separate roads, advanced toward Columbia. As they destroyed railroads along the way, they isolated Charleston and compelled its abandonment on February 18.

These Yankee veterans were intent on punishing South Carolina. When a soldier in the XIV Corps crossed over the bridge into the state, he yelled back, "Boys, this is old South Carolina, let's give her hell," at which his comrades cheered. Without authorization, they burned parts or most of 18 towns and plundered or wrecked all sorts of private property. Sherman's troops would have their revenge.

After some skirmishing, the army entered Columbia on February 17, where the troops discovered that Confederates and civilians had begun looting shops and had left stacked bales of cotton on fire. That night, the wind kicked up and revived the flames, floating these burning projectiles to nearby buildings. In their revelry, Sherman's soldiers actively spread the fires. By morning, after the winds had died down, military officials had restored some order. A third of the city lay in ashes. Yet Sherman's troops had not had their fill. They torched parts of five more towns in South Carolina.

Once the army crossed over into North Carolina, officers issued orders to remind the soldiers that North Carolina had been the last state to secede and had a strong Unionist minority. They urged troops to distinguish between the people of the Tarheel State and South Carolina. The army destroyed the arsenal in Fayetteville, and some firebugs burned several blocks. Generally, though, Sherman's men behaved themselves much better in North Carolina. In an army of 65,000, men plundered, especially soldiers who acted as foragers, but most soldiers eased up on their destructiveness.

By the time Sherman's troops reached North Carolina, the Confederates had begun to accumulate some forces to resist the advance. South Carolinian Lieutenant-General Wade Hampton brought cavalry from Lee's army and superseded Wheeler. Remnants of Hood's Army of Tennessee augmented Hardee's command that escaped from Savannah, and as the army fell back, they collected various coastal garrisons. On the advice of Lee, Davis restored Joe Johnston to command them all.

Despite Johnston's weakness in manpower, he had to try to block Sherman's movements. Implementing a plan devised by Hampton, he directed Hardee to delay the advance by fighting at Averasborough, which he did successfully on March 16, 1865, at a loss of 800 men. This bought more time to accumulate additional troops and set the trap. Hampton devised a fishhook-shaped position, and some Federals walked right into it. On the morning of March 19, when some bluecoats reported resistance, Sherman brushed it aside as nothing more than cavalry in their front. Suddenly, Confederates sprung the trap and rocked back the advancing Federals, but as additional Union units rushed to the sound of gunfire, the Yankees stiffened. Two days later, a Union counterattack cut through the Rebels and threatened their rear, until Sherman recalled the troops. Sherman was convinced that the end was near, and he loathed the idea of spilling any more blood. The Battle of Bentonville ended, with Johnston losing 2,606 men in the attack and Sherman suffering 1,527 casualties.

The Carolinas campaign, February–March 1865.

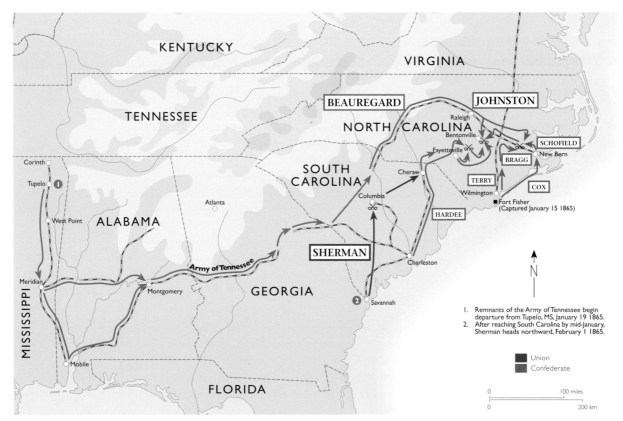

1. Remnants of the Army of Tennessee begin departure from Tupelo, MS, January 19 1865.
2. After reaching South Carolina by mid-January, Sherman heads northward, February 1 1865.

Union
Confederate

0   100 miles
0   200 km

Three days later, on March 24, Sherman marched into Goldsboro, North Carolina, where his troops ended their part in the campaign. His army had marched 470 miles (756km), destroyed hundreds of miles of rail, wrecked an arsenal, burnt towns, and terrified civilians along the route. Yet like the Savannah Campaign, the impact of the march through the Carolinas extended far beyond those who experienced it. Even Southerners who avoided the destruction suddenly confronted the reality that the Confederacy could no longer protect its citizens. In effect, Southerners were at the mercy of Yankee hordes. By destroying railroads, Sherman's army impaired the ability of Robert E. Lee to draw supplies to Richmond, inflicting greater hardship on those beleaguered Confederates. The disruption of communication caused widespread anxiety about loved ones in those regions. And perhaps most importantly, Sherman's march encouraged massive desertion from Confederate armies by forcing Rebel soldiers to choose their ultimate responsibility, between their country and their family. When Confederate troops learned how their loved ones were suffering, many veterans deserted the ranks to care for them, and quite a number of their officers could not blame them. The problem reached such epidemic proportions in the Rebel army of Northern Virginia that Lee himself wrote the governor of North Carolina, alerting him that letters from home were promoting desertion and imploring him to rally the people of the Tarheel State to support the Rebel cause. In the end, neither the governor nor Lee could stem the tide of desertion. More than a campaign against an army, Sherman targeted a hostile people. Through his destructive marches, he shattered Confederate resolve to continue the rebellion.

This sketch, prepared by an eyewitness and published in *Harper's Weekly*, April 1, 1865, shows men in the XIV Corps crossing the Catawba River at Rock Hill, South Carolina. (Joseph T. Glatthaar)

The Battle of Fort Fisher and the arrival of Schofield's command

Although the Union blockade had reduced much of the traffic flow on the high seas, the Confederacy continued to bring in goods and military supplies through Wilmington, North Carolina. A massive Rebel bastion called Fort Fisher protected the mouth of the Cape Fear River, with Wilmington just 20 miles (32km) upriver. After the débâcle on the Red River, Admiral Porter, the new commander of a flying squadron on the Atlantic, suggested to his old friend

Grant a joint expedition in December 1864 to knock Fort Fisher and Wilmington out of the war. Grant assigned Major-General Godfrey Weitzel, a clever engineer, to work with Porter, but Fort Fisher was part of Major-General Benjamin Butler's department, and Butler took over direction of the project. Butler proposed a scheme to explode a ship loaded with gunpowder under the fort, which he thought would demolish it. On December 25, when the ship explosion failed to damage the fort, Butler sent only 2,500 men ashore and then canceled the attack.

As Porter fumed, Grant dispatched a more capable officer, Major-General Alfred Terry, and an additional brigade. Porter and Terry cooperated brilliantly. After heavy naval gunfire softened the defenses, Terry's troops and 1,000 sailors and marines landed on the beach on January 14, 1865. The next day, again under cover from naval gunfire, Terry's men stormed the timber and sand bastion. By nightfall, Fort Fisher had fallen into Union hands.

To assist Sherman and secure the fall of Wilmington, Grant pulled Schofield and his XXIII Corps from Thomas's army and injected them into North Carolina with Terry's men. The combined force captured Wilmington on February 22, and in late March, Schofield rendezvoused with Sherman's army at Goldsboro, North Carolina, bringing 40,000 troops and ready access to some much-needed supplies.

COMMON SOLDIERS: BLACK SOLDIERS AND POWS

"For a man to enjoy the service, he must not be averse to much strong drink, must not be encumbered with morals & must possess an insatiable appetite for confusion," quipped a Minnesotan. The soldier was one among some three million who responded to the call of their governments. Almost all of them volunteers, they entered military service wide-eyed, anticipating glory and rapid success. Instead, they experienced a world of hardship, heartache, and frustration.

Like the America from which they came, most Civil War soldiers were from farming or rural backgrounds. These men were an industrious, self-reliant lot, an unusual blend of idealism, individualism, and practicality. They depended on their own labor and judgment for survival, which fostered confidence in their decision-making ability. Accustomed to forming their own opinion about matters, and resistant to regimentation from the outside, their sense of independence proved both the boon and bane of their military existence.

While all sorts of pressures – family, friends, community, perceptions of manhood, quests for glory – worked on them, in the end it was that ability to decide for themselves that led most to enlist. Southerners entered military service to protect hearth and home and to defend their "rights" – to own slaves, to take those slaves wherever they saw fit, and to live without fear of others

Assault on Fort Fisher. (Anne S. K. Brown Military Collection, Brown University Library)

encouraging servile insurrection. Since the US government seemed opposed to protecting those rights, they seceded and formed a new government, one that would protect them. Yankees, by contrast, believed in the permanence of the Union. Barely 80 years old, the United States was the great experiment in a democratic republic. "It was," so argued an Indiana sergeant, "the beacon of light of liberty & freedom to the human race." Secession trampled on an inherent principle of any democratic government that all would abide by the outcome of a fair election. They went off to war to sustain that government and the underlying concept because, one Yankee reasoned, "constitutional liberty cannot survive the loss of unity in the government." Only a minority early in the war fought for abolitionism. Although many Northerners disliked slavery, most also believed that African-Americans were inferior beings.

In 1861, soldiers rushed off to war amid celebrations and cheers. Believing the war would be short, most had the misplaced fear that the fighting would end before they saw any action. Few of them anticipated just how difficult prolonged military service would be, and how demanding life in uniform could be. Most soldiers did not know how to cook or care for themselves in camp and on the march. They loaded themselves down with excess baggage, never realizing how burdensome it was on a 15- or 20-mile (24–32km) hike. Then, when winter rolled around, they shivered through cold days and nights, cursing that Indian summer day when they had discarded their overcoats. Rather than enemy bullets, they succumbed to diseases in staggering numbers. Childhood illnesses had seldom afflicted people in rural communities, but once they gathered in large armies, these pathogens spread throughout camps, and farm boys had no resistance to them. Failure to enforce proper sanitary practices took unanticipated tolls, as camps bred pestilence and promoted the transmission of diseases at epidemic rates. As one Iowan wryly concluded, "There is more reality than poetry in a life on the Tented field."

Nor did they correctly anticipate the scale and scope of combat. Entering battle with severe misperceptions, the killing, the maiming, and the destruction caught men on both sides unprepared. Many had visions of personal and group glory, which realities abruptly banished from their minds. "I can inform you that I have Seen the Monkey Show at last," a Confederate penned home after Stones River, "and I dont Waunt to see it no more." He went on to describe, "Som had there hedes shot of[f] and som ther armes and legs Won was Shot in too in the midel." He then concluded with exasperation, "I can tell you that I am tirde of Ware."

They were nothing more than livestock in a butcher's pen, herded forward for the slaughter by what seemed like uncaring and incompetent generals. Men in the prime of their lives were cut down indiscriminately. Friends and comrades fell on their left and right, leaving those who survived to puzzle over the question: why them? And while they may have won the battle, rarely did they advance the cause dramatically. There seemed to be no end in sight.

Eventually, that experience in camp, on the march, and in battle hardened men on both sides. They learned how to conduct themselves better on the battlefield and in camp, to husband valuable resources and to discipline themselves on important matters. Soldiers accrued some emotional immunity to the randomness of the killing and the brutality of warfare, realizing that fear and intensive examination would produce no results. They resigned themselves to the idea that it was either God's will or their time.

The men of 1861 and 1862 had become veterans, with a vast warehouse of military knowledge based on personal experience or observation. "The experience of twenty years peaceful life," noted a veteran on the anniversary of his first battle, "has been crowded into three years." After just a few years, so stated another enlisted man, he and his comrades "had learned nearly all that was worth knowing, at least far more than [our] generals knew three years before."

Since early childhood, family and society had taught them to make decisions for themselves, to act as they saw best. Veterans did not hesitate to put those hard-earned military lessons to good use, even without supervision of their officers. They mastered the art of selecting excellent tactical positions and throwing up breastworks to shield their bodies from the accurate fire of rifled muskets. Engineers marveled at the positions and fortifications that enlisted men built quickly and on their own initiative. While killing was an inextricable component of warfare, soldiers learned how to take steps to reduce risks, to preserve themselves and their comrades for another day. Early in the war, they advanced elbow to elbow, as the tactics manual had instructed them. As veterans, they realized that the purpose was to concentrate firepower and strength, but they could accomplish that by dispersing themselves a little more and exploiting terrain features and cover. Yet they retained the important objective: to focus their fire on specific targets and areas. In camp and on the march, they knew "just what to do and what not to do." They practiced good hygiene, and supplemented their diet from the countryside. As one sergeant in Sherman's army commented, "I believe if we were as green as we were when we first came out – (as the 'Vets' say) we would starve to death." Almost as important, veterans could teach these lessons to new troops. While they liked to play pranks and mislead newcomers, the hardened soldiers also understood that their own lives depended to some degree on how well the green soldiers performed, and they would not neglect the instruction of any who would listen.

Along with changes in behavior, veterans embraced new attitudes about the war. They began to see both soldiers and civilians as the enemy, and they recognized the destruction of property as a powerful tool in fighting the war. Rebel cavalry commander Nathan Bedford Forrest proved himself master of the destructive cavalry raid, wreaking such havoc on garrisons, railroads, and supply depots that Sherman called him "that devil Forrest." Confederates, too, paid less credence to notions of "civilized warfare," especially when it came

The overwhelming majority of black soldiers, perhaps 150,000 of the nearly 180,000, came from slavery. Often they fled from the fields as Union armies passed nearby, or they undertook a risky trek to locate Federal lines. Here two photographs expose the uplifting nature of military service. In one, we see a boy in his slave clothes; in the other, he has transformed into a drummer boy for the United States Army. (Left, Library of Congress; Right, US Army)

to black soldiers. Both they and the black troops fought under the black flag, signaling their opponent that they would give no quarter, nor expect any. All too often, they executed those they captured.

While Confederates in the Western Theater exhibited that change in attitude about the war, they did not have nearly as many opportunities as the Federals to implement it. Union soldiers campaigned throughout the South and, eventually, they came to the conclusion that by making Southern whites suffer, they could contribute mightily to the war effort. In part, Northerners felt a sense of hostility over secessionists' efforts to destroy a wonderful union, but as veterans they also came around to see the linkage between the home front and the men in the field. Confederates certainly exhibited tremendous loyalty to their cause, fighting for years under adverse conditions on meager rations and in skimpy clothing. Yet the Yankees realized that many Rebel opponents had a greater loyalty than that cause – the one to their families. If Federal troops could make life miserable for loved ones at home, they would force Confederate soldiers to choose between their responsibility to their families and their obligations to their government. As Union armies penetrated deeper into the Confederacy, consuming food, confiscating slaves and other property, and terrifying the Southern people, more and more Rebels left the ranks to care for their loved ones.

By the last year and a half of the war, these Union and Confederate troops had mastered the art and science of soldiering. Those who remained in ranks had toughened their bodies by fighting off diseases. They had learned to deal with harsh elements, to march great distances and to live amid plenty or on little subsistence. In short, these citizens had learned to think, to act, to feel, and to fight like veteran soldiers.

Black soldiers

Early in the war, abolitionists and African-Americans urged the Lincoln administration to accept African-Americans for uniformed service. The President declined. He had more white volunteers than he was authorized by Congress to accept, and the Union was walking a tightrope with the Border states. Black enlistment might have driven them to the Confederacy.

Blacks, however, began to take matters into their own hands. By the end of April 1861, several slaves whom Rebels had employed in constructing defense works slipped away and sought sanctuary at Fort Monroe, Virginia. When a Confederate officer came to retrieve the runaways, Brigadier-General Benjamin Butler, a prewar lawyer and politician, refused. Federal law did not apply to Rebels, Butler explained. Furthermore, slaves had aided the Confederate army and were subject to confiscation as contraband of war. Butler then employed the runaways to build a bakery for Federal troops. In one decisive moment, Butler had freed slaves and hired them to work for the Union army. Four months later, Congress endorsed Butler's policy in the First Confiscation Act.

Aware that Federal forces were their ticket to freedom, slaves began fleeing to Union troops whenever they approached nearby. Often they grabbed whatever they could carry, but in this case the refugees were able to use a wagon and horses to convey them to freedom. (Library of Congress)

As the Union forces penetrated into the Confederacy, more and more slaves entered their camps. Many Federal officers objected to the idea of returning slaves, especially to owners in seceded states, and the practice distracted military personnel from their primary duty of suppressing the rebellion. In early 1862, the War Department prohibited the use of soldiers in retrieving slaves. The institution of slavery broke down a bit more.

After the failure of McClellan's campaign against Richmond in mid-1862, Lincoln reevaluated his approach to the war. Recruiting had slowed to a trickle, and the largest untapped resource, African-Americans, was not being exploited. Slavery, moreover, had been the basis of secession, and the enemy had used slaves to help their cause. If the Union planned to prosecute the war fully, it must take slaves away from the Rebels and employ them for the Federal Government, both in and out of uniform. And if Northerners hoped eventually to bring the seceded states back into the Union, they must put that one unsolvable problem, slavery, on the road to extinction. Lincoln determined to issue an emancipation proclamation and to recruit blacks as soldiers.

For these controversial decisions, the President had tacit support from Congress. On July 17, 1862, Congress passed the Second Confiscation Act, which authorized the President to confiscate all slaves of Rebels. That same day, Congress adopted the Militia Act, which permitted Lincoln to employ African-Americans for any military duties that he believed they were competent to perform. Lincoln also justified emancipation by his powers as commander in chief. Slaves aided the Rebel war effort. Surely he could deprive them of their use. As it turned out, Lincoln decided to await the next major Union victory, which did not occur until September 1862 at Antietam, before issuing the proclamation. But that summer, he began bringing African-Americans into uniform.

The first black soldiers came from a New Orleans militia unit, the 1st Louisiana Native Guards. The Native Guards had black company-grade officers and even a black major. In January 1863, the Union recruited the first black regiment from scratch, the 1st South Carolina (Colored) Infantry, later called the 33rd US Colored Infantry, with all white officers.

OVERLEAF:
The Andersonville Stockade, the most notorious of Civil War prison camps. It was originally planned to hold 10,000 but it was home to more than three times that number which resulted in severe overcrowding, sanitary problems, and disease. (Anne S. K. Brown Military Collection, Brown University Library)

The idea of putting blacks in uniform was extremely controversial. To increase the policy's acceptability, the administration sought competent whites to command these soldiers. By the end of the war, well over 7,000 whites had received commissions in the United States Colored Troops, while only 125 or so blacks were made officers.

Although black abolitionist Frederick Douglass and others promised that blacks would make excellent soldiers, it was essential for these first regiments to fight well. And they did. At Port Hudson, the 1st and 3rd Louisiana Native Guards charged Confederate works valiantly, and suffered heavy losses. After a *New York Times* newspaperman witnessed the attack, the paper declared, "It is no longer possible to doubt the bravery and steadiness of the colored race, when rightly led."

In June 1863, black soldiers participated in a brutal fight at Milliken's Bend, Louisiana. The black regiments had only a few days of training and many had never fired their rifles. In a vicious assault by overwhelming Confederate numbers, the white soldiers fled but the black troops stood fast. Even though they could not reload and fire effectively, they fought hand to hand and ultimately repulsed the Rebels. One black regiment suffered the highest percentage of men killed in a single battle for the entire war. "I never more wish to hear the expression, 'The niggers wont fight,'" proclaimed a white officer in the fight.

The final event that secured a place for black soldiers was the intrepid assault by the 54th Massachusetts (Colored) Infantry on Fort Wagner, South

Carolina, on July 19, 1863. The 54th was the brainchild of the governor of Massachusetts, and it was raised in the North with tremendous publicity. Abolitionists or their sons served as officers. Among the enlisted ranks were two of Douglass's sons. Its colonel, Robert Gould Shaw, volunteered the regiment to spearhead the attack on the fort that helped to guard Charleston harbor. Against a withering fire, the 54th carried up to and into the fort, yet, ultimately, the defenders repulsed them. Among the 40 percent casualties that the 54th suffered was its commander, Shaw, whom Rebels gleefully announced was "buried with his niggers." For the second time, newspapermen witnessed the attack, and the battle received extensive coverage in the North.

Having proved their worth on the battlefield, black soldiers began to convert detractors in and out of the army into supporters. By the end of the war, almost 179,000 blacks had served in the Union army and another 20,000 had enlisted in the navy. Military service was a thrilling event in their lives, especially for former slaves. "I felt like a man," recalled one black soldier, "with a uniform on and a gun in my hand." It gave blacks, free and slave, a sense of belonging to the United States.

Black soldiers and sailors fought to destroy slavery and restore the Union, and they hoped that a grateful nation would reward them for their devotion by giving them full and equal rights in the postwar world. Their sense of commitment sustained them through extensive discrimination by the Union army and acts of brutality, such as the Fort Pillow massacre in Tennessee, by Confederates.

At peak, one in every eight Union soldiers was black; the percentage of black sailors was even higher. Black troops fought on 41 major battlefields and in 449 minor engagements. Sixteen soldiers and seven sailors received Medals of Honor for valor. Some 37,000 blacks in an army uniform gave their lives, and untold sailors did, too. Lincoln paid them high compliments when he declared that black soldiers fought as well as whites, and that their service was indispensable to victory. "Keep it and you can save the Union," he wrote. "Throw it away, and the Union goes with it."

Perhaps the greatest tribute to black soldiers, though, was paid by their opponents. Desperate for manpower, the Confederacy narrowly elected to enlist its own black soldiers in the waning months of the war. Critical in the adoption of the policy was a statement from General Robert E. Lee, in which he argued that the Union had employed black troops with success and he believed they would make "efficient soldiers."

Prisoners of war

In a strange way, both Grant's Vicksburg campaign and the recruitment of black soldiers negatively influenced conditions in Civil War prison camps. Neither the Union nor the Confederacy had prepared well for the massive influx of prisoners that occurred in the last two years of the war. In the first year, only a small number of soldiers were captured. Numbers escalated in the second year of fighting, and both governments threw up prison camps until they could exchange them. In 1863, however, this exchange broke down. Confederates refused to treat black soldiers and their white officers as prisoners of war, insisting that former slaves return into bondage and their officers be prosecuted for inciting servile insurrection. The unwillingness of Confederates to include black troops in any exchange program dissolved the cartel. Confederates, moreover, declared the paroles issued by Grant to Rebel soldiers at Vicksburg invalid and placed quite a number of these parolees back in the ranks without exchanging them properly. In protest, the Federal Government refused to swap prisoners, and for much of the next two years, the number of prisoners on both sides mounted.

Since no one anticipated the breakdown of the cartel, the huge influx of captives from the 1863 and 1864 campaigns caught them unprepared. The Confederates, for example, erected Andersonville because they feared the Union army might overrun the camp on the James River in Virginia. They chose the Andersonville location for its isolation. Originally laid out on 16 acres (6.5ha) for 10,000 prisoners, they eventually expanded it to 26 acres (10.5ha). Ultimately, Andersonville served as the home for 45,000 Union soldiers, with a peak number at 33,000. Amid the filth, congestion, lack of shelter, and poor water supply, some 13,000 died there.

Large Federal prison camps existed at Point Lookout, Maryland; Elmira, New York; Camp Chase, Ohio; and Johnson's Island, Illinois. Although Elmira earned the worst reputation among Confederate prisoners, the conditions there were better than at Andersonville. Elmira housed less than a third of the number of inmates on over 60 percent more acreage. The Union also erected barracks to shelter the inmates from the brutal cold of a Central New York winter. Still, Elmira had a staggering 24 percent death rate for Rebel soldiers incarcerated there.

No doubt, more intelligent planning and effort on both sides would have alleviated much of the misery in these camps. Of the 195,000 Union prisoners of war, more than 30,000 died. Federals held 215,000 Confederates, 26,000 of whom perished. Nor did these figures include all those who endured severe or chronic ailments from prolonged hardships and exposure. Yet despite postwar accusations, neither the Union nor the Confederacy deliberately intended to inflict horrible suffering on their captives. Rebel prison camps tended to be worse than Federal pens, but Confederate soldiers fared worse than Yankees. If the Confederacy struggled to feed and clothe its own fighting men, it should have surprised no one that its prisoners would fare poorly.

PORTRAIT OF A SOLDIER: WILLIAM WILBUR EDGERTON

"What storyes I shall have to tell when I get home," announced Private William Wilbur Edgerton to his mother. Born and reared in Central New York, the third of four children to Dorothy Doud and John Leffingwell Edgerton, Wilbur had enlisted in the 107th New York Volunteer Infantry illegally in July 1862, just one month shy of his 17th birthday.

From a tender young age, Wilbur had been on his own. His father was a ne'er do well who wandered about, searching for success and happiness, never to find it. Wilbur's two older sisters married, and his mother, financially abandoned, took the youngest boy to Sparta, Wisconsin, where she had friends. Wilbur had bonded well with his mother, recalling, "When I was a little boy, I tought nothing was so nice as to sit on mothers lap and I have not exatly [gotten] over that."

The best thing that ever happened to him, he believed, was being thrown out to his own devices at such an early age. Wilbur started kicking around at various jobs at 12 – fiddle playing, a cooper, a farm hand, a factory worker, and then a blacksmith. Neither fiddling nor work as a cooper paid much, so he took on employment with a farmer. When the man ripped him off of nearly half his pay, he stormed off and entered factory labor. Wilbur left that to apprentice with a blacksmith, which at the time offered a much better career track. "Blacksmithing is black work," he conveyed to his mother in racially charged language common in that day, "but it brings white money so I dont care." Unfortunately, the blacksmith's explosive temper and vulgar ways convinced him to quit. He then linked up with another blacksmith; this time a good, decent man.

Edgerton enlisted for the simple reason that everyone kept asking him why he did not soldier. He was a young man, without family, in good health, and because he had been on his own so long, everyone assumed he was older than he really was. "I made up my mind that it was my duty to fight for my country and I did so," Edgerton justified.

Just two and a half months after the regiment was formed, the 107th New York "saw the elephant" in the single bloodiest day of the war, at Antietam in Maryland. Lee had raided into Maryland, but his plans fell into Federal hands. When Union forces moved more aggressively against him than he anticipated, Lee retreated to the north bank of the Potomac River, near a town called Sharpsburg and a creek named Antietam. On the morning of September 17, 1862, the 107th advanced through the North Woods and into the timber, where they came under fire for the first time. As they rushed into the East Woods, a Rebel volley struck down men on either side of Edgerton. You "have no idea what it is to be a souldier off in a strang country whare your comrades are a dieing off fast and no[t] noing how soon before your time will come," he explained to his younger brother. In the course of passing through the woods, "I run over a good maney ded and wounded *Rebels*."

A couple of hours later, the 107th advanced to protect an artillery battery. "The balls flew around my head like hail stones and sounded like a swarm of bees," he described to his brother. "O Johney I tell you that you can have no conception of the thouths [thoughts] that run through a mans head about thouse times it made a man think of the good and the bad things that he ever did in his life. I know my head was full of thoughts." People who had been in combat had tried to prepare him for it, but the experience was nothing like anything he had ever witnessed. "I have heard it said that after the first volley that you forged [forget] all the dainger," he elaborated. "Unless a man is scart out of his rite sences he knowes what is going on as well as he did at first." Still, combat affected him. "I know that my flesh tickeld and flinched all the time expecting to feel a ball pierce it."

Two days later, his regiment had to cross over the hotly contested battlefield in pursuit of the Rebels. "Sutch a odor (politely speaking) I never heard tell of *nor ever do I want smell it again*," he confessed. "The dead layed in heaps well it made me so sick that I had to fall out and laydown beside the road." Despite this vivid depiction, the young private felt he had failed to convey a true sense of the experience. "It is no usee," he insisted, "woords have not enuf meening."

In mid-1863, the 107th New York fought in two of the greatest battles of the war, Chancellorsville and Gettysburg, and Edgerton was right in the thick of them. At Chancellorsville, Confederate General Stonewall Jackson launched a brilliant flank attack that rolled up the Union XI Corps and threatened the rear of the XII, to which the 107th was assigned. In the course of the fighting, Edgerton had his percussion cap box shot off, and a Rebel ball passed through his cap. "I wouldent sware that I kiled aney body," he admitted to his father, "but I am prety shore that a good maney were hit buy me fore the most of the time they were not more than 10 or 15 rods [55–82½ yards; 50–75m] off and I know that I can hit a hat 20 rods off every time for I have tride it so you can judg for your self."

At Gettysburg two months later, the battle was "as hard if not harder than aney other that I have been in." At one point, a shell fragment knocked his rifle right out of his hand. Having fought in several major battles, Edgerton had begun to develop some seasoning in combat. "I mad[e] up my mind that if *they* wanted me to stop fighting *hit me* fir they couldent *scare* me aney," he told his mother after Gettysburg.

Just before Antietam, his best friend, John Wiggins, deserted, only to return under Lincoln's amnesty the next April. Edgerton helped his friend, who had a family at home, by lending him money, but he would never have entertained that kind of conduct himself. "I dont care about fighting," he confessed after Chancellorsville. "I would willingly give all I am *worth* and a *good deal more if I had it to be out of this scrape*, but never the less I am no *coward* and I *never* will *disgrace* the *name* of *Edgerton* by *desertion* or *Sneeking* out of *danger* like some have."

That fall of 1863, after the Union disaster at Chickamauga, the War Department transferred the XI and XII Corps under Major-General Joseph Hooker to Chattanooga. It was an extraordinary logistical achievement; Edgerton and his comrades endured the "rufiest rideing" and a derailment, but they made it in time to witness the rout of Bragg's army. For a change, the

107th saw little action, but the regiment's arrival marked a dramatic change for its men. Not until the war's end would they return to Virginia. They soon became part of the Western Army, with the XI and XII merged to form the XX Corps under Hooker.

Because of his service in both theaters, Edgerton offered some valuable insights into the way that the enemy fought. Federal commanders, he noticed, preserved the lives of their men better by placing greater emphasis on artillery fire. The Rebels, with inferior artillery, compensated with aggressive infantry. "There is one thing that our goverment does that suits me to a dot," he instructed his mother, "that is we fight mostly with Artillery, The Rebls fight mostly with Infantry. They fight as though a mans life was not worth one sent or in other words with desperration." He also believed that the western Rebels did not fight as well as Lee's troops. Around Chattanooga, he knew that the Federals confronted what he described as two-fifths of Lee's army, including two of Longstreet's divisions, "the best fighting men the World ever saw." Weeks after the Union crushed Bragg's army without Longstreet's troops present, Edgerton measured the performance of Confederate eastern and western troops and concluded, "The rebels in this country are not such fighting men as they are in Va. [Virginia]."

The hardships of campaigning and general military service wore him out, yet he refused to let them drag his morale down too far. "Oh if I ever do get home I know I will enjoy myself," he vowed to his mother. "You will never hear me grumble." Food was always substandard. He estimated to his sister that rain-soaked clothes, blankets, and knapsacks weighed about 100lb (45kg), and that a soldier on the march hauled a woolen blanket, a rubber blanket, a change of underclothes, a tent, a knapsack, three days' rations, a belt, and a rifle. In addition to combat, everyday duty exacted quite a toll from the men. As Edgerton walked guard duty in rain, high winds, and hail, "I would satisfy my self buy saing, that it was all for the *union*."

As he traveled more and more throughout the South, the New Yorker gained greater exposure to the institution of slavery. "It looks horrible," he wrote his mother. He detested the idea of people held in bondage, some of whom were as white as he was. Slavery, he felt, made Southern whites somewhat lazy. "I am and always was an Abolitionist," he claimed, "and I guess I am on the right side."

That spring, 1864, the Union army under the overall leadership of Grant determined to press the Confederates on every front, with the two major operations targeting Richmond and Atlanta. As campaign season approached, Edgerton did not want to go forward, but duty compelled him to do so. "Of course we dont like to fight but then, if nesesary, why, there is no body knows how aney better than we do," he elaborated to his mother. "I shant expose myself unnesisaryly, neither shall I shirk from doing my duty as a soldier." Just before the campaign opened, he and Wiggins had their photograph taken together. "I dont feel very patriotic this morning for we

Sherman's troops foraging in South Carolina. William Edgerton must have been successful at foraging for his food since he reported to his mother, "some have went hungry for a long time but Will has had plenty to eat." (*Battles and Leaders of the Civil War*)

have got to march to morrow to the frunt & I dont want to go," he admitted to his brother. But go he did.

Sherman had to maintain continual contact with the Rebel army under Johnston, to prevent wide flank attacks or the movement of reinforcements elsewhere, while at the same time enabling the Federals to turn the Confederates from their defensive positions. As a result, Edgerton and his comrades remained under fire nearly the entire campaign, occupying positions anywhere from 200 to 500 yards (180–450m) away. In the fight at Dallas on May 28, 1864, Edgerton declared it "the hottest plase I was ever in" – strong words from someone who had fought in the thick of battle at Antietam, Chancellorsville, and Gettysburg. His regiment lost 168 men that day. Throughout June, he reported numerous close calls. "I have again been preserved from the leden missles of death, while so maney of my comrades have fallen," he alerted his mother in late June. After assessing the hardships of the campaign, he announced, "It is a wounder [wonder] to me that I am alive."

On June 14, a cocky Wilbur Edgerton notified his mother, "The rebls here dont know how to fight & they never will." Less than two months later, a Confederate sharpshooter drilled him in the right shoulder with a minie ball outside Atlanta. Edgerton went to the field hospital, where he recovered in short order and returned to his command, just in time to participate in the fall of Atlanta. When Sherman swung his army to the southwest of the city, to sever the last open rail connections, he left the XX Corps to guard his own railroad supply line. As Hood vacated the city, the Federals pushed into Atlanta, with the 107th among the first to enter. "Atlanta is ours," Edgerton crowed to his mother, knowing full well the consequences of that victory.

Throughout the Atlanta campaign, the upcoming presidential election seldom strayed far from the minds of Edgerton and his comrades. Nearly all of them supported Lincoln's reelection bid, even if they were too young to vote, as was Edgerton. "Our army is full of animation, patriotism &c. [etc.]," he assessed to his mother in early July. "[We] have a determination to settle this war before next Presidential election for fear of copperhead being elected." He predicted, "if Lincoln is reelected next fall the War will end." Several weeks later, he announced, "I am for the administration as it is & for an unconditional surrender or extermination of the rebles." The fall of Atlanta virtually assured that reelection. Still, he pledged his commitment to the Union and all for which it stood. "I would die far sooner than have it destroyed," he wrote.

By mid-November 1864, Edgerton and the other 65,000 men in Sherman's two armies had begun their lengthy trek to Savannah. The 107th passed through Milledgeville, the capital of Georgia, where some men held mock proceedings and left the capitol building a mess. Foraging parties gathered food and fodder from the countryside, while soldiers wrecked railroads and anything else of military value. By Christmas time, they had seized Savannah.

Throughout the Georgia campaign and the occupation duty in Savannah, Edgerton expanded his contacts with Southern women. Generally, he had few problems. Their penchant for chewing tobacco disgusted him, and he felt they lacked the intellectual snap of Northern women, but if Union soldiers behaved properly, they responded with respect. In Savannah, they sold meals and other items to soldiers, and the interactions were quite informative. Most Southern white women supported the rebellion, Edgerton thought, because they believed the Federal army would take away their slaves, which of course was true. "Now that they are going to lose their niggers they dont know what to do," he explained.

In late January 1865, after a much-needed rest, the army set out once again, this time northward for North Carolina, a campaign that proved much more demanding than the march to Savannah. In addition to stronger Confederate opposition, the topography, winter rains, and scarcity of food took a greater toll on Edgerton and his comrades. After a few days in South Carolina, he announced, "This country is nothing but swamps, swamps, swamps." Along the way, he saw old, worn-out plantations overgrown by woods and underbrush. Although his regiment marched around Columbia, he passed through Fayetteville, North Carolina, which housed a major Confederate arsenal. There, he assessed the campaign as "the hardest of the war." Throughout South Carolina, the troops had to forage for their food in a land of scattered farms and plantations. "Some have went hungry for a long time," he commented to his mother, "but Will has had plenty to eat." At Averasborough, North Carolina, the 107th exchanged shots with the Rebels, suffering 27 men wounded. The only other men the regiment lost in the Carolinas campaign were 19 foragers whom Confederate cavalry and guerrillas captured.

Several days after the army reached Goldsboro, North Carolina, Edgerton announced to his mother, "I am so sick of soldering that my patriotism is below par." Fortunately, the war did not last much longer. In April, Sherman's army advanced, and just as

This is the scene of the Battle of New Hope Church, or Dallas, in late May 1864 during the Atlanta campaign. Private Wilbur Edgerton, a veteran of Antietam, Chancellorsville, and Gettysburg, declared it "the hottest plase I was ever in." (Library of Congress)

quickly it halted for negotiations. By the end of the month, the Confederates had surrendered, and the 107th New York began its march for Washington, DC. On May 24, it proudly participated in the Grand Review along Pennsylvania Avenue, with the President, Grant, Sherman, and others in attendance. Three and a half weeks later, Wilbur Edgerton had purchased a new suit of civilian clothes and began work in a store. He received an honorable discharge on June 18, 1865.

In the years after the war, Edgerton tried his hand at a variety of occupations. He graduated from medical school and practiced in Kansas and Missouri. Eventually, he gave that up for jobs as a merchant and a banker in Wheeling, Missouri. The father of three children, he became a prominent member of the community, even serving as mayor of the town. Fittingly, he died on Armistice Day (now called Veteran's Day), November 11, 1931.

PORTRAIT OF A CIVILIAN: EMMA LeCONTE

"Reunion! Good Heavens!" exclaimed 17-year-old Emma LeConte about the prospects of peace with those vandals, the Yankees. "How we hate [them] with the whole strength and depth of our souls."

Born in Georgia and raised in Columbia, South Carolina, Emma was the daughter of a science professor at the College of South Carolina, later renamed the University of South Carolina. From this privileged background, she received a world-class education for a young woman in her day. Her upbringing bound her intricately to the cultural trappings of Southern society, and her youthful and unyielding passion for the Confederacy reflected broad sentiments among the well-to-do people in South Carolina.

Just a handful of blocks away from her home on campus grounds, South Carolinians celebrated secession from the Union. Emma recalled with delight the moment she and her neighbors learned that Fort Sumter had capitulated. They were seated in her father's library when the bell at the marketplace clanged, announcing a momentous event. Everyone rushed outside, where they heard the news. "The whole town was in joyful tumult," she described. Men rushed off to war. Women filled the void in all sorts of ways and contributed to the war effort by supporting the cause, caring for the ill and injured, and enduring any sacrifice necessary for victory.

Emma never doubted the justice of the Confederate cause. Despite her exceptional education in mathematics, science, French, German, philosophy, literature, and history, she did not challenge the notions that blacks were inferior beings and that slavery benefited the African race. The Northern states threatened to undermine the institution of slavery and impose themselves and their ideas on the Southern people. No self-respecting individual, no free person, could justly endure such a humiliation. The North attempted to enslave them, and Southern whites dissolved their connection to the Union. God and justice – inseparably intertwined in her mind and those of fellow secessionists – were on their side.

But by the end of 1864, the prospects looked bleak. Lee and his valiant army had locked in a life-and-death struggle outside Petersburg and Richmond. Sherman's army had swept through Georgia, leaving desolation in its wake. Savannah had capitulated. And "Sherman the brute avows his intention of converting South Carolina into a wilderness," she feared.

Even before the Federal army turned northward, it threatened Emma's family. Her 15-year-old sister Sallie, her aunt, and two cousins resided on a plantation 25 miles (40km) south of Savannah. In December, Emma's father, who worked during much of the war for the Nitre and Mining Bureau, embarked on a lengthy trek to find and bring them back to Columbia. While she waited, reports reached her ears on the conditions in Georgia. How would they survive without provisions, she wondered. In her diary, she worried over "how dreadfully they must have been frightened." With her father traveling into harm's way, the thought of his death instilled a sense of terror in her. By February 7, 1865, he had brought them all back to Columbia, but in doing so, he had unwittingly moved them from an area beyond Sherman's swath to a primary target.

The war had taken its toll on the LeConte family's quality of life, too. Although they were well off financially, skyrocketing inflation, a relatively tight Union blockade, and limited supplies forced them to cut back drastically. The family ate two meals a day. They had two plates of bread for breakfast, usually made from corn meal. Dinner consisted of a small piece of beef, some corn bread, potatoes, and hominy. Fortunately, they had two cows that furnished milk and butter. "We have no reason to Complain," Emma noted, "so many families are so much worse off."

Her clothing, too, had declined in quality and quantity. She wore homespun undergarments, more coarse than they gave to slaves in prewar times. She knitted her own stockings, and a pair of heavy calfskin shoes covered her feet. Emma owned two calico dresses and a black and white plaid homespun for everyday use. She also had a few old silk outfits from prewar days which were wearing out rapidly. Those she saved for special occasions.

Each January, the community women held a bazaar at the state house to raise money for the care of soldiers. Emma helped arrange the booths. Despite the wartime shortages, the decorations looked elegant and the tables were loaded with niceties that slipped through the blockade. Cakes, sweets, and other items sold at exorbitant prices. One large doll went for $2,000. Her astonished uncle commented, "Why one could buy a live negro baby for that!" In the three previous years, the bazaar had lasted two weeks. Within four days, though, it closed because of Sherman's advance into South Carolina.

Since early January, Emma had feared for the loss of Columbia. "The horrible picture is constantly before my mind," she confessed in her diary, yet she refused to evacuate the city. By the time they closed the bazaar, everyone felt the city was doomed. The Confederacy had no viable force to oppose the

Yankee march. Mounting anxiety reached such a peak that Emma, who always found great solace in her books, could no longer concentrate when she tried to read. The War Department ordered her father to pack up the Nitre Laboratory and move it out of danger, which left Emma, her two younger sisters, her mother, and the household slaves to brave it together.

Distant cannon booms alerted locals to the approaching bluecoats. People panicked throughout the city. Crowds, trying to flee from Sherman's path, tangled in traffic snarls. Others, like Emma, awaited the onslaught with no clear picture of how awful it would be. All those tales of brutality and destruction by Sherman's troops played on their imagination. Two days before they reached the city, Emma's sister sobbed hysterically all morning. The next day, they presented a composed front, but "our souls are sick with anxiety." When Union shells fell into the city, the family hunkered down in the basement. Emma felt nauseous and faint. Her mother, who had held together all that time, broke down in utter terror when she heard gunfire in the streets.

Once the Rebel cavalrymen evacuated, the shooting died down. There was a calm, and then Emma could hear shouts and finally, some Yankee troops raised the Stars and Stripes over the state capitol. "Oh, what a horrid sight," she wrote, that "hateful symbol of despotism." Emma could not look upon the Yankees without "horror and hatred, loathing and disgust."

That evening, the wind picked up, and by nightfall fires had begun to spread throughout the city. Smoldering cotton bales ignited by Rebel cavalrymen and fanned by the high winds initiated the blaze, but Union troops, drunk on alcohol or intoxicated by their success, and fueled by their hatred of South Carolina, the hotbed of secession and in their minds the cause of this unholy rebellion, spread the flames. "Imagine night turned into noonday," described Emma in her journal, so bright and extensive were the fires. With hospitals that housed Union and Confederate soldiers nearby, the LeConte home escaped the ravages. Others – men and women, elderly and infant alike – did not. Except for a handful of clothing and a few morsels of food, they escaped with only their lives. The flames consumed everything else.

The inferno destroyed a third of the city, including much of the heart of old Columbia. Charred brick walls and scorched chimney stacks were all that remained of entire city blocks. Several days after the Federal army left, Emma wandered about the town. Only a foundation and chimney remained from the old state house, where just a month earlier she had witnessed such gaiety at the bazaar. At the market, she saw the old bell, nicknamed "secessia," which had chimed as South Carolina and each succeeding state seceded. Now it lay half buried amid the ashes.

Emma's father escaped. He and another official narrowly avoided capture and, after enduring considerable hardships, worked their way back home. His appearance lifted her spirits tremendously.

To feed the people, Sherman left 500 scraggly head of cattle. While many slaves took off with the Federals, quite a number stayed behind, and refugees from outlying areas flocked to the city for sustenance. Government officials, Emma's father among them, traveled far and wide in search of food to supplement the cows. Each day, Emma drew some rancid salt pork or stringy beef and a pint of corn meal as rations.

Even though Federal troops had marched right through her state, and were at least partially responsible for the destruction of much of their city (Emma, like most locals, blamed Sherman exclusively), Emma remained defiant. She so detested the Yankees, and believed so strongly in the righteousness of the cause, that she could not imagine a just God would allow the Federals to win. She had no confidence in Johnston, who was restored to command. When she learned he had fallen back to Raleigh, North Carolina, Emma predicted that he would retreat all the way to Lee, who "may put a stop to his retrograde movement." All her faith rested in Lee and his army, "an army that has never suffered defeat, a contrast to the Western army." When word of Lee's surrender arrived, she was so overwhelmed that, "there seemed no ground under my feet." She resisted to the last, but Jefferson Davis's capture and the surrender of all western troops brought an end to her dreams. Her only consolation was the assassination of Abraham Lincoln, which elicited cheers from her and her family and friends.

In the immediate aftermath of the war, occupation soldiers irritated Emma, and the prospect of black soldiers overseeing them outraged her. Dreams of emigration to a different land or hopes that the next generation could wage a more successful war nourished her spirit.

Emma's father moved the family to California, where he taught at the University of California. Emma remained east. She married a Citadel cadet who entered the army with his classmates. They settled on a 1,000-acre (400ha) farm. Emma bore two girls. When the older daughter was 12, Emma's husband died. Not surprisingly, Emma ran the farm on her own and still managed to raise and educate her daughters.

This is a photograph taken by George N. Barnard of the ruins of Columbia, South Carolina, from the capitol. Emma LeConte walked past this place regularly and described the destruction all around it. (NARA)

HOW THE WAR ENDED: PEACE IS DECLARED

On March 27 and 28, 1865, Sherman visited Lincoln, Grant, and Porter at City Point. After his long travels, Sherman regaled them with tales of the trek. But this was not all fun. Grant and Sherman discussed the closing campaign, and Lincoln instructed both officers on the terms of surrender they could offer.

Before Sherman had reached North Carolina, Grant had turned Lee out of his defenses around Petersburg. Both Union generals were wary that Lee would somehow unite with Johnston and attack Sherman. With 100,000 troops, Sherman felt confident he could withstand any onslaught, but he accelerated the pace of replenishing his supplies to get his army into the field as soon as possible. The march against Johnston began on April 10, and within two days, he learned that Lee had surrendered to Grant on the 9th. His army celebrated wildly.

Johnston had hoped that Lee could elude Grant and unite with him. While his army waited to see the results of Lee's desperate move, Johnston gathered with President Davis and other cabinet members at Greensboro, North Carolina. During the meeting, they received confirmation of the rumors that Lee had surrendered. Davis urged them to keep fighting, but Johnston announced his opposition. The people were whipped and his army was deserting in large numbers. The war was over.

With Davis's reluctant consent, Johnston contacted Sherman to open negotiations for peace. On April 17, the two generals who had opposed each other in Mississippi, in Georgia, and again in North Carolina, assembled at the home of James and Nancy Bennett, not far from Durham Station. On April 18, Sherman, forceful in war and soft in peace, offered Johnston mild terms that clearly overstepped his bounds. He permitted Confederate soldiers to take their arms home and deposit them at state capitals; he recognized state governments, restored the franchise, and said nothing of emancipation.

Had Lincoln been president, he no doubt would have corrected his general's excessive generosity. By then, however, an assassin named John Wilkes Booth had shot and killed him, an event which occurred on April 14. At the moment when Sherman's terms arrived, Washington officials were in near hysteria. The new President, Andrew Johnson, and the cabinet unanimously rejected the terms, and Secretary of War Stanton intimated in a letter published in the *New York Times* that Sherman was a traitor.

Grant volunteered to resolve the problem. President Johnson directed Grant to supersede Sherman, but Grant refused to insult his friend that way. He traveled down to North Carolina with little fanfare and instructed Sherman to offer the same terms as he gave Lee, that they would stack arms and sign paroles, and as long as they behaved themselves and obeyed the laws, the Rebels could live undisturbed by Federal authorities. The two wrangled a bit, but Johnston, confronted with the reality of a collapsed war effort, signed on April 26.

On April 12, Union forces under Major-General E. R. S. Canby had battled their way into Mobile. For two years, Grant had sought its capture, and as Grant ruefully noted, it finally happened when its fall meant nothing. Two weeks after Sherman and Johnston concluded the surrender agreement, Union cavalrymen captured Confederate President Jefferson Davis in Georgia. By May 26, General Edmund Kirby Smith had surrendered the Rebel forces in the trans-Mississippi west. The war was over.

CONCLUSION AND CONSEQUENCES – UNITED STATES

The Union army demobilized in rapid order, from one million strong at the end of the war to 80,000 men a year later. Yankee soldiers returned to their rendezvous point, received back pay, signed documents, and were officially mustered out of service. Others viewed the delay as another ridiculous government policy and simply walked home. Several decades later, when they applied for veterans' pensions, that decision proved nettlesome.

Confederate soldiers simply headed home. Men who owned their horses were allowed to take them. Some received railroad transportation as far it would take them, which in the aftermath of Sherman's marches was not usually very far. For the men from Texas, it took up to two months to make it back home.

Scholars and military experts have posited a host of reasons why the Confederacy lost. Immediately after the war, a prominent Virginia journalist and numerous military leaders blamed Southern defeat on Jefferson Davis's incapacity as commander-in-chief. Hatred of Davis motivated most of these early critics. Later scholars who attributed Rebel defeat to Davis lacked the hatred of that earlier generation. They derived their criticism of Davis largely by comparing him with Lincoln. Yet all American presidents pale whenever they are juxtaposed with Lincoln, and recent military historians and biographers of Davis have demonstrated clearly that, despite some weaknesses, Davis was certainly a competent commander-in-chief. Other students of the Civil War

The End of the Rebellion in the United States. (Anne S. K. Brown Military Collection, Brown University Library)

have argued that internal dissension undid the Confederacy, or that Southern whites lost the will to resist. But by comparison, dissension in the North was at least as powerful, and every nation that suffers a defeat ultimately loses the will to continue the fight.

In more recent years, some scholars have embraced the idea that the Confederacy should have adopted a guerrilla war. Brigadier-General Edward Porter Alexander, perhaps the most thoughtful young officer in the Confederacy, proposed the idea to Robert E. Lee in the waning days of the war. At the time, Lee rejected it, insisting that the Confederacy had borne the battle for four long years, and a guerrilla war would only extend and increase the suffering on both sides, with no real benefit. Nonetheless, a handful of historians have challenged Lee's assessment as faulty. They draw on the partisan success of the Rebels in the American Revolutionary War, and the triumph of North Vietnam against the United States in the 1960s and 1970s. These scholars point out how vexing the guerrilla war was in Missouri, and how much difficulty the Federal army encountered in trying to protect Unionists in Tennessee and Kentucky.

Each of these views, however, suffers from serious flaws. During the War of Independence, partisans in the South performed successfully because they served in conjunction with traditional armies. Nathanael Greene and his Continentals fought alongside the guerrillas, and George Washington in New York and later Virginia commanded a standing army. In contrast to the American Revolutionary War, which was fought in a pre-industrial era, warfare in an industrial age requires mass production, either by the nations at war or by sponsor nations that provide it to them. When a nation adopts guerrilla warfare, it exposes its people and land to enemy invasion, thereby endangering its ability to produce munitions and other materiel that are necessary for war. Vietnam received massive support from the Soviet Union and the People's Republic of China; the Southern Confederacy had no such patron. In Vietnam, moreover, the United States imposed restrictions on where its ground troops could advance. No massive ground invasion took place in North Vietnam, and the United States only blocked supply shipments by water in the late stages of the war. During the Civil War, the Confederacy was the primary battleground, and an ever-tightening blockade, working in conjunction with land troops, had choked off imports to the Confederacy almost completely by 1865.

Selected scholars have argued that the difficulty of quelling the guerrilla war in Missouri and Tennessee demonstrates just how effective it could have been on a larger scale. But two factors undercut that assertion. First, Missouri remained in the Union, and an overwhelming percentage of its people opposed the Confederacy. Three of every four men from Missouri who entered the army donned the Union blue. Federal authorities had to deal with the people of Missouri respectfully, because so many supported the Union. Tennessee also had a strong pro-Union contingent, especially in the eastern part of the state. In other seceding states, Federals had no reason to protect the people, except for pockets of hill-country Unionists.

Second, by the late stages of the war, the Union had begun to adopt the raiding strategy, which targeted civilians and property, along with soldiers in the field, as the enemy. This was ideally suited to crushing guerrilla activities by destroying or confiscating property and making life a hell for Confederate civilians and soldiers alike. As Emma LeConte recorded in her diary, when her Uncle John, a prisoner of war, discussed the possibility of guerrilla fighting with a soldier in Sherman's army, the Yankee replied, "Well, I hope the South won't do anything of that kind, for of course in that event we would not spare or respect your women." Beneath his bluster, the soldier's comments suggested both the hardened nature of Union troops and their growing callousness toward Southern civilians. They possessed just the right attitude to combat guerrillas.

National approaches to war are products of social structure, economy, technology, and culture. Confederate whites were a propertied people, who seceded from the Union in order to protect what Mississippi called "the greatest material interest of the world." Their constitution attempted to secure two elements of that society, white persons and property, and they entered military service to defend both of those elements. A guerrilla war policy would have exposed their families and that property to Federal destruction or abuse, a strategy that would have undercut the very reasons for a Southern Confederacy. And by drawing food and supplies from the Southern people, while at the same time exposing their homes and property to Union destruction, Confederate guerrillas would have alienated them from the cause as well.

In organizing for war, Confederates drew on what they perceived as the Southern military tradition. They aspired to build armies along Washington's model, which would exploit martial aspects of Southern character and establish for the Confederacy a credibility with other nations of the world that guerrilla forces would not. Their heritage, secessionists believed, would more than compensate for any manpower advantages that the Union possessed.

When asked some years afterward why the Confederates lost at Gettysburg, George Pickett replied, "I think the Yankees had something to do it with." That same argument best explains why the Confederacy lost the war. For all the sacrifices, for all the losses, for all the hardships, for all the narrow defeats, the Confederacy simply could not overcome the Union. Internal strife, patchy leadership, and many other factors hindered its war effort. The same, of course, could be argued for the Yankees. But in the end, the Union defeated the Confederacy; the Confederacy did not defeat itself.

Many scholars believe that the Union won because of overwhelming numbers, what one scholar has called "the heaviest battalions." There is truth to the North's preponderance of strength. Federals employed over two million soldiers, while the Confederacy mustered close to 900,000. Despite having one million men in uniform at once, the Northern states grew enough food to feed civilians and soldiers and still market huge amounts overseas. By the end of the war, the Union had over 700 navy vessels, many of them ironclads; the Confederacy had almost none. From November 1862 to late October 1863, the Union army purchased from Northern factories as many field artillery guns as the Confederacy's principal producer, Tredegar Iron Works, manufactured in the entire war. That same year, the Federal Ordnance Department bought over 1,400,000 artillery rounds and 260 million small-arms cartridges from Northern munitions makers. For the entire war, the Confederacy produced only 150 million small-arms cartridges, and the Richmond Arsenal, the Confederacy's largest manufacturer, made 921,000 artillery rounds. Nor were these lopsided statistics simply anomalies. The same overwhelming advantages existed in weapons, clothing, and other military accouterments. But as the Vietnam experience demonstrated, overwhelming superiority in equipment, population, and even technology do not assure victory.

Ultimately, three critical factors enabled the Union to win the war. First, it possessed overwhelming resources in population, industrialization, agriculture, and transportation, and a slight edge in technology. Second, the Union benefited from political and military leaders who harnessed those resources, transforming them into military might and focusing that power on the critical aspects of the Confederacy. Finally, the Federals had a home front that remained committed enough to the war to see it through to its conclusion, despite all the losses, hardships, and sacrifices.

What were the consequences of the war? Several were obvious. More than 260,000 Confederate soldiers and over 360,000 Federals died in the war. The preponderance lost their lives to disease. An additional 500,000 suffered wounds, and hundreds of thousands more endured ailments and disabilities from their days in the service. According to the best estimate, the total cost of the Civil War exceeded $20 billion, a figure 31 times larger than the federal government's budget in 1860. In fact, so devastating was the war to the Confederacy that it took some six decades for the Southern states to reach their 1860 level in agricultural productivity.

Once and for all time, the war removed the scourge of slavery from the American landscape. Well over four million African-Americans had been held, sold, and controlled as chattel. The war destroyed that institution. Hundreds of thousands entered Federal lines on their own. Others followed the Union armies to freedom. Still many more waited until the fighting ceased before securing their liberty. Passage and ratification of the Thirteenth Amendment to the US Constitution on January 31, 1866, abolishing slavery forever, made certain that wartime measures freeing slaves could not be overturned in peacetime.

While the achievement of freedom was a wondrous thing for blacks, white society prevented them from exploiting its benefits fully. The Fourteenth Amendment secured citizenship and equal protection and due process of law. The Fifteenth Amendment granted black males the right to vote. But in time, Southern whites resurrected their power and stripped African-Americans of many of their rights. Northerners, tired of war and struggles over power in the South, yielded Southern control to Southern whites. Although African-Americans in the South and the North were better off after the destruction of slavery, it took more than a century for them to achieve their Civil War goal of basic civil rights.

By winning the war, too, the Northern vision of the United States took precedence over the more local, states' rights, agriculturally oriented version of the South. No longer were they states united, but a United States. The federal government established its preponderance over the state governments, a trend that has continued ever since. The nation moved on an accelerated course of industrialization and urbanization. And finally, the Northern version of freedom, with aspirations of egalitarianism and economic opportunity for all, prevailed for white Americans.

Although Southern whites howled over Reconstruction policies, they were under the circumstances quite mild. There were no wholesale land confiscations, no widespread imprisonments, no mass executions for treason. Only Major Henry Wirz, Commandant of Andersonville Prison, was put to death. Among Rebel leaders, Jefferson Davis alone was held in jail for two years, but Northerners never had the stomach for a trial. After his release, Davis lived a long life in the United States. By 1877, the US government had removed all soldiers from the former Confederacy, and the last of the secessionist states had returned as full and equal partners in the Union.

After the war, word circulated that the great Prussian general Helmuth von Moltke had said of Sherman's army that there was nothing one could learn from "an armed mob." When asked about it, Sherman replied that he knew Moltke but never questioned him on the story, "because I did not presume that he was such an ass as to say that."

From a military standpoint, the Civil War offered an extremely valuable legacy for thoughtful analysts. American military leaders realized that rifles, artillery, and field fortifications weighed heavily on the side of defenders. Over the next few decades, United States army officers sought to restore the tactical offensive to warfare through single-line formations with greater dispersion and mobility, to reduce the impact of defensive weapons.

Most European analysts dismissed the war as one conducted by bumbling amateurs. They insisted that breech-loading small arms of the late 1860s made lessons from all previous wars obsolete. In the minds of most foreign experts, the lightning offensives and decisive campaigns of the Austro-Prussian and Franco-Prussian Wars readily cast a dark shadow over any insights into future conflicts from the American Civil War. Yet the Civil War proved more prophetic of the First World War than either of those clashes between European powers. Analysts failed to grasp the enhanced power of the defensive and the value of good field works. They also missed valuable lessons from cavalry serving as mounted infantry, a combination of mobility and firepower that proved so decisive in the Second World War.

Lieutenant-General Philip Sheridan, the hard-charging general who had arrested a corps commander for arriving with his men 12 hours late, observed the Franco-Prussian War from the Prussian side. In a letter to Grant in 1870, he thought that the battles were actually not that distinct from the Civil War, and "that difference is to the credit of our own country." Sheridan believed, "There is nothing to be learned here professionally, but it is a satisfaction to learn that such is the case." He insisted that Europeans could benefit from studying Americans' more effective use of cavalry and rifle pits, better protection of their lines of communication, and more efficient staff departments. By the end of the century, some European officers had extracted valuable lessons from studying the Civil War, particularly tactics, but not enough to anticipate the unparalleled bloodshed in the First World War.

Little more than a month before his death, Lincoln had called for the nation to complete its undertaking and then bind its wounds. Several decades later, survivors on both sides attempted to do just that, to set aside old grudges and to shake hands at several battlefield commemorations. In their youth, they had been touched by fire. By middle and old age, that passion and animus had largely flickered out. And while veterans retained many fond memories, and preferred to emphasize those aspects in their letters and conversations, they never forgot the harsh side of war.

In 1864, an Illinois officer assessed, "There is no God in war. It is merciless, cruel, vindictive, un-christian savage, relentless. It is all that devils could wish for." Few veterans would have disagreed.

FURTHER READING

PRIMARY SOURCES

Alexander, E.P., *Fighting for the Confederacy*, Chapel Hill, NC, 1989.

Basler, R.F. (ed.), *Collected Works of Abraham Lincoln*, 8 vols, New Brunswick, NJ, 1953.

Beatty, J., *The Citizen Soldier; or, Memoirs of a Volunteer*, Cincinnati, OH, 1879.

Berlin, I., and others (eds), *Free at Last: A Documentary History of Slavery, Freedom and the Civil War*, New York, 1992.

Brown, V.D. (ed.), *A Colonel at Gettysburg and Spotsylvania*, Columbia, SC, 1931.

Chesnut, M.B., *A Diary from Dixie*, New York, 1905.

Davis, K.F., *George N. Barnard: Photographer of Sherman's Campaigns*, Kansas City, MI, 1990.

Delbanco, A. (ed.), *The Portable Abraham Lincoln*, New York, 1993.

William W. Edgerton Papers, University of Houston.

Edmondston, C.A.D., *Journal of a Secesh Lady*, Raleigh, NC, 1979.

Grant, U.S., *Personal Memoirs of U. S. Grant*, 2 vols, New York, 1885.

Holt, D., *A Mississippi Rebel in the Army of Northern Virginia*, Baton Rouge, LA, 1995.

Johnson, R.U. and C.C. Buel (eds), *Battles and Leaders of the Civil War*, 4 vols, New York, 1887.

LeConte, J., *'Ware Sherman: A Journal of Three Months' Personal Experience in the Last Days of the Confederacy*, Berkeley, CA, 1938.

Lee, R.E., *The Wartime Papers of R. E. Lee*, Boston, MA, 1961.

McClellan, G.B., *The Civil War Papers of George B McClellan*, New York, 1989.

McClure, A.K. (ed.), *The Annals of the War Written by Leading Participants North and South*, Philadelphia, PA, 1879.

Meade, G.G., Jr, *The Life and Letters of George Gordon Meade*, 2 vols, New York, 1913.

Miers, E.S. (ed.), *A Rebel War Clerk's Diary*, Baton Rouge, LA, 1993.

Miers, E.S. (ed.), *When the World Ended: The Diary of Emma LeConte*, New York, 1957.

Nevins, A., *Diary of George Templeton Strong*, 4 vols, New York, 1952.

Record Group 94, National Archives.

Sherman, W.T., *Memoirs of W. T. Sherman By Himself*, 2 vols, New York, 1891.

Stone, K., *Brokenburn: The Journal of Kate Stone, 1861–1868*, Baton Rouge, LA, 1955.

Wainwright, C.S., *A Diary of Battle*, New York, 1962.

War of the Rebellion: Official Records of the Union and Confederate Armies, 128 vols, Washington, DC, 1880–1901.

Williams, F.D., *The Wild Life of the Army: Civil War Letters of James A. Garfield*, East Lansing, MI, 1964.

Worsham, J.H., *One of Jackson's Foot Cavalry*, New York, 1912.

SECONDARY SOURCES

Ambrose, S.E., *Halleck: Lincoln's Chief of Staff*, Baton Rouge, LA, 1962.

Ash, S.V., *Middle Tennessee Society Transformed, 1860–1870*, Baton Rouge, LA, 1988.

Ash, S.V., *When the Yankees Came: Conflict and Chaos in*

the Occupied, South, 1861–1865, Chapel Hill, NC, 1995.

Bailey, A.J., The Chessboard of War: Sherman and Hood in the Autumn Campaigns of 1864, Lincoln, NE, 2000.

Ballard, M.B., Pemberton: A Biography, Jackson, MI, 1991.

Barney, W.L., Battleground for the Union: The Era of the Civil War and Reconstruction, 1848–1877, Englewood Cliffs, NJ, 1990.

Barney, W.L., The Passage of the Republic, Lexington, MA, 1987.

Bearss, E.C., The Vicksburg Campaign, 2 vols, Dayton, OH, 1985–86.

Boatner, M.M., III, The Civil War Dictionary, New York, 1959.

Bradley, M.L., Last Stand in the Carolinas: The Battle of Bentonville, Campbell, CA, 1996.

Carter, S., The Final Fortress: The Campaign for Vicksburg, 1862–1863, New York, 1980.

Castel, A., Decision in the West: The Atlanta Campaign of 1864, Lawrence, KA, 1991.

Castel, A., William Clarke Quantrill: His Life and Times, New York, 1962.

Catton, B., A Stillness at Appomattox, New York, 1953.

Catton, B., Glory Road, Garden City, NY 1952.

Coddington, E.B., The Gettysburg Campaign, New York, 1968.

Connelly, T.L., Autumn of Glory: The Army of Tennessee, 1862–1865, Baton Rouge, LA, 1971.

Connelly, T.L., Army of the Heartland: The Army of Tennessee, 1861–1862, Baton Rouge, LA, 1967.

Cooling, B.F., Fort Donelson's Legacy: War and Society in Kentucky and Tennessee, 1862–1863, Knoxville, TN, 1997.

Cooling, B.F., Forts Henry and Donelson: The Key to the Confederate Heartland, Knoxville, TN, 1987.

Cooper, W.J., Jr, Jefferson Davis, American, New York, 2000.

Cooper, W.J., The South and the Politics of Slavery, 1828–1856, Baton Rouge, LA, 1978.

Coulter, E.M., The Confederate States of America, 1861–1865, Baton Rouge, LA, 1950.

Cozzens, P., The Darkest Days of the War: The Battles of Iuka and Corinth, Chapel Hill, NC, 1997.

Cozzens, P., This Terrible Sound: The Battle of Chickamauga, Urbana, IL, 1992.

Cozzens, P., No Better Place to Die: The Battle of Stones River, Urbana, IL, 1990.

Crook, D.P., The North, the South, and the Powers: 1861–1865, New York, 1974.

Curry, L.P., Blueprint for Modern American; Nonmilitary Legislation of the First Civil War Congress, Nashville, TN, 1968.

Daniel, L., Shiloh: The Battle That Changed the Civil War, New York, 1997.

Daniel, L.J., Soldiering in the Army of Tennessee: A Portrait of Life in a Confederate Army, Chapel Hill, NC, 1991.

Davis, W.C., "A Government of Our Own": The Making of the Confederacy, New York, 1994.

Davis, W.C., Jefferson Davis: The Man and His Hour, New York, 1991.

Davis, W.C., Battle at Bull Run, Garden City, NY, 1977.

Davis, W.C., The Battle of New Market, Garden City, NY, 1975.

Donald, D., Lincoln, New York, 1995.

Dowdey, C., Lee's Last Campaign, Boston, MA, 1960.

Dyer, F.H., A Compendium of the War of the Rebellion, Des Moines, IA, 1908.

Engle, S.D., Struggle for the Heartland: The Campaigns From Fort Henry to Corinth, Lincoln, NE, 2001.

Engle, S.D., Don Carlos Buell: Most Promising of All, Chapel Hill, NC, 1999.

Fellman, M., Inside War: The Guerrilla Conflict in Missouri During the American Civil War, New York, 1989.

Frank, J.A. and G.K. Reaves, 'Seeing the Elephant': Raw Recruits at the Battle of Shiloh, New York, 1989.

Freeman, D.S., Lee's Lieutenants, 3 vols, New York, 1942–44.

Furgurson, E.B., Not War But Murder: Cold Harbor 1864, New York, 2000.

Gallagher, G.W. (ed.), The Antietam Campaign, Chapel Hill, NC, 1999.

Gallagher, G.W. (ed.), Three Days at Gettysburg: Essays on Confederate and Union Leadership, Kent, OH, and London, 1999.

Gallagher, G.W. (ed.), The Spotsylvania Campaign, Chapel Hill, NC, and London, 1998.

Gallagher, G.W., The Confederate War, Cambridge, MA, 1997.

Gallagher, G.W. (ed.), The Fredericksburg Campaign: Decision on the Rappahannock, Chapel Hill, NC, 1995.

Glatthaar, J.T., Partners in Command: Relationships Between Leaders in the Civil War, New York, 1994.

Glatthaar, J.T., "Lord High Admiral of the US Navy," Military History Quarterly, vol. 6, no. 4 (summer 1994), pp. 6–26.

Glatthaar, J.T., Forged in Battle: The Civil War Alliance of Black Soldiers and White Officers, New York, 1990.

Glatthaar, J.T., The March to the Sea and Beyond: Sherman's Troops in the Savannah and Carolinas Campaigns, New York, 1985.

Grimsley, M., The Hard Hand of War: Union Military Policy Toward Southern Civilians, 1861–1865, Cambridge, England, Cambridge University Press, 1995.

Hagerman, E., *The American Civil War and the Origins of Modern Warfare*, Bloomington, IN, 1988.

Hattaway, H. and A. Jones, *How the North Won: A Military History of the Civil War*, Urbana, IL, 1983.

Henderson, G.F.R., *The Science of War*, London, 1905.

Hennessey, J.J., *Return to Bull Run: The Campaign and Battle of Second Manassas*, New York, 1993.

Hess, E., *Banners to the Breeze: The Kentucky Campaign, Corinth, and Stones River*, Lincoln, NE, 2000.

Humphreys, A.A., *The Virginia Campaign of '64 and '65: The Army of the Potomac and the Army of the James*, New York, 1883.

Johnson, L.H., *Division and Reunion: America, 1848–1877*, New York, 1978.

Klement, F.L., *The Limits of Dissent: Clement L. Vallandigham and the Civil War*, Lexington, MA, 1970.

Lamers, W.M., *The Edge of Glory: A Biography of General William S. Rosecrans, USA*, Baton Rouge, LA, 1999.

McDonough, J.L., *War in Kentucky: From Shiloh to Perryville*, Knoxville, TN, 1994.

McDonough, J.L., *Shiloh: In Hell Before Night*, Knoxville, TN, 1977.

McMurry, R.M., *Atlanta 1864: Last Chance for the Confederacy*, Lincoln, NE, 2000.

McPherson, J.M., *For Cause and Comrades: Why Men Fought in the Civil War*, New York, 1997.

McPherson, J.M., *Battlecry of Freedom: The Civil War Era*, New York, 1988.

McWhiney, G., *Braxton Bragg and Confederate Defeat*, New York, 1969.

Marszalek, J.F., *Sherman: A Soldier's Passion for Order*, New York, 1993.

Marvel, W., *A Place Called Appomattox*, Chapel Hill, NC, and London, 2000.

Marvel, W., *Andersonville: The Last Depot*, Chapel Hill, NC, 1994.

Massey, M.E., *Bonnet Brigades: American Women and the Civil War*, New York, 1966.

Massey, M.E., *Refugee Life in the Confederacy*, Baton Rouge, LA, 1964.

Mitchell, R., *Civil War Soldiers*, New York, 1988.

Paludan, P.S., *'A People's Contest': The Union and the Civil War, 1861–1865*, New York, 1988.

Pfanz, H.W., *Gettysburg: Culp's Hill and Cemetery Hill*, Chapel Hill, NC, and London, 1993.

Pfanz, H.W., *Gettysburg: The Second Day*, Chapel Hill, NC, and London, 1987.

Potter, D.M., *The Impending Crisis: 1848–1861*, New York, 1976.

Rable, G., *The Confederate Republic: A Revolution against Politics*, Chapel Hill, NC, 1994.

Rhea, G.C., *The Battle of the Wilderness*, Baton Rouge, LA, 1994.

Robertson, J.I., *Soldiers Blue and Gray*, Columbia, SC, 1988.

Rogers, H.C.B., *The Confederates and Federals at War*, London, 1973.

Roland, C.P., *The American Iliad: The Story of the Civil War*, Lexington, KY, 1991.

Roland, C., *Albert Sidney Johnston: Soldier of Three Republics*, Austin, TX, 1964.

Sears, S.W., *Chancellorsville*, Boston, MA, 1996.

Sears, S.W., *Landscape Turned Red: The Battle of Antietam*, New York, 1983.

Silbey, J.H., *A Respectable Minority: The Democratic Party in the Civil War Era, 1860–1868*, New York, 1977.

Simpson, B.D., *Ulysses S. Grant: Triumph Over Adversity, 1822–1865*, Boston, MA, 2000.

Smith, C., *Fredericksburg 1862*, Oxford, 1999.

Smith, C., *Chancellorsville 1863*, Oxford, 1998.

Sword, W., *Embrace an Angry Wind: The Confederacy's Last Hurrah: Spring Hill, Franklin and Nashville*, New York, 1992.

Symonds, C.L., *Stonewall of the West: Patrick Cleburne and the Civil War*, Lawrence, KA, 1997.

Symonds, C.L., *Joseph E. Johnston: A Civil War Biography*, New York, 1992.

Tanner, R.G., *Stonewall Jackson in the Valley: Thomas J. Stonewall Jackson's Shenandoah Campaign, Spring 1862*, Mechanicsburg, 1996.

Thomas, E.M., *The Confederate Nation, 1861–1865*, New York, 1979.

Trudeau, N.A., *The Last Citadel: Petersburg*, Boston, MA, 1991.

Warren, R.P., *The Legacy of the Civil War*, New York, 1964.

Wert, J.D., *From Winchester to Cedar Creek: The Shenandoah Campaign of 1864*, Carlisle, PA, 1987.

Wiley, B.I., *Confederate Women*, Westport, CT, and London, 1975.

Wiley, B.I., *The Life of Billy Yank: The Common Soldier of the Union*, Indianapolis, IN, 1952.

Wiley, B.I., *The Life of Johnny Reb: The Common Soldier of the Confederacy*, Indianapolis, IN, 1943.

Wilson, E., *Patriotic Gore: Studies in the Literature of the American Civil War*, New York, 1962.

Woodworth, S.E., *Jefferson Davis and His Generals: The Failure of Confederate High Command*, Lawrence, KA, 1990.

ABOUT THE AUTHORS

Gary W. Gallagher is the John L. Nau III Professor in the History of the American Civil War at the University of Virginia. He is the author of several books, among them *The Union War, Lee and His Generals in War and Memory, The Confederate War*, and *Causes Won and Forgotten*. He also serves as editor and co-author of the *Military Campaigns of the Civil War* series, which includes titles on nine operations.

Stephen D. Engle is Professor of History at Florida Atlantic University. He is the author of many books and articles on the Civil War, particularly the war in the western theater including *Struggle for the Heartland*, a volume in the "Great Campaigns of the Civil War," focusing on the early phase of the Civil War in the West. His articles have appeared in *Civil War History, Journal of Negro History*, and *Yearbook of German-American Studies*. He is the recipient of numerous teaching and research awards and in 1995–96 was a Fulbright Scholar at Martin Luther University in Germany. He has lectured both in the United States and in Germany and his most recent work, *Gathering to Save a Nation: Abraham Lincoln, War Governors, and Preserving the Union*, is forthcoming with Johns Hopkins University Press.

Robert K. Krick grew up in California, and has been responsible for the preservation of several battlefields in Virginia for more than 30 years. He is the author of 18 books and more than 100 published articles. His 1990 title *Stonewall Jackson at Cedar Mountain* won the Douglas Southall Freeman Award for Best Book in Southern History.

Joseph T. Glatthaar is currently Professor of History at the University of North Carolina. Among his publications are *General Lee's Army: From Victory to Defeat, Forged in Battle: The Civil War Alliance of Black Soldiers and White Officers*, and *Partnerships in Command: The Relationships between Leaders in the Civil War*.

INDEX